Empowering Project Teams

Using Project Followership to Improve Performance

Empowering Project Teams

Using Project Followership to Improve Performance

Marco Sampietro
Tiziano Villa

Foreword by Russell D. Archibald

CRC Press
Taylor & Francis Group
Boca Raton London New York

CRC Press is an imprint of the
Taylor & Francis Group, an **informa** business
AN AUERBACH BOOK

CRC Press
Taylor & Francis Group
6000 Broken Sound Parkway NW, Suite 300
Boca Raton, FL 33487-2742

International Standard Book Number-13: 978-1-4822-1755-1 (Hardback)

Library of Congress Cataloging-in-Publication Data

Sampietro, Marco.
　Empowering project teams : using project followership to improve performance /
Marco Sampietro, Tiziano Villa.
　　pages cm
　Includes bibliographical references and index.
　ISBN 978-1-4822-1755-1 (hardcover : alk. paper)
　1. Project management. I. Villa, Tiziano, 1953- II. Title.

HD69.P75S3225 2014
658.4'022--dc23
　　　　　　　　　　　　　　　　　　　　　　　　　　　　　　2013048180

Visit the Taylor & Francis Web site at
http://www.taylorandfrancis.com

and the CRC Press Web site at
http://www.crcpress.com

Contents

SECTION II Project Followership during Project Initiation

SECTION III   Project Followership during Project Planning

SECTION IV   Project Followership during Project Execution and Control

SECTION V   Project Followership during Project Closure

Foreword

By taking the perspective of *project followership* in this unique and intriguing book, Professors Marco Sampietro and Tiziano Villa convey an interesting, useful, and somewhat different view of what project management is all about. Essentially all of the many books in this field (including my own) present views of the project management (PM) world from either the project manager or the executive level perspective. The project world does indeed look different to project team members, whether as functional specialist experts, specialist team leaders, knowledge workers, or members of the "project controls" supporting staff included in the smaller project management team for a given project.

Recognition in recent years that the project team is a key player and stakeholder for each project demands that project team members also must have PM skills, team knowledge, and skills in addition to their specialist skills. But these PM skills are not identical to those that a successful project manager possesses. Indeed, a project cannot come to life and will not progress to completion until both the project manager and the project team members are assigned to the project. Outstanding teamwork demands that every member of the team be a good follower, a good leader, and a good collaborator within their areas of responsibility and with due regard for the total project. The concept of project followership encompasses all of these attributes. Good, and especially high-performance, teamwork depends predominantly on the human behavior of the team members, and secondarily on their technical skills—without which they would not be on the team. We all know that a high-performance sports team can usually defeat an all-star team, and the same is true for a business or project team.

Providing the required and appropriate PM understanding and collaborative skills to all project team members has now been identified by Sampietro and Villa as a necessary step to achieving excellence in planning, executing, and controlling projects, especially when those projects involve transformational change in, or unusual risks to, the enterprise, or when the projects are unusually complex. Key project team members must contribute to the project planning, scheduling, risk analysis, cost estimating, controlling, and related activities, thereby increasing their commitment to the project and the probability of its success. I have long advocated project team planning, especially during project start-up but also when starting up a new major phase of the project, and I have demonstrated the practicality and power of team planning on a number of large, complex projects.*

The logical sequence of the chapter topics, the clear and direct writing style, the use of numerous graphics and illustrative examples, and the many authoritative references all combine to make *Empowering Project Teams: Using Project Followership to Improve Performance* a valuable addition to project management knowledge and the published literature. The authors walk the project team member through each of the important PM topics and clearly explain what the team members' roles are in regard to each of them. One caveat that I must convey is that the book describes the ideal situation where the right team members are actively and appropriately involved in each of the PM topics presented in each chapter. Unfortunately, in many actual situations the right team members are not given the opportunity to be active contributors as described here. Too often a group of "planners, estimators, and schedulers" (who may not even become members of the project team!) creates the project plan and hands it over to the project manager and project team for execution. This approach may be acceptable for some commercial or delivery projects, but when new, high-risk, or transformational projects are involved, the project team members must be directly involved. Perhaps armed with the knowledge conveyed in this book, the key project team members can properly assert themselves and take their rightful place in their next project!

This book gives the reader a complete picture and sound knowledge of all the PM essentials in a manner that is easily understood from the project team member's point of view. In fact, many—perhaps most—project managers will benefit from reading this book as well, since by studying these clear explanations from the project followership viewpoint, even experienced project managers will gain valuable insights into how to improve the teamwork and overall success on their projects.

Russell D. Archibald

PhD (Hon) in strategy, programme, and project management; MSc mechanical engineering, BSME; PMI Fellow and founding trustee;

---

* Archibald, R.D., *Managing high-technology programs and projects*, Wiley, Hoboken, NJ, 2003. See Chapter 11.

About the Authors

Marco Sampietro earned an MSc in economics at the University of Insubria, Italy and a PhD at the University of Bremen, Germany. Since 2000 he has been a professor at SDA Bocconi School of Management at Bocconi University in Milan, Italy. SDA Bocconi School of Management is ranked among the top business schools in the world (*Financial Times* rankings).

Dr. Sampietro is a core faculty member at SDA Bocconi School of Management and teaches project management in the following programs: Master of Business Administration (MBA), Executive Master of Business Administration (EMBA), and Global Executive Master of Business Administration (GEMBA). He is also responsible for the executive education course, IT Project Management. Dr. Sampietro is a faculty member at MISB Bocconi—Mumbai International School of Business Bocconi, the Indian subsidiary of SDA Bocconi School of Management.

Since 2001 he has been a contract professor at Bocconi University where he teaches project management, IT management, and computer skills for economics. In 2008 and 2009 he was vice-director of a master's degree program in IT management at Bocconi University. He is also contract professor at the Milano Fashion Institute, where he teaches project management. Some of Dr. Sampietro's international experiences include speaker at the NASA Project Management Challenge 2007, 2008, and 2011, United States; speaker at the PMI Global European Congress, 2010; speaker at the IPMA–GPM Young Crew Conference, 2008, Germany; and visiting instructor at the University of Queensland, Australia.

Dr. Sampietro is coauthor of 8 books on project management and 7 books on IT management. He is the author of internationally published articles and case studies.

Tiziano Villa, PMP,® CMC,® started his career at IBM as an organizational analyst in the manufacturing plant of Vimercate, Italy. Subsequently he worked in the IT area of insurance companies, first as a project manager and later as PMO coordinator. Since 1989 Villa has worked in the management consultancy field, mainly on project management–related topics as a trainer and consultant.

In 2002 he founded the Project Management LAB®, an Italian consulting and training company which is also a PMI® REP. From 2003 to 2007 he was a member of the board of directors of the PMI®–Northern Italy Chapter (NIC). He is a past director of PMI®–NIC. In this role he coordinated PMI®–NIC research, workshops, and events. Villa is project management contract professor of the Master IT Governance and Compliance program in the School of Business Administration (SAA) at the University of Turin.

Introduction

This book aims to fill a gap in international publications on project management. Most publications are in fact aimed at project managers and, more generally, the people responsible for coordinating complex and innovative initiatives. In recent years, it was understood that without the support of senior management, a project manager had greater difficulty managing the project. For this reason, other publications targeted to senior management, which commissions and sponsors the projects (West 2010, Englund and Bucero 2006, Love and Brant-Love 2000), appeared. Other publications instead recognize the importance of the project team as a key player in project environments, and they provide hints to the project managers on how to lead, motivate, and manage project teams (DeMarco and Lister 2013, Brown and Hyer 2009, Wong 2007). It was only very recently that some companies and training providers realized it is necessary to work on the whole team in order to achieve positive results. The trend is moving toward widespread project management where the project leadership is shared among the entire project team. Shared leadership is required whenever a corporation deals with very complex and critical challenges that demand a level of skills beyond a single person's capacity (Pearce and Barkus 2004).

This is why the team, if it becomes a key player, must be supported by providing project management skills. However, these skills are not identical to those that a project manager must have; the level of knowledge of project management methodologies and the most appropriate conduct are different, and traditional project management books and training are not fully aligned to meet these needs.

Despite an understanding that the success of the project is directly proportional to the entire project team's ability to assume the role of and act as a managerial center of excellence, so far no publication has been exclusively dedicated to individuals who participate in projects.

This book is therefore specifically aimed at those who are regularly required to work in projects, as members of a project team.

Each member of a project team is required to provide a twofold contribution: on the one hand, a technical and specialist contribution related to his or her area of expertise, and on the other, a managerial contribution in the key stages of the project.

The technical and specialist contribution considers the team member as a point of reference for a particular subject area (knowledge of a product, experience in a specific technology, familiarity with a particular customer environment, mastery of a complex regulatory framework). The managerial contribution instead refers to a set of project management actions for which the expert's contribution is crucial. For instance, think of schedule/cost estimates on certain project activities, the identification of the main project risks, the analysis of variances during the work progress review, the handling of change requests to the initial plan, and capitalizing on the experiences gained from the project.

According to this perspective, the project team member interacts with the project manager and the other members of the team even on managerial aspects, sharing assessments, proposals, and actions that help to strengthen the project management system.

We propose to define the managerial contribution of the project team members' "project followership." *Project followership* means proactive participation in all managerial aspects of the project work within an individual's visibility horizon.

The term *followership* does not have negative connotations (Boccialetti 1995, Chaleff 1995, Kelley 1992) and should not be seen as disparaging for the following reasons:

- A follower's role in supporting the achievement of objectives should not be read as "facilitating the careers of others"; instead, it means supporting the group in achieving higher levels of performance, which have a positive impact on all.
- Being a good follower does not mean being inferior to the leader; a leader without good collaborators could not be a good leader, and vice versa, collaborators without a good leader to coordinate them would have less chance of success, less space to express themselves, fewer career opportunities, and fewer opportunities to engage in motivating activities.
- In our working lives we all play both leader and follower roles; so we should not associate these labels with power, but rather conduct that is appropriate in some situations and less so in others.

This is the raison d'être of project followership: to provide individuals who work in project teams with tools and skills to produce better-performing projects on the one hand and increase their personal satisfaction on the other.

This book explores the application of project followership in the key stages of the project; methods and techniques that a project team member should know and apply are covered for each stage.

The book is divided into 5 sections and a total of 12 chapters.

Section I, composed of Chapters 1 and 2, is devoted to the introduction and exploration of the concepts of project management and project followership. More specifically, the basic concepts of project management are explained, which are necessary to define the typical profile of a project, its organizational environment (the stakeholders and interests at play), and the increasing importance of project followership. We then focus on the specific actions of project followership that must be put into effect at the key stages of the life of the project in order to increase the chances of success.

Section II, which includes Chapters 3 and 4, is dedicated to the project start-up, namely, that very often underestimated set of activities that make it possible to start working in the best way and make future phases less problematic. The basic idea is that "well begun is half done," and in fact, this famous saying can also be safely used in project management.

Of course, managing a project well is essential, but correctly managing a project that started off badly would be like putting a professional driver at the wheel of a three-wheeled instead of four-wheeled vehicle: it would undoubtedly do better than other unfortunate three-wheeled vehicles, but it will not be able to compete for victory (and may not even cross the finish line).

A project that has been set up badly will require an enormous effort to stabilize and provide a return on the efforts of the participants. In order to start the project off on the right foot, there are various aspects to evaluate and establish. Of these, the kickoff meeting and a requirements analysis are particularly important. These two types of activity meet different but complementary needs. The purpose of the requirements analysis is to detect and express, clearly and intelligibly, the needs that different stakeholders wish to meet through the project. The purpose of the kickoff meeting is to create the project team through the presentation of the team members and the objectives that, together, they will have to pursue.

Project team members have an active and important role to play in these two types of activities. In fact, the team members directly contribute to the collecting of information on project requirements, and they are the key players in the kickoff meeting, both as observers (receiving information about the project) and as active participants (communicating additional information and also expectations). This part of the book is given over to the requirements analysis and project kickoff meeting, and specifically to the added value they can provide to the success of the project.

Section III, which includes Chapters 5 to 8, deals with the subject of project planning, a fundamental element for proper project management (Pinto and Slevin 1988). In fact, just like any complex action, a project is very rarely successful on account of pure chance or external events. Success cannot be based on luck alone: it must be planned, and if fortune then favors, so much the better. Unfortunately, team members are often left on the sidelines of the planning process.

The project team member should instead be an integral part of the planning process insofar as

- Only the expert of a specific domain has the knowledge to assess whether a proposal is feasible or not (in terms of the schedule, costs, or technical solutions).
- Only the expert of a specific domain can correctly identify and assess the risks in a specific area.
- Only through debate and sharing a plan is it possible to reach the point where the plan represents the ideas of all those involved, and therefore everyone will make a proactive contribution to its achievement.
- Only team members' commitment to a shared plan will lead to immediate reactions in the case of adversity.

Section IV, which includes Chapters 9 and 10, deals with the execution and control of the project, emphasizing how projects are dynamic environments in which changes are more the rule than the exception.

However, this dynamism should be understood better. It is one thing to change in order to improve project performance and another to change without generating any impact, or possibly making the situation worse. The former changes may also be welcomed; the latter, however, should be eliminated. Moreover, change is not something that comes from outside, something that has been imposed; to a large extent, it also comes from those directly involved in the project, such as the project team. Project team members therefore have a double role: on the one hand, they acknowledge change requests, and on the other, they are the very source of change.

To better understand how the project is changing and to react appropriately, it is, however, necessary to monitor the status of the project and then predict its evolution. Team members very often have a negative perception of project control as it is proposed from a purely bureaucratic point of view (Wolinsky 2010, Keung 2007, Klein 1990): filling in time sheets. In fact, controlling is more noble and useful, as it makes it possible to understand what has been done, what has changed, why it changed, and therefore to suggest actions for constant improvement. Again, the role of the project team member is key, as direct contact with project activities makes it possible to define their current status accurately and suggest feasible improvement actions.

Finally, Section V, which includes Chapters 11 and 12, deals with project closure and transfer. From a company point of view, project closure and transfer are understood as the implementation of all those activities that leave no situation in suspense and make it possible for future users to immediately appreciate the benefits of the implemented solution. In this book, however, we shall stray from this vision, useful and correct as it may be, to embrace another, which sees the project end as an important moment to "take stock" and evaluate whether the effort invested has been rewarded by the satisfaction received.

While individual projects certainly have a definite start and finish, it is also true that the working life of many people can be described through a series of projects. In this situation, project team members should consider the intelligent closure of a project to be one that makes it possible to increase their wealth of experience and knowledge so that it can be reused and transferred in future projects.

We will then discuss lessons learned as methodology and as occasions for debate useful for future improvement, both from a rational point of view as an increase in project performances and from an emotional point of view as satisfaction that comes from having contributed to innovation activities that, if carried out well, have also led to a personal improvement.

Finally, we will attempt to draw conclusions from this journey along a project life cycle by proposing a personal assessment of the project team member that, unlike a company's financial statements, will not measure economic aspects, but will help to assess whether it is worth a project follower's while to participate enthusiastically and proactively in projects.

Each chapter contains case studies, and exercises for the reader on the topics covered in the various chapters can be found at the back of the book. This is to alternate between the theory and practice of project followership.

To get the most from the content, we suggest reading the book in the order the chapters are listed in the table of contents.

REFERENCES

Boccialetti, G. 1995. *It takes two: Managing yourself when working with bosses and other authority figures.* San Francisco: Jossey-Bass.

Brown, K., and N. Hyer. 2009. *Managing projects: A team-based approach with student CD.* Columbus, OH: McGraw-Hill/Irwin.

Chaleff, I. 1995. *The courageous follower: Standing up to and for our leaders.* San Francisco: Berrett-Koehler Publishers.

DeMarco, T., and T. Lister. 2013. *Peopleware: Productive projects and teams.* 2nd ed. New York: Dorset House Publishing Company.

Englund, R.L., and A. Bucero. 2006. *Project sponsorship: Achieving management commitment for project success.* San Francisco: Jossey-Bass.

Kelley, R.E. 1992. *The power of followership.* New York: Doubleday.

Keung, J. 2007. Software engineers' view of software metrics in Australia: A survey. Presented at the International Workshop on Accountability and Traceability in Global Software Engineering, Nagoya, Japan.

Klein, A.R. 1990. Organizational barriers to creativity ... and how to knock them down. *Journal of Consumer Marketing* 7, 1: 65–66.

Love, A.L., and J. Brant-Love. 2000. *The project sponsor guide.* Newtown Square, PA: Project Management Institute.

Pearce, C.L., and B. Barkus. 2004. The future of leadership: Combining vertical and shared leadership to transform knowledge work. *Academy of Management Executive* 18, 1: 47–59.

Pinto, J.K., and D.P. Slevin. 1988. Project success: Definitions and measurement techniques. *Project Management Journal* 19, 1: 67–72.

West, D. 2010. *Project sponsorship.* Burlington, VT: Gower Publishing Company.

Wolinsky, H. 2010. B for bureaucracy. *EMBO Reports* 11: 664–666. Accessed from http://www.nature.com/embor/journal/v11/n9/full/embor2010121.html.

Wong, Z. 2007. *Human factors in project management: Concepts, tools, and techniques for inspiring teamwork and motivation.* San Francisco: John Wiley & Sons.

Section I

Project Followership

Section 1

Project Follow-up

1

Introduction to Project Management

KEYWORDS

Critical success factor (CSF)
Project
Project followership
Project management
Project management team
Project manager
Project sponsor
Project team
Stakeholder

READER'S GUIDE

This chapter allows you to

- Understand the growing importance of projects in today's society
- Deepen your understanding of the key characteristics of a project
- Deepen your understanding of project life cycle and project management processes
- Examine the elements that contribute to the success of a project
- Define the key stakeholders of the project

Note: The purpose of this chapter is to introduce the key elements of project environments. If you already have knowledge on project management topics (see the keywords for reference) you can skip directly to Chapter 2.

1.1 PROJECTS, PROJECTS, AND MORE PROJECTS!

The pervasiveness of a word underlines its importance. In May 2013, the word *projects* returned 2,640,000,000 search results on one of the most important search engines. *Project* receives more hits than *sex* (1,610,000,000) but fewer than *love* (4,080,000,000). Many buzzwords receive far fewer hits: *tablet* (514,000,000), *smartphone* (319,000,000), *apps* (1,230,000,000), *WiFi* (804,000,000); the same can be said for other common topics: *environment* (1,160,000,000), *tax* (1,180,000,000), *ethic* (31,200,000), *globalization* (40,600,000), *labor* (275,000,000).

Surprising isn't it? These simple facts lead us to state that projects, in all their forms and purposes, are now an integral part of our daily life, in a society increasingly characterized by marked and widespread planning. In fact, there are many and diverse interpretations of the concept of project: ways of organizing work, personal lifestyle, a tool for social development, an element of innovation, change perspective, results-oriented business, looking to the future, a challenge to face, and opportunities to be seized.

But what exactly do we mean by *project*?

The word *project* comes from the Latin word *projectum* from the Latin verb *proicere*, "to throw something forward," which in turn comes from *pro-*, which denotes something that precedes the action of the next part of the word in time (paralleling the Greek πρό), and *iacere*, "to throw." The word *project* thus actually originally meant "something that comes before anything else happens."

When the English language initially adopted the word, it referred to a plan of something, not to the act of actually carrying this plan out. Something performed in accordance with a project became known as an object. More pragmatically, the PMI® (Project Management Institute) defines a project as "a temporary endeavor undertaken to create a unique product, service or result." This definition highlights two dimensions: a project has a start and an end (temporary), and every project is different from another (unique).

Today projects lend themselves to countless applications in all areas and have the most diverse purposes.

Examples of projects are the construction of a bridge, putting on a large sporting event, the development and launch of a new product, the reorganization of a company, the repairing of a computer system, moving from one city to another, opening a shop, the definition of a new treatment protocol, the reconstruction of an area struck by an earthquake, the search for

TABLE 1.1

Project Examples

Human Genome Project. Completed in 2003, the Human Genome Project (HGP) was a 13-year project coordinated by the U.S. Department of Energy and the National Institutes of Health to sequence the 3 billion basepairs that make up human DNA.

GNU Project. The GNU Project is a free software, mass collaboration project, announced on September 27, 1983, by Richard Stallman at MIT. It initiated GNU operating system development in January 1984. The founding goal of the project was, in the words of its initial announcement, to develop "a sufficient body of free software … to get along without any software that is not free."

Project Mercury. Project Mercury was the first human spaceflight program of the United States. It ran from 1959 through 1963 with the goal to be the first nation to put a human in orbit around the earth.

Project A.L.S.™ The mission of Project A.L.S. is to recruit the world's best research scientists and clinicians to work together toward an understanding of and the first effective treatments for amyotrophic lateral sclerosis (ALS), also known as Lou Gehrig's disease.

The Million Dollar Homepage™. Citing the founder, the idea is simple: to try and make US$1 million by selling 1,000,000 pixels for $1 each—hence the name. "The main motivation for doing this is to pay for my degree studies, because I don't like the idea of graduating with a huge student debt. The pixels you buy will be displayed on the homepage permanently. The homepage will not change. Using some of the money I make from the site, I guarantee to keep it online for at least 5 years."

Satellite Sentinel Project (SSP). SSP launched on December 29, 2010, with the goals of deterring a return to full-scale civil war between northern and southern Sudan and deterring and documenting threats to civilians along both sides of the border. SSP focuses world attention on mass atrocities in Sudan and uses its imagery and analysis to generate rapid responses on human rights and human security concerns.

The Atlantis Project. The Atlantis Project, which proposed the creation of a floating sea city named Oceania, began in February 1993, receiving nationwide publicity from many magazines. The project ended due to lack of interest in April 1994.

Ohio River Bridges Project. The Ohio River Bridges Project addresses the long-term transportation needs of the Louisville–Southern Indiana region. Its purpose is to enhance safety, reduce traffic congestion, and improve transportation connections throughout the growing metropolitan area.

LHC Project. The project's purpose is to smash protons moving at 99.999999% of the speed of light into each other and so re-create conditions a fraction of a second after the big bang. The LHC experiments try to work out what happened.

Source: Google Search, May 2013.

renewable energy sources, adventure travel to a distant country, a traveling art exhibition, wedding preparations, a social awareness campaign, an archaeological expedition, a humanitarian mission, and the strengthening of a sales channel.

Table 1.1 shows a random list of projects, the result of simple research on the Internet centered around the word *project*.

To actively participate in a project and come out satisfied, we must have some familiarity with project work and project management.

1.2 TEN KEY CHARACTERISTICS OF A PROJECT

Table 1.2 lists the ten characteristics that distinguish the profile of a project. The list is a summary of various contributions in the project management field, and the order does not indicate their level of importance, insofar as all the characteristics are assumed to be equally significant. A brief comment on each characteristic follows:

1. Unique. The decision to start a project is something outside of the ordinary, where ordinary means the normal, orderly, and efficient flow of things, be they business activities or individual lifestyles. A project provides us with a different kind of goal, which we have often never faced before. The project is therefore an element of discontinuity that requires us to get into the right mindset to tackle the new challenge. Projects may be similar to each other, but they are never identical. The project is a "one-off" initiative that represents the best contingent solution in relation to a specific "here and now." The same project may not turn out to be the best solution following changes in the reference context. Therefore, organizations that work on projects are technically called "adhocracies," where each project is an ad hoc adventure.

TABLE 1.2

Ten Key Characteristics of a Project

1.	Unique	Ad hoc
2.	Targeted	Results meet the requirements and it is actually useful
3.	Limited	In compliance with the assigned constraints
4.	Innovative	The world, before and after the project
5.	Visible	On the stage, for better or worse
6.	Temporary	Start, end, milestones
7.	Progressive	Becomes clear and is adjusted along the way
8.	Risky	Uncertain by nature
9.	Reusable	Extraordinary source of knowledge
10.	Collaborative	Team over hierarchy

2. Targeted. A project's raison d'être is the tangible results that it must necessarily produce. These results are the justification for starting the project. The project must be able to rely on a firm intention and clear direction in order to achieve results that meet the specifications and that are capable of generating benefits higher than the costs incurred to achieve them.

3. Limited. Each project, independently of its degree of importance, is subject to implementation constraints. Constraints are often formalized by contract and concern, for example, schedule, budget, quality of results, regulations, and technologies. It follows that the project must be planned and carried out with respect to these constraints. The project constraints are agreed in the project mandate at the beginning when the project is awarded, and their validity is then systematically verified during the execution of the project. There is no such thing as a project without constraints: the constraints should be brought to the surface as soon as possible so the project's actual feasibility can be assessed.

4. Innovative. By its nature a project changes "a part of the world," be it small or large. The project inevitably involves a certain degree of innovation, in terms of the product, process, people, culture, and so on. It changes the existing situation into a situation to work toward. The project therefore is a tool for organizational, social, and cultural change.

5. Visible. A project is in itself visible in the frame of reference. The project stakeholders, internal or external to the performing organization, know that the project is active and expect tangible results. The progress and outcome of the project are plain for everyone to see, as are the actions of the project team.

6. Temporary. While ordinary activities (for example, the process of manufacturing a consumer good) are by nature repetitive and permanent, a project has a limited life marked by a beginning, an end, and intermediate deadlines. The project has its own life cycle, made up of seasons, each with its own characteristics. The temporary nature of the project necessarily forces the stakeholders involved to work together for a limited time, focusing on a common objective and the results associated with it.

7. Progressive. A project is specified by defining, through the step-by-step results, new alternatives that arise as the work progresses, the analysis of variances from the initial plan, and change requests. It is physiological for a project to become clear and undergo alterations along the way. Progressive elaboration, which refines the project in increments

during its progress, is the most appropriate method to effectively manage a project, especially if it has a high degree of innovation and instability (Collyer and Warren 2009).

8. Risky. Risk is "an uncertainty that matters" (Hillson 2009), and the project is by definition uncertain. Project risk management is a topic of growing importance in the field of project management models. The risks (as both threats and opportunities), if managed well, will turn out to be a keystone for the success of the project. The project risks paradigm is radically changing: from managing project risks (risks as another issue to deal with) to managing the project by risks (risks as the main perspective around which to plan and control the project).

9. Reusable. Projects may be considered as arenas for renewal and learning processes (Lundin and Midler 1998). In fact, each project offers several learning opportunities to the point of generating new knowledge, increasing the expertise of individuals, and enriching the organization's wealth of key skills. Project knowledge should be considered and managed in all respects, like other project variables (schedule, costs, results, quality, people, risks, procurement, etc.).

10. Collaborative. A project is necessarily a collective effort. The project cuts across organizational charts and companies, while bringing together people from different companies, organizational positions, specializations, and cultures to focus on the project idea. The project team therefore is a key ingredient of the project, where defining the right roles, competencies, and management methods is fundamental for project success.

The ten key characteristics as a whole lead us to state that the project is by nature an initiative that has high organizational and relational complexity. For instance, think of the levels of complexity in risk management, the progressive development of work plans, compliance with constraints and contractual specifications, collaboration in the project team, and acquiring project stakeholders.

As projects become larger and more complex, the effective management of them becomes proportionally more significant (Wideman 2001). Normally the project manager is mentioned as the person capable of strongly influencing a project's probability of success. While this is acceptable, it is, however, correct to say that success comes from the expertise and collaboration of the individuals that form the project team.

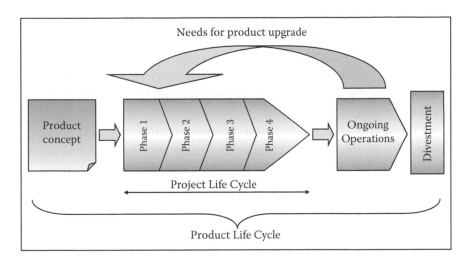

FIGURE 1.1
Product life cycle and project life cycle.

1.3 PROJECT LIFE CYCLE

The first distinction to make is between the product life cycle and the project life cycle. The diagram in Figure 1.1 shows this distinction.

The product life cycle can be defined as "a collection of generally sequential, non-overlapping product phases whose name and number are determined by the manufacturing and control needs of the organization. The last product life cycle phase for a product is generally the product's retirement" (PMI 2008).

The product (or service) life cycle, in its different variations, includes ideational phases in which the product is conceived; design phases in which the project is developed, engineered, and launched; production phases in which the product is made and the planned number of units distributed; a product relaunch phase in which the product is revisited and offered to the market again; and final phases involving product disposal once the product's reason for existing on the market has been exhausted.

The duration of the product life cycle varies depending on the market sector and the success of the product itself. There are long-lived products (for example, the Moka coffee maker, designed in 1933 and still on the market today, appropriately redesigned but faithful to the operating principle and the original design) and more ephemeral products (for example, any type of mobile phone, whose life expectancy is about 18 months, if not less).

The product life cycle contains one or more project life cycles; for example, there is the initial project life cycle involving the creation and launch of the first version of the product, and then subsequent project life cycles involving the creation and launch of subsequent versions of the product. The longer the life of the product, the more project life cycles there are in the same product's life cycle.

An important aspect that should be emphasized is: a project does not always aim to create a new product that must then be produced in the planned volumes. In the case of a sporting event, wedding, relocation, or company reorganization, for example, the project product is unique and not expected to be repeated. In these cases it makes little sense to talk about the product life cycle: the project begins and ends as such, and is not part of a broader life cycle.

Project life cycle means "a collection of generally sequential and sometimes overlapping project phases whose name and number are determined by the management and control needs of the organization or organizations involved in the project, the nature of the project itself, and its area of application" (PMI 2008).

Note the following:

- There is no such thing as a generalized life cycle that can be applied indiscriminately to any kind of project. The life cycle of an individual project is determined by its content, the market sector it belongs to, and the organizational environment in which the project must be produced. For example, in the pharmaceutical sector projects to develop new drugs have a very long life cycle extending over several years, divided into several phases, and characterized by significant technical times dictated by the social and healthcare implications in play and control body regulations. In other sectors project life cycles are very short and have a much simpler phase structure. For example, think of product development projects in the consumer goods sector.
- Costs and workloads are low at the start of the project, significantly increasing when the project is running, and then decreasing when the project nears its closure.
- The level of uncertainty and therefore risk associated with the project is highest at the beginning and then gradually tends to reduce as the project proceeds.
- The ability to influence the quality of results produced by the project follows the same trend.

- The life cycle of the project provides for specific mandatory reviews along the way. These reviews are usually scheduled at the end of each phase or at key points within a single phase. Based on specific evaluation criteria, the purpose of the review is to decide whether to continue, opening the next phase of the project, whether to continue with changes to the initial choices, or whether to halt the project, insofar as the situation arrived at to date does not justify its continuation. The phase reviews, if well planned, managed, and shared, make it possible to identify the projects that will succeed in advance, and likewise to postpone or cancel projects that have little chance of success.

Except for very simple projects, structuring a project into phases is recommended.

A project phase is defined as "a designated group of activities that normally result in a deliverable or a milestone" (PMI 2008). Phases are part of the project life cycle and may be sequential, overlap, and be repeated many times during the project life.

Each project phase should be carefully managed, applying specific project management processes. The project management processes are combined into specific groups. A project management process group is a logical grouping of processes with a common purpose; for example, the planning processes group encompasses all the project management processes aimed at planning all the aspects of a project (schedule, costs, risks, procurement, communications, resources, etc.). Project management processes are typically combined into five groups, as shown in Table 1.3.

It should be clearly emphasized that project management process groups are independent from the market sector and type of project managed. They therefore represent generalized processes focused on the management of the project as such. The processes groups are linked to each other by the logical sequence in the diagram shown in Figure 1.2.

Another important aspect to stress is that project management process groups are not the phases of the project life cycle. The five project management process groups should be carried out in the sequence shown in Figure 1.2, as many times as there are phases of the project life cycle. Each project phase should therefore be managed by applying project management process groups. This substantial difference is well represented in the diagram shown in Figure 1.3.

TABLE 1.3

Project Management Processes Groups

Project Management Processes Group	Purpose
Initiating	To define a new project or a new phase of an existing project through the formal authorization to start up the entire project or a phase of the project
Planning	To refine the project objectives, define the scope of the project, and develop an appropriate plan of action to achieve these objectives
Executing	To carry out the project work as defined in the plan of action and achieve the expected results
Monitoring and controlling	To monitor, review, and regulate the project progress and performances, identify any areas that require changes to the initial plan, and start implementing the corresponding changes
Closing	To complete all the activities included in all the processes groups and formally close the entire project or a phase of the project

Source: Elaboration of the authors based on Project Management Institute, *A Guide to the Project Management Body of Knowledge*, 4th ed., PMI, Newtown Square, Pennsylvania, 2008.

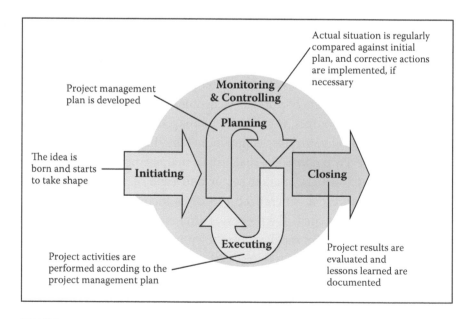

FIGURE 1.2
Framework of the project management process groups. (Based on Project Management Institute, *A Guide to the Project Management Body of Knowledge*, 4th ed., PMI, Newtown Square, Pennsylvania, 2008.)

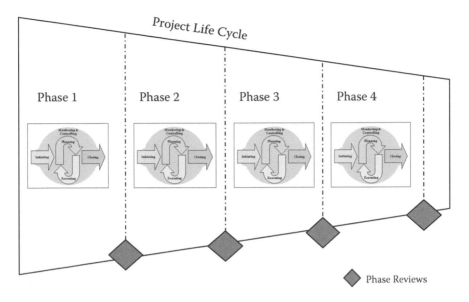

FIGURE 1.3

Phases of the project life cycle and project management process groups. (Based on Project Management Institute, *A Guide to the Project Management Body of Knowledge*, 4th ed., PMI, Newtown Square, Pennsylvania, 2008.)

1.4 PROJECT ENVIRONMENT AND THE STAKEHOLDERS

1.4.1 Project's Key Stakeholders

The project environment is the organizational context in which the project is carried out.

The project environment involves different organizational structures referred to one or more companies (the client, supplier, third parties, professional organizations, and so on). The project environment is populated by players, who by nature are numerous, diverse, and geographically dispersed. They are known as project stakeholders.

Stakeholder can be defined as "individuals and organizations that are actively involved in the project, or whose interests may be positively or negatively affected by execution of the project or project completion" (PMI 2008). As well as being influenced by the progress and outcome of the project, stakeholders can influence the project by exercising different forms of power. It is therefore vitally important, for the success of the project, to fully understand the environment in which it is carried out, in terms of the stakeholders and interests at play.

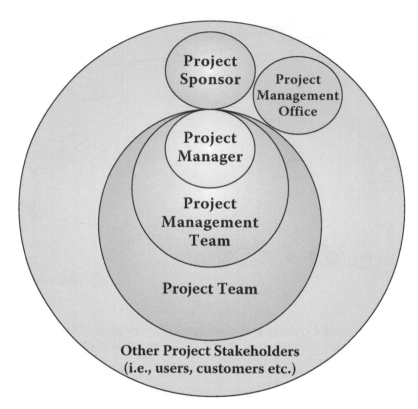

FIGURE 1.4
The different types of project stakeholders. (Based on Project Management Institute, *A Guide to the Project Management Body of Knowledge*, 4th ed., PMI, Newtown Square, Pennsylvania, 2008.)

Figure 1.4 helps us to classify the project environment and the different stakeholder categories. The diagram highlights five types of stakeholder.

1.4.1.1 Project Sponsor

The project sponsor is "is the person or group [of people] that provides the financial resources, in cash or in kind, for the project" (PMI 2008). This figure belongs to the project performing organization and has the formal power to officially open the project and support it over time.

The project sponsor in all respects becomes the functional boss of the project manager for the entire duration of the project. The project manager agrees to the project mandate with the project sponsor and must report to the said sponsor on the progress and outcome of the project. The project sponsor and project manager share the same interest: the success of the project. Therefore, they must know how to establish and maintain close collaboration over time, which, although hierarchically unbalanced (delegator and delegate), must be based on a dialectic, constructive, and mutually supportive relationship.

The role of the project sponsor is typically held by a senior figure within the company's permanent organization. In some cases the project sponsor may be the project manager's permanent hierarchical boss, or a figure from an even higher hierarchical level, to whom the project manager reports directly, bypassing the intermediate hierarchical levels, on the strength of the special mandate received.

The project sponsor answers to the company for the business case of the project, in other words, its initial economic justification and its sustainability during the progress of the project.

For this reason the project sponsor in turn reports to a higher hierarchical level. This may be a permanent body that already exists within the company independently from the project in question, for example, the management committee or a business committee, or it may be a temporary organization especially established to provide direction to the specific project. In these cases we are speaking about project boards and project steering committees. The choice to establish an ad hoc committee for the project is made when the project is big, complex, and innovative, and when it is strategic for the organizations involved. Nothing prevents people "registered under different VAT numbers" from sitting on the project committee, such as figures from the organization awarded the project, the client organization, and third parties to whom the organization awarded the project subcontracts' parts, and even large parts, of the project.

It should be pointed out that the customer organization may be another company (external market) or another part of the same company (internal market). Formalization of the project between the two organizations varies depending on the type of market in which the project is carried out (offer and relative contract between the client and supplier in an open market, framework agreement between companies of the same group, internal agreement between divisions of the same company, etc.). In the case of the external customer, the project is defined as a *job order*, while in the case of an internal customer the project is defined as an *investment*.

In some projects the internal customer and the external customer overlap, i.e., when the project starts and ends within the same company. For example, the sales department of a company could self-commission a project for the radical redesign of its sales network.

1.4.1.2 Project Manager

The project manager is the role around which the entire project revolves.

The project manager is a temporary figure called upon to manage all the variable aspects of the project (scope, schedule, costs, quality, risks, procurement, human resources, communications, etc.) in order to achieve the objectives set in the project mandate. The project manager is therefore the "film director" throughout the entire life cycle of the project.

An individual may fill the role of project manager in a specific project while at the same time maintaining his or her permanent role in the organization. In this case the individual plays an additional fixed-term role for the duration of the project. As they say in the jargon, an individual can "wear more than one hat."

The project manager position could be part-time or full-time. In the first case an individual dedicates a portion of his or her time, for the entire duration of the project, to coordinating a specific project. In the second case an individual dedicates all his or her time to coordinating the project. In the case of part-time positions, an individual may find himself or herself acting as the project manager of different projects at the same time.

In organizations whose business is largely established around projects, the project manager role becomes a permanent organizational position established in the company organizational chart. In other words, some people in a company have the status of project manager, at various levels of seniority, and therefore hold that role on a permanent basis and are assigned each time to coordinate specific projects. When a particular project ends, the project manager ceases to act as such for that project but continues to hold that status while waiting for other project assignments. This structural solution assumes the company has a portfolio of projects that would justify the creation of the permanent status of project manager and the presence in the company of a certain number of people that hold that role.

For the duration of the project the project manager functionally coordinates all the individuals that make up the project team.

1.4.1.3 Project Management Team (PMT)

The term *project management team* (PMT) means the limited number of people who possess all the skills and all the authority to directly perform or have others perform the work necessary for the project. PMI defines the PMT as "the members of the project team who are directly involved in project management activities" (PMI 2008). The next section will explain the typical composition of the PMT. From here on it is assumed that the project follower is a member of the PMT.

1.4.1.4 Project Team

The project team is the team expanded to all individuals that will work, even for limited periods of time, on the project activities. The project team typically includes the project manager, the members of the PMT, and the other individuals called upon to provide a specialized and operative contribution to the project.

In the case of projects with limited scope, the PMT and the project team overlap.

1.4.1.5 PMO

The project management office may support the project manager and the project team in different ways: schedule development and control, budget development, cost control, risk assessment, etc. Project management offices are becoming quite popular, especially for medium to large projects. They allow project teams to delegate the methodical side of project management so that they can focus more on people management and problem solving.

1.4.1.6 Other Project Stakeholders

This includes all the other figures involved in the project. They are people from the performing organization (for example, the functional or line managers) or other organizations involved who, while not having to work on the project, are influenced by it or can influence it. For instance, think of the end users of a new computer system, the residents of an area that will be crossed by a new high-speed railway line, the representatives of control bodies with whose directives the project must comply, and other project managers of projects related to the project in question.

1.4.2 Focus on the Project Management Team

Modern project management practices highlight the centrality of the PMT as a center of excellence of project management.

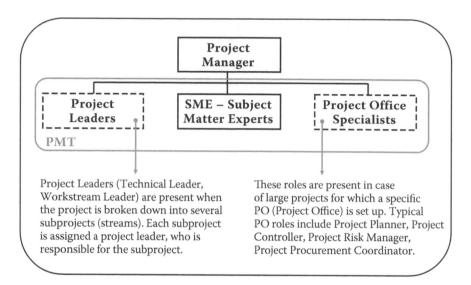

FIGURE 1.5

Composition of the Project Management Team (PMT).

Let us examine the typical composition of a PMT, using the diagram in Figure 1.5.

The PMT is first comprised of experts in a subject matter, in the jargon known as subject matter experts (SMEs). Each expert brings his or her specialist expertise to the project. The expert therefore becomes the official point of contact for all issues relating to a specific subject matter (a particular technology, a product line, a specific type of business, mastery of a complex regulatory framework). The expert must obviously be a person with proven skills and be recognized as authoritative in the context of the project. The expert is usually transferred from his or her own permanent organizational unit and formally assigned, full-time or part-time, to the project coordination team. Experts perform specialist project work directly or can in turn enlist other specialists from their subject area, acting as a point of reference for them.

In its minimum size, the PMT is limited to a few subject matter experts, functionally coordinated by the project manager. For larger projects, the PMT usually provides for two other types of members: the project leader and the project office specialist.

When the project is of a significant size, it is usually broken down into subprojects, for greater managerial efficiency and effectiveness. Each subproject is assigned a project leader. The project leader is to the subproject what the project manager is to the overall project.

The extent of the project management activities grows in proportion to the size and complexity of the project. The quantity of data and information to be collected, processed, and distributed, together with the need to use advanced project management techniques for the various managerial issues to be dealt with (project risks, for example), leads to the establishment of a specific project office. Its function is to assist the project manager in the project management activities. Thus, specialized project management roles are created, with full- or part-time assignments. For instance, we talk about the role of a project planner, focused on planning the project (work packages, responsibilities, work performance sequence, schedule and cost estimates, etc.); a project controller, for all aspects concerning the technical and economic performance of the project; a project risk manager, centering around the integrated management of the project risks portfolio; and a project procurement coordinator, for issues concerning problems relating to project procurement (definition of supply contracts, purchasing procedures, the administration of contracts, etc.).

1.5 SUCCESS OF THE PROJECT

1.5.1 Frame of Reference

Successfully completing a project is no easy task. For this reason, it is appropriate to analyze elements influencing the success of the project.

A lot of work has been done on defining project success (see the systematization of this topic in Lavagnon (2009)) and the antecedents of project success (Baker et al. 2008, Belassi and Tukel 1996, Hughes 1986).

Figure 1.6 summarizes the aspects we shall consider. There are three: First, we should define the system that will be used to evaluate the success of the project. The system is divided into different evaluation perspectives, each distinct and complementary. For example, the success of the project can be assessed on the basis of compliance between the products/services actually produced and the assigned schedule and cost constraints. However, the success of the same project could also be assessed from another perspective, referring to the project team, as regards the degree of collaboration between the members of the team and the individual level of satisfaction. The evaluation system should be formalized and shared among the stakeholders so that it is clear to everybody from the start

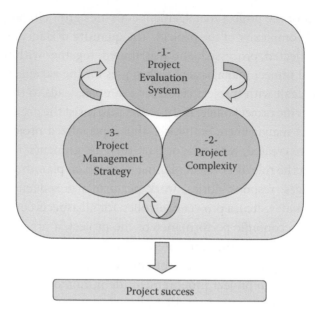

FIGURE 1.6
Variables influencing project success.

which parameters will be used to define whether the project has been a complete success, a partial success, a partial failure, or a total failure.

Second, we should define the degree of complexity associated with the project. Some projects are simpler, and others are more complex. Each project, insofar as a unique initiative, has its own degree of complexity. The level of managerial difficulty increases proportionally to the project's degree of complexity. In this case too, it is appropriate to measure the project's degree of complexity by using a set of objective and shared criteria. This makes it possible to officially attribute the relative complexity profile to the project, raising awareness among stakeholders on the type of shared adventure that awaits them. Team members play a key role in this aspect. Very often, in fact, the project manager does not have technical or specialized expertise on all elements of the project, and therefore cannot adequately assess its complexity. Team members thus have the right/duty to inform the project manager of the level of complexity in their area of responsibility.

The third and last step is identifying the project management strategy considered most appropriate for its level of complexity. Simple projects require a basic management strategy based on a few rules to be applied for the entire duration of the project. Complex projects, on the other hand, require a much more complex management strategy that should be skillfully adjusted as the works progresses. In other words, the project management system to be used to manage the project should be carefully measured, avoiding oversimplification on the one hand, and excessive managerial complications on the other. On this aspect the debit/credit balance often shows a loss from the point of view of team members. There is the feeling of having to respect a set of excessive rules. In fact, the benefit of following numerous rules is not always apparent to an individual expert, while it is clear to the person with overall responsibility for the project. Very often, however, project management rules, if applied well, generate benefits for everyone, reducing the error rate and therefore decreasing the need for so-called rework (editing documents, clarification meetings, reworking parts, managing customer dissatisfaction, etc.).

Let us now analyze the three aspects linked to the success of the project in more detail.

1.5.2 Project Evaluation System

Projects and their results can be evaluated from different perspectives. Just think of project evaluation:

- From a contractual point of view, concerning whether the results meet the formally agreed requirements
- From a commercial point of view, as regards the level of customer satisfaction
- From an economic point of view, in terms of the profitability of the project for the performing organization
- From the relations point of view, as regards the level of collaboration in the project team
- From the business point of view, in relation to the benefits generated by the project

From these simple examples it is clear that the project, insofar as a complex initiative, should be assessed using systemic logic, taking into consideration all the variables that contribute to determine its success. What should be avoided is limiting the project evaluation to a single perspective, however important it may be. Many projects have been painstakingly completed in accordance with the project mandate (schedule, costs, scope), but have not generated any benefit in terms of business!

The criteria with which to evaluate the success of the project should also be shared by the stakeholders. In a project the stakeholders involved are

TABLE 1.4

Evaluation Perspectives of the Success of the Project

Evaluation Perspective	Meaning
Project governance	This perspective aims to evaluate the project on aspects more typically connected with its organizational management. This perspective in fact measures, on the basis of a series of specific parameters, the project management skills brought into play by the project team during the management of the project. The assessment parameters relate, for example, to the management of change requests, risk management, and the involvement of key stakeholders.
Project team	This perspective aims to evaluate the project based on the operation of the project team, as an engine of the project itself. This perspective in fact measures, on the basis of a set of parameters, typically relational aspects related to the individuals that make up the project team and their interactions. The assessment parameters relate, for example, to the degree of collaboration within the project team and the personal satisfaction of the individual members of the team.
Project results	This perspective aims to evaluate the project in terms of the results produced compared to the agreed-upon requirements. This perspective, in fact, is based on a series of parameters, measuring the compliance of the project in terms of the schedule, cost, and scope. It can be summarized in the slogan "do the project right."
Business outcomes	This perspective aims to evaluate the project in terms of the positive effects arising from the project results. This perspective, based on a series of parameters, measures the value of the project from a business point of view, independently from its level of conformity. The assessment parameters relate, for example, to customer satisfaction and achieving business benefits. It can be summarized in the slogan "do the right project."
Future developments	This perspective aims to evaluate the project in terms of its contribution to future developments. This perspective, based on a series of parameters, measures the contribution that the project experience can provide in terms of knowledge, innovation, and new opportunities.

Source: Adapted from Atkinson, R., *International Journal of Project Management*, 17, 6, 1999, 337–342; Shenhar, A. J. et al., *Project Management Journal*, 28, 2, 1997, 5–13.

usually numerous, diverse, and geographically dispersed. It is also understandable that each stakeholder would assess the project from its own point of view: each point of view is neither right nor wrong, but it is valid as such, like all the other points of view. Each stakeholder sees in the project what it wishes to see. The project, therefore, is a sum of local viewpoints.

It is clear that an understanding focused only on a single area of the progress and outcome of the project does not promote the overall result. It is difficult to reconcile several incentives to move in different directions with the uniform direction that should be given to the project. In the absence of an integrated evaluation model, the risk is to waste resources and energy, as well as lower the project's overall level of success. This aspect is related to the way in which team members should address a project: if it is true that it is right to protect and enhance their area of responsibility, it is not right to apply evaluation methods that are too "exotic," based on their needs only; instead, it is right to encourage strong integration between the different areas that make up the project.

It is therefore in everybody's interests to have a uniform evaluation system aimed at integrating local points of view.

Table 1.4 lists the main perspectives that are usually used to assess the success of a project.

1.5.3 Degree of Complexity of a Project

The project's degree of complexity is based on a set of diversified variables. Different models have been developed to define project complexity (Vidal et al. 2011, Maylor et al. 2008, Vidal and Marle 2008).

Figure 1.7 shows a diagram that is useful to determine a project's degree of complexity, on the basis of four variables:

- The dimension of the project, which in turn is divided into the time dimension (the longer the project lasts, the more complex it is to manage), the economic dimension (the more the project costs, in money and other resources, the more complex it is to manage), and the organizational dimension (the more numerous, diverse, and geographically dispersed the stakeholders are, the more complex the project is to manage).
- The innovation associated with the project, in terms of both product innovation (the degree of novelty introduced by the solution implemented by the project) and process innovation (the degree of novelty introduced in the methods of implementing the project).
- The instability connected with the project, as regards both the initial vagueness of the project scope (boundaries, requirements, underlying assumptions, priorities, etc.) and the variability of the scope

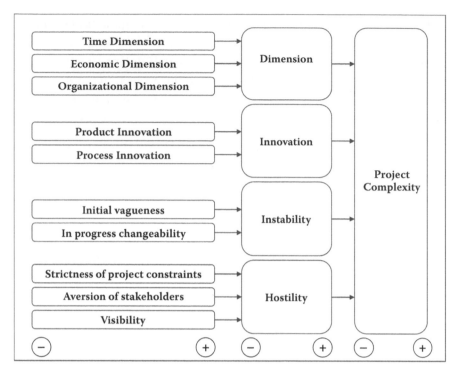

FIGURE 1.7
Criteria to determine a project's degree of complexity. (From Villa, T., *Management by Projects*, IPSOA, Milan, Italy, 2008.)

as the work progresses (instability of requirements, changes in perspective, contractual variations, etc.).

- The hostility of the context in which the project must be implemented. This variable refers to the strictness of the implementation constraints, the aversion of stakeholders, in particular those with greatest influence on the key decisions, the visibility, and therefore the expectations placed on the project.

It is clear that the larger, more innovative, unstable, and hostile the project is, the more complex it will be.

1.5.4 Project Management Strategy

When the complexity is similar, one difference is how the project is managed. The management strategy is therefore another element on which the success of the project depends.

TABLE 1.5

Project Management CSFs

1. **Project mission:** Initially clearly defined goals and directions.
2. **Top management support:** Willingness of top management to provide the necessary resources and authority/power for project success.
3. **Project schedule/plan:** A detailed specification of the individual action steps for project implementation.
4. **Client consultation:** Communication, consultation, and active listening to all impacted parties.
5. **Personnel:** Recruiting, selection, and training of the necessary personnel for the project team.
6. **Technical tasks:** Availability of the required technology and expertise to accomplish the specific action steps.
7. **Client acceptance:** The act of "selling" the final project to its ultimate intended users.
8. **Monitoring and feedback:** Timely provision of comprehensive control information at each stage in the implementation process.
9. **Communication:** The provision of an appropriate network and necessary data to all key actors in the project implementation.
10. **Troubleshooting:** Ability to handle unexpected crises and deviations from plan.

Source: Pinto, J. K., and Slevin, D. P., *Project Management Journal*, 19, 1, 1988, 67 72.

The project management strategy must obviously account for the project's degree of complexity, but it must also be built around specific critical success factors.

A critical success factor (CSF) is "a measurable factor that when present in the project environment is most conducive to the achievement of a successful project" (Wideman 2009). The CSFs are therefore those few conditions that, if present, determine much of the success of a project and, if absent, lead to most of its failure.

Table 1.5 sets out the ten CSFs to be used as starting points to establish the project management strategy (Pinto and Slevin 1988).

It is the project manager's job to assess which CSFs are particularly important for the success of the project, and thus define the relative project management strategy.

This strategy should, on the one hand, be agreed to with the project customer (usually identified with the term *project sponsor*), and on the other, it should be discussed and refined with the project management team, in order to be able to count on a course of action that is understood and shared by those who will be called upon to provide a managerial contribution critical for the success of the project.

The evaluation of which CSFs are particularly important for the success of the project is of course the responsibility of the project manager.

Nevertheless, the team members, with their specialist knowledge on certain aspects of the project, can and should contribute to the definition of the most appropriate project management strategy.

1.6 CONCLUSIONS

Projects are tools for implementing complex and innovative solutions, in all sectors and with the most diverse purposes. Today we legitimately live in a society of projects.

To be successful, a project should be understood well and just as well managed. A project is characterized by ten key characteristics: unique, targeted, limited, innovative, visible, temporary, progressive, risky, reusable, and collaborative.

The project life cycle is the set of steps that make it possible to carry out a project in a progressive and controlled way. The structure of the project life cycle (number of phases, sequence of phases, project duration) depends on its contents and on the reference sector.

At the end of each phase there should be a formal review to decide whether and how to proceed with the execution of the project.

The project life cycle (one or more) is an integral part of the product life cycle, where the purpose of the project is to create a product or service that must be produced or provided when the project is operating regularly.

Project management processes make it possible to manage the project life cycle. These processes are grouped into homogeneous groups: initiating, planning, executing, monitoring and controlling, and closing. Project management processes should be applied to each phase of the project.

Project management processes are not the phases of the project life cycle. The project is carried out in a specific contingent organizational environment, which is created in relation to the project profile. This environment is crowded with numerous, diverse, and geographically dispersed players, reflecting the interfunctional and intercompany value of the project. These players are known as stakeholders. The backbone of the project organization is represented by the project sponsor, the project manager, and the PMT. A relationship of close collaboration must be established and maintained among these three stakeholders for the entire duration of the project.

The success of a project is desired by all, and it must therefore be carefully planned and controlled. In this regard there are three aspects to examine: (1) the system of assessing the success of the project, based on different measurement perspectives, each distinct but complementary; (2) the degree of complexity associated with the project, which depends on the dimension, innovation, instability, and hostility associated with the project; and (3) the project management strategy built around the CSFs of the project, such as customer consultation, the communication system, and the management of critical situations.

See page 249 for the exercise relating to this chapter.

REFERENCES

Atkinson, R. 1999. Project management: Cost, time, and quality, two best guesses and a phenomenon, it's time to accept other success criteria. *International Journal of Project Management* 17, 6: 337–342.

Baker, B.N., D.C. Murphy, and D. Fisher. 2008. Factors affecting project success. In *Project management handbook*, ed. D.I. Cleland and W.R. King. 2nd ed. Hoboken, NJ: John Wiley & Sons.

Bellassi, W., and O.I. Tukel. 1996. A new framework for determining critical success/failure factors in projects. *International Journal of Project Management* 14, 3: 141–151.

Collyer, S., and C.M.J. Warren. 2009. Project management approaches for dynamic environments. *International Journal of Project Management* 27: 355–364.

Hillson, D. 2009. *Managing risk in projects.* Burlington, VT: Gower Publishing Company.

Hughes, M.W. 1986. Why projects fail: The effects of ignoring the obvious. *Industrial Engineering* 18: 14–18.

Lavagnon, A.I. 2009. Project success as a topic in project management journals. *Project Management Journal* 40, 4: 6–19.

Lundin, R.A., and C. Midler. 1998. Projects as arenas for renewal and learning processes. Boston: Kluwer Academic Publishers.

Maylor, H., R. Vidgen, and S. Carver. 2008. Managerial complexity in project-based operations: A grounded model and its implications for practice. *Project Management Journal* 39, 1: 15–26

Pinto, J.K., and D.P. Slevin. 1988. Project success: Definitions and measurement techniques. *Project Management Journal* 19, 1: 67–72.

Project Management Institute. 2008. *A guide to the Project Management Body of Knowledge.* 4th ed. Newtown Square, PA: Project Management Institute.

Shenhar, A.J., O. Levy, and D. Dvir. 1997. Mapping the dimensions of project success. *Project Management Journal* 28, 2: 5–13.

Vidal, L.A., and F. Marle. 2008. Understanding project complexity: Implications on project management. *Kybernetes* 37, 8: 1094–1110.

Vidal, L.A., F. Marle, and J.C. Bocquet. 2011. Measuring project complexity using the analytic hierarchy process. *International Journal of Project Management* 29, 6: 718–727.

Villa, T. 2008. *Management by projects. I progetti come leva strategica di business.* Milan: IPSOA.

Wideman, M. 2001. Total project management of complex projects. Improving performance with modern techniques. http://www.maxwideman.com/papers/performance/performance.pdf.

Wideman, M. 2009. Firsts principles in project management. Part 1. http://www.maxwideman.com/papers/first_principles/success.htm.

2

Project Followership in Action

KEYWORDS

Deliverable
Kickoff meeting
Lessons learned
Product life cycle
Project charter
Project life cycle
Project management processes
Project phase
Schedule network diagram
Work breakdown structure (WBS)
Work package (WP)

READER'S GUIDE

This chapter allows you to

- Define the meaning of widespread project management and the vital importance of the contribution of each project team member for the success of that project
- Deepen your understanding of the meaning of project followership and its distinctive features
- Assess the real benefits that can be obtained from the systematic and staunch practicing of project followership
- Examine the main actions of project followership
- Contextualize such actions in the key stages of project management

- Assess the importance of the six distinct features of project follower-ship in relation to the specific project situation to be tackled
- Analyze actual examples of project followership

2.1 TOWARD WIDESPREAD PROJECT MANAGEMENT

Why doesn't project management only concern project managers? The chapter opens with this question, which acts as a guide to the entire book.

The question mainly concerns those required to participate in a project as members of the project team. "What degree of familiarity with project management must I have, and more importantly why?"

The practice requires that each project be assigned to a project manager. The project manager, or project leader, is the key figure around which the entire project revolves and is the person formally responsible for completing the project in accordance with the objectives set in the project mandate.

The project manager is required to coordinate all the project management activities, from the start-up to closing, by way of planning and control. Project management is therefore inextricably linked to the project manager's ability to coordinate.

Coordinating the project, performing the necessary project management activities, does not mean acting alone. A project, even of limited complexity, necessarily requires a shared managerial effort that goes well beyond the personal contribution provided by the project manager.

Working on projects is by nature a transversal activity.

The project spans the performing organizations in order to build inter-functional teams based on a variety of professional expertise that differs in terms of specialization, organizational position, and culture.

This "horizontal cut" across the organization leads to the weakening, and sometimes even the undermining, of hierarchical relationships within the company; in fact, it is said that working on projects leads to a flattening of the hierarchy (Gareis 1991).

On the one hand, the project manager must act as an integrator (Crawford 2000)—thus not the *deus ex machina* of the project, but rather a wise catalyst who solicits contributions from all those who possess knowledge of the project, technology, business, and productive processes covered in the project. This is to give the project direction, adjust it as work progresses, and keep all the stakeholders informed on a regular basis.

On the other hand, members of the project team also have a responsibility to play an integrating role, avoiding the classic purely reactive attitude represented by thoughts such as: "Nobody tells me what to do and I suspect the project manager understands little about this product," "In any case the project manager is responsible for the results and will get any credit," and "For better or worse, the project will end sooner or later and I'll go back to my original department."

Nowadays, every team member should play a role that can be defined as project follower. This expression refers to the ability to follow the project actively and consciously by contributing to task completion and by achieving assigned objectives through cognitive, relational, and professional skills. Project followership does not mean challenging the project manager's authority, but neither does it mean unconditionally obeying the project manager's orders. Effective project followership is assertive, but without diminishing the role of the project manager.

Project followership therefore means proactive participation in all aspects of project work, both technical and managerial, within an individual's visibility horizon.

Glossary Note: In this book we will use the following expressions interchangeably: *project follower, project team member, team member, subject matter expert, expert, specialist, project specialist, and member of the project team.*

2.2 PROJECT FOLLOWERSHIP: A REFERENCE MODEL

Project followership is based on several different fields of study (project management, followership, shared leadership, boundary spanning, proactive behaviors). The most relevant resources are reported in the bibliography of this chapter.

Figure 2.1 presents the distinctive features of project followership.

Global vision is the ability to construct and maintain an overview of the project, broken down into existing situations and situations to work toward. Kelley (1988) maintains that an important quality of followers is to determine one's own goals within a large context and to decide what role to take at any given time. Global vision means being able to go hunting for the facts: if you do not know or understand something relating to

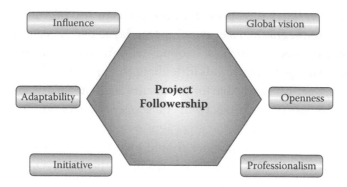

FIGURE 2.1
The distinctive features of project followership.

your work in the project, or more generally to the rationale of the project itself, ask. If you are trying to understand a problem or a situation, try to reconstruct the overall picture and find the causes; do not stop at the first clues or data and information taken for granted.

Global vision plays an important role in self-motivation. In fact, a key to motivating followers is the concept of having them realize how important their function is in a broad sense. Blanchard and Bowles (1998) relate the story of what was considered a meaningless job—dishwashing at a college cafeteria: "Dishwashing in a college cafeteria—it just doesn't get more important than that … think of the impact those students were going to have on the world. Business leaders, doctors, social scientists, world leaders, researchers. One load of unclean, bacteria-infected dishes could have wiped out a whole class. Look at it in terms of human impact…. Students arrived tired, hungry, and likely lonely. You were an important part of the chain that provided joy and nourishment…. What a wonderful gift to give another human being" (p. 33).

Openness is the ability to encourage and sustain a dialectic discussion with other members of the project team and the project manager, paying genuine attention to the viewpoints of others, with a view to achieving a common goal. Openness derives from the fact that nobody has the knowledge to solve all the problems in a project and from the interdependencies that exist among project tasks. In interdependent systems, the behavior of an individual has an impact not only on the effectiveness of that individual, but also on the effectiveness of others, including groups, teams, and the organization as a whole. The potential for an individual to contribute to effectiveness at a team or an organizational level depends on the embeddedness of his or her work role in the social context (Murphy and Jackson

1999). When the activities of a work role are independent of others, then there is a simple link between an individual's behavior and effectiveness as an employee. When the activities of a work role are interdependent with other roles, the link between behavior and effectiveness is more complex. For these reasons, exchanging ideas and asking support is fundamental in a project environment. Chaleff (1995) also claims that effective followers are cooperative and collaborative, qualities that are essential to all human progress. Try to be curious, exchange views with others, and better still, learn from them and ensure that others can learn from you.

Professionalism is the ability to assume the role and act on the basis of professional, behavioral, and ethical models considered to be of reference in an individual's field. Professionalism means:

- Having specialized knowledge on a particular subject matter. This is an essential requirement for a good follower and a typical success factor (Pinto and Slevin 1988): in order to interact "on a par" with the project manager and the other members of the project team, it is essential to provide a solid and tangible contribution of professional expertise.
- Having specialized knowledge on project management relevant for project team members. A good project follower should know what are the most important project management topics and how to apply them in order to be integrated with the other project participants.
- Ethics. Kelley (1988) suggests that on top of the most important characteristics of an effective follower may be the willingness to tell the truth. As the quantity of available information has increased exponentially, it has become imperative that followers provide truthful information. In addition, ethics is an important component of project management professional development (see the Project Management Institute (PMI) Code of Ethics and Professional Conduct (PMI 2006)).

Initiative is the ability to take action on key issues of the project even in the absence of instructions or a precise order. Initiative means being proactive: do not wait to be told what to do; if you notice project situations that need to be revised or fixed, inform others of them, and propose and, if possible, implement solutions without hesitation. Chaleff (1995), in his five unique behaviors of courageous followers, mentions: "They generate new ideas and initiate actions to improve external and internal processes. Courageous followers seek solutions and encourage others to do the same" (p. 6).

Proactive behaviors normally produce positive results (Frese and Fay 2001); however, other authors (Belschak et al. 2010) acknowledge that personal initiative (as one type of proactivity at work) does not always have positive consequences; in combination with low skills, personal initiative may often lead to negative consequences. A type of initiative is to proactively establish relationships with stakeholders external to the project team (the so-called boundary spanning behavior; see Marrone et al. 2007) in order to gain useful information, to influence the stakeholders' decisions, and to control the stakeholders' satisfaction.

Adaptability is the ability to be flexible in project contexts that are constantly changing. Workers need to be increasingly adaptable, versatile, and tolerant of uncertainty to operate effectively in these changing and varied environments (Pulakos et al. 2000). Adaptability means knowing how to change perspective: projects are inherently uncertain and become clear along the way. So you must bear in mind that a good dose of creativity, lateral thinking, and breaking patterns will be required.

Influence is the ability to get other people involved in solutions to be adopted or actions to be taken in the overall organization of the project. Influence means being assertive; while it does not mean that you have formal or hierarchical authority in the project group, sometimes results are obtained simply by influencing, collaborating, and supporting one's point of view with solid arguments. Influence is an exercise of shared leadership; in fact, "shared leadership occurs when all members of a team are fully engaged in the leadership of the team and are not hesitant to influence and guide their fellow team members in an effort to maximize the potential of the team as a whole. Simply put, shared leadership entails a simultaneous, ongoing, mutual influence process within a team that is characterized by 'serial emergence' of official as well as unofficial leaders. In this sense, shared leadership can be considered a manifestation of fully developed empowerment in teams" (Pearce 2004, p. 48). Finally, Bjugstad et al. (2006, p. 310) by commenting on Kelley (1992) define exemplary followers as "willing to question leadership. This type of follower is critical to organizational success. Exemplary followers know how to work well with other cohorts and present themselves consistently to all who come into contact with them."

Each member of the project team will be required to apply this model of followership systematically on the different occasions the project presents.

To summarize, if you find yourself participating in a project as a project team member, remember that you are required to provide a twofold contribution to the "common cause":

- First, it is obviously a "specialized" contribution as an expert in a particular subject addressed by the project (applicative, technological, organizational, legal, business, etc.). This first type of contribution aims to ensure that planned project activities are carried out on an informed basis, with skill and strict content so as to produce the expected output quality.
- Added to this is another type of more "managerial" contribution. This second type of contribution aims to ensure that the project is planned in detail, executed in line with the plans, that its inevitable development is monitored with respect to the original plans, and finally, that it is closed in a manner beneficial to the organization and at the most appropriate time. You will therefore be required to provide, in some key stages of the project, assessments, estimates, data, and information essential for good project management. For instance, think of the key contribution that experts can and must provide in defining the activities to be performed, estimating the timing and costs of activities, identifying the project risks, analyzing deviations from the initial plans, evaluating change requests, and producing the lessons learned from the project.

2.3 PROJECT FOLLOWERSHIP ACTIONS

Project followership, in order to be such, must be translated into project management actions during the key stages of managing the project. This is the only way the principles of project followership can receive a tangible response in the field.

Project followership should be firmly linked to project management processes. In fact, project followership actions are nothing more than project management activities for the use and consumption of project team members.

A good solution is to connect the main project followership actions to each project management processes group (PMI 2008), as indicated in Table 2.1.

2.3.1 Project Followership during Project Initiation

The start-up marks the story of the entire project. The high-level profile of the project is in fact defined during initiation, through a document known

TABLE 2.1

The Main Project Followership Actions in Project Management Processes

Project Management Process Group	Project Followership Actions
Initiating	Share the project mandate (kickoff meeting)
Planning	Collect or formalize requirements
	Develop the WBS
	Specify the characteristics of the individual WP each team member is responsible for
	Contribute to the definition of the logical relations between the different project tasks
	Identify, analyze, and respond to project risks
	Develop make-or-buy assessments
	Describe the profile of the products/services to procure externally
Executing—monitoring and controlling	Coordinate the work of internal specialists and external suppliers
	Assess execution problems and suggest their solutions
	Circulate information on the execution of the project
	Report the actual values for both time and cost of each individual WP
	Assess development during the project progress reviews
	Assess the change requests to the initial plan
	Provide advice on replanning the project
	Assess the compliance of project deliverables
	Supervise the acceptance of deliverables by the customer
Closing	Support the delivery stage of the project
	Describe the project experiences (lessons learned)

as the project charter. The project charter is first officially approved during initiation and is then presented to the stakeholders.

In jargon we talk about the kickoff meeting, meaning a meeting (or series of meetings) aimed at kick-starting the project. Specifically, the kickoff is intended to inform and align the stakeholders most interested in the project. The project management team (PMT) is undoubtedly one of them.

As previously pointed out several times, the success of the project is significantly influenced by the managerial contribution provided by the PMT as a whole. The initiation of the project is crucial in this regard. The PMT is in fact formed during initiation and reinforced through the mandate.

We might ask what actual contribution individual members of the PMT, as project followers, can honestly provide during the project initiation. The confusion comes from the fact that the "important decisions" have already been made: whether to carry out the project or not; if yes, with what objectives, with respect to what constraints, with what implementation logic. The answer is that the project team member can and must provide an original contribution during the project initiation.

The project team member, even when facing a preestablished scenario, must in fact perform a very important action, namely, understanding and sharing the mandate (see Section 2.2). The precise understanding and sharing of the mandate is without a doubt a necessary step in order for the PMT to operate well. It is one thing to passively adapt to the project, as decided upon earlier in the process, and another to ask questions and demand answers on the origin of the project, its profile, and the organizational and business implications arising from it. Essentially, it means being an active part of the kickoff meeting.

2.3.2 Project Followership during Project Planning

Planning represents the project's script. In fact, during planning the project mandate is transformed into a plan that can be executed. As stated in almost every book on project management, the PMT is the author of this fundamental step.

Project planning envisages members of the PMT working side by side, directed by the project manager. Planning involves a series of face-to-face meetings and using means for remote contact, in order to define the different elements representing the project plan.

The stakeholders' needs are translated into project requirements that, in turn, must be broken down into the project's work structure, known as the work breakdown structure (WBS). An accountable person from within the PMT should be appointed for each element of the WBS, called work package (WP) in jargon, and schedule and cost estimates should be documented that are as reliable as possible and shared. The sequence the project will be carried out in, the so-called project schedule network diagram, should also be agreed on, and the logical dependencies between the different activities clearly defined. The same care should be taken to identify the project risks, select the priority risks, and define the actions to respond to these risks. It should also be established which parts of the project will be done in-house (make) and which parts will be procured from outside (buy), providing details of their contents and enlisting specific suppliers for their implementation.

Is it possible to plan the project without the contribution of experts in the different subject matters covered? The answer is obviously no! Method and expertise are the basic ingredients of successful planning. The mere application of planning methods, in the absence of solid specialized expertise, represents a content-poor work plan. Vice versa, proven but poorly organized and even less targeted skills lead to a waste of resources and poor quality results.

The real capacity of the PMT to implement widespread project management is unequivocally measured in project planning. Each project follower is required to provide a twofold contribution: specialized expertise on the one hand, and project management method on the other.

2.3.3 Project Followership during Project Execution and Control

The execution is the project's testing ground. The planned aspects will meet, come up against, and collide with the reality of the facts.

The project management plan is implemented by the PMT, effectively involving all the people forming part of the project team. Most of the resources allocated to the project, in order to carry out the tasks provided for in the plan, are used during execution.

Monitoring and control activities are also performed at the same time as the execution. Execution and control are two sides of the same coin. Project execution results feed the control system, which in turn determines an initial review of the plan, with the consequent impact on the activities to be completed.

The PMT is at the heart of project execution and control. The members of the PMT, led by the project manager, coordinate the execution of different project strands, directly perform some of the set tasks, and play a key role in controlling the project. Execution and control feed on project followership.

As regards execution, individual members of the PMT, as project followers, are required to distribute the work among the stakeholders interested in their project strand, circulate the necessary information, and intervene in the event of problems, proposing and implementing solutions.

As regards control, project team members are required to actively contribute to the project progress report, in terms of collecting data and information on what has been accomplished, assessing the situation to date, formulating estimates to complete, and developing corrective actions, where necessary.

The management of change requests to the initial plan is another area in which project followership is exercised. Change requests are numerous and unfortunately often ambiguous. These requests should be systematically collected, categorized, assessed, and approved/rejected. In any case, the applicant should be informed of the final decision, complete with explanations on the matter. The specialist and managerial skill of the project team member makes a difference in how change requests are managed.

In jargon project results are called deliverables. Deliverables should be assessed in terms of their compliance with the initial plan specifications; they should then be presented to the customer and formally accepted. The assessment, presentation, and acceptance of deliverables require the indispensable contribution of project specialists, as "guardians" of the value of the deliverables in the overall economy of the project.

2.3.4 Project Followership during the Project Closure

Project closure confirms the outcome of the project, be it negative or positive. During closing, activities and contracts are formally interrupted and stock is taken of what has been done and produced.

The project follower's contribution during closing is twofold: to support the transition into operation of the solution implemented by the project and to contribute to the production of lessons learned.

The project is a temporary initiative, and its results should be incorporated within the organizations that participated in it. The project manager and PMT positions are temporary, as is the project. The project achievements are handed over to specific permanent roles in the organizations involved. For instance, think of the need to enable the network of distributors to sell the new product created by the project. In many cases this step is costly, wasteful, and produces conflict.

As regards the mandate received, the project manager and members of the PMT typically assume an attitude clearly focused on deliverables: what counts is producing deliverables that conform with the specifications indicated in the project mandate. Once the mandate has been fulfilled, the project is finished and, after due consideration, the promised rewards can be expected. This is a good thing, but what of the solution implemented by the project: Will it be used? If yes, what will the operating costs be? Will it generate the expected benefits? Will it improve the client's business? Will it justify the investment?

Modern project management practices argue that the PMT cannot fail to respond. The change in perspective is significant: from a deliverable-oriented approach to a business-oriented approach. It follows that the project team member must facilitate the handover, supporting the recipients of the solution provided by the project. In other words, the project team member must be familiar with the context of use, understand its distinct features and the priorities, operating in sync with it.

The other area requiring project followership during closing is the production of lessons learned. Experiences gained in the performance of the project should be revisited, distilled, and modeled in order to produce a condensed set of rules, suggestions, and ideas for the future, known as lessons learned. Without the experts, the production of lessons learned is practically impossible. The valuable experience of the project is effectively thrown away. The project team member is required to actively contribute to the production of lessons learned: he or she must bring his or her wealth of project experiences to the PMT and know how to compare his or hers with the experiences of others, in order to incorporate the most valuable elements in the project lessons learned.

2.3.5 Importance of the Distinctive Features of Project Followership

Project followership is characterized by six distinctive features, explained in Section 2.2. These features highlight the skills the project team member must have and know how to bring into play.

All the features are important, but not always to the same extent. For instance, during project start-up the global vision is without doubt the most important, while during project execution adaptability is essential. This means the importance of a project followership feature varies depending on at which point in the project it must be applied.

Table 2.2 summarizes the degree of importance of each distinctive feature of project followership in the key stages of project management.

The figure is useful to guide the reader in the application of project followership: What is most important at any given time and what is less important? "What features should I concentrate my energies on if I find myself in a particular project situation?"

During project initiation the most required project followership trait is global vision. It could not be otherwise. In project initiation it is essential to fully understand the context in which the project started and in which the results must be placed. Global vision not only concerns the project manager, but involves all members of the PMT. Project followership is only effective if the project follower has embraced the so-called big picture of the project. To a lesser extent, but in any case significant, other distinctive features of project followership are also called for, namely, openness

TABLE 2.2

Importance of the Distinctive Features of Project Followership in Managing the Project

Project Followership Feature	Initiating	Planning	Executing— Monitoring and Controlling	Closing
Global vision	•••	••	•	••
Openness	••	•••	••	•••
Professionalism	•	•••	••	••
Initiative	•	••	•••	•
Adaptability	•	••	•••	•
Influence	••	•••	••	•

Note: The highest importance is represented with the symbol •••, while the symbol •
   indicates the lowest importance.
Source: Elaboration of the authors.

and influence. As regards openness, the project specialist's ability to spark a dialectic exchange with the project manager and the other members of the PMT, who will be the adventure companions during the project, is highlighted. The plot has already been defined, but the project's punctuation still has to be written. Influence during the project initiation means asking basic questions and soliciting the answers from the project manager and the PMT. If you are not convinced about an important aspect of the project, you should express your concerns and assertively argue your point of view. Taking a determined position may pay off, even in the early stages of the project, resulting in the clarification of issues that have been dealt with too broadly.

Below is a case of project followership focused on the global vision and referred to the project initiation.

FROM A PARTIAL VISION TO A GLOBAL VISION

During the first meeting of the ohm project, concerning the development of a new technology for the electric propulsion of cars, the project manager went on about the positive environmental impact aspects resulting from the project. Given that the ohm project, compared to other solutions on the market, also brought other benefits, a participant of the project team asked to speak: "Our solution can certainly bring huge environmental benefits. However, we must not forget the significant reduction in weight, which will provide electric cars with a more agile and satisfying driving performance, as well as lower maintenance costs. Finally, our solution has a much less drastic impact on planning criteria for car manufacturers compared to combustion engine propulsion. In a period of strong focus on costs, this is a highly relevant issue for car manufacturers, who are the first clients of our project."

During planning other traits become more important: openness, professionalism, and influence. Planning thrives on heated debate between members of the PMT. Openness and influence are the fuel in this debate. These are, in fact, the essential ingredients to package a project plan that is consistent in all parts and shared by those who must then implement it. Planning cannot exist on debate alone, but it also requires professionalism. For instance, specialized evaluations on schedule and cost estimates must be justified by solid professional arguments based on standards and models of reference. Personal intuition unsupported by proven practices and experiences won't solve any problems. It might even be counterproductive, radicalizing positions unsupported by facts. It should also be pointed out that project planning is a watershed moment for the PMT: the project plan is in fact the first collective result produced independently by the PMT.

Below are another three cases of project followership during project planning. The first refers to openness, the second to modeling, and the third to influence.

A SOMEWHAT CLOSED OPENNESS

It was the first time the company SmartTechy had faced an interdivisional project that involved practically all the company divisions. Usually each division developed its own projects independently. As a company decision, some products of the various divisions were also competing on the market, in order to encourage continuous improvement. During a project planning meeting it became clear there was a need for strong interdependence between two divisions on some project activities. To coordinate themselves better, the project manager asked the divisions to provide more detailed schedules than the high-level ones that had been provided up to that point. One participant gave an absolutely unexpected response: "I think collaboration is essential, but I'd rather sell the information to another company than give it to the other division. They mustn't know how long we take to complete that activity; otherwise, they'd be able to understand if they are competitive or not." Perhaps it is superfluous to add that this behavior was swiftly chastised and the team member taken off the project.

A NOT ENTIRELY PERFECT MODEL

During the project development, the project manager asked a team member to estimate the duration of an activity he was in charge of. The task was to "install and configure 200 new PCs in the three company locations." The response was immediate: "Well, it'll take at least 30 working days." The project manager was amazed but also unhappy with the answer, and replied: "Look, I understand you're a professional in your sector, but how can you give such a quick estimate without knowing where the locations are and, above all, what type of applications will be installed during the initial configuration." The team member, not having a valid response, said in a subdued tone: "I based it on my experience."

SORRY, BUT IF …

The project plan is practically complete. The project team is satisfied with the work performed. It involves a series of four theatrical performances to be held outdoors on midsummer evenings in little-known historical locations in the province—one performance in each location. It is the first time an initiative of this kind has taken place. During planning the project team rightly considered the possible risks (What if it rains? What if few people attend? What if the main actor gets sick? What if the light system breaks? etc.) and defined the response actions. "For each threat we have the answer ready," the project manager said proudly. Everyone agreed except for the youngest and least experienced team member, who said: "But what if more people come than we have seats for?" "We haven't thought of that;

we'll be lucky if more than 500 people attend each evening, it's still a local event and there are no famous names," answered the project manager. The team member went on: "OK, but if more people than expected do turn up, what kind of problems are we going to face? Crowds, lines, traffic jams, complaints, security, etc." The insistence was silenced: "It would be great to think about this public success, but it's pure fantasy. We'll deal with it at the time!" The project plan was approved without taking into consideration the possibility feared by the young team member. The first performance, which was held in a small ancient courtyard in the countryside, was attended by over 1000 people—good weather in conjunction with a food and wine fair held in the vicinity, and the fact that the week before a tourism magazine had published an article on the most beautiful courtyards in the countryside, including the one in question, all played their parts. In a nutshell, crowds, shoving, police intervention, panicked actors, and so on. "Damn it, if only they had listened to me," the young team member thought to himself. "Damn it, if only you had insisted they listen to you more," we add.

The execution and control of the project emphasize professionalism, initiative, and adaptability. The project plan formulated during planning never corresponds to the reality of the situation. It may seem like a paradox, but it isn't. Change as the work progresses is a physiological fact for a project. Initiative and adaptability are therefore the testing ground of project followership during the course of the project. The project team member is regularly faced with situations that are different from those planned, with contingent problems that should be swiftly analyzed and resolved, with changes in perspective caused by the myriad competing interests. The project team member is faced with three alternatives: passively accept the changes and the unexpected events, retreat behind the starting lines, or intelligently adapt to the change. The last alternative is obviously the right one and should be pursued with great conviction. Adaptability refers to the ability to assess changes in project priorities and exploit them for the benefit of the project, or at least to find solutions that reduce the negative effects as much as possible. Initiative means taking action even in the absence of specific instructions, where waiting would make the situation worse. Initiative means the capacity to make proposals and take action in the interest of the project. The drive for personal initiative turns out to be truly effective during execution, provided that at the start the PMT shared a common vision of the project and was able to dialectically discuss the drafting of the project plan. Otherwise, personal initiative during the execution of the project becomes sterile and further confuses an already confused project. Finally, professionalism is fundamental during execution and control since executing and controlling a project means also applying the technical knowledge that a person has.

Below are two more cases of project followership, referring to the execution and control of the project. The first concerns adaptability, and the second initiative.

ADAPTABILITY YES, BUT FOR OTHERS

The company Laby had succeeded in becoming the supplier of a prestigious multinational company that, in brand and size, differed greatly from Laby's usual clients, which were typically small. During the later stages of the project to develop the intranet portal for the sales force, the new client informed Laby's project manager of its dissatisfaction with some activities; in particular, the user support documentation was not considered adequate to clearly explain the system features. The project manager and the project sponsor of Laby, analyzing the situation, decided that the client was right to be dissatisfied. The project manager then spoke with the team member responsible for the system documentation, who replied: "Our clients are always satisfied with the documentation we provide. It's hardly our fault if this client has difficulty understanding. At most they'll take a little longer to understand the system, but then they'll adapt. Everybody can adapt. You just have to be willing."

THE WEAK INITIATIVE

Again, the company Laby, during the same project to implement the intranet portal for the sales force, noticed that the testing activities would have been more complex than those planned. A solution therefore needed to be found because, for such a strategic client, it was imperative to respect the end date agreed. So a meeting was called to evaluate how to proceed, and in the end it was decided to pull in some outside consultants to work alongside the internal resources for the testing activities. During the meeting many people said they had contacts in this area. After four days a second meeting was organized to assess the different alternatives and then choose the consultancy firm. In practice this was not necessary: only one person had taken the trouble to speak to his or her contact; the others had not done anything. Given the emergency, it was decided to "choose" the firm suggested, not knowing, however, if the price was fair or if other firms might have better references.

The project closure, finally, focuses on openness as the dominant feature of project followership. During the project closure the PMT is called upon to assess the progress and outcome of the project and produce the lessons learned. Assessing the project from a constructive point of view means openly discussing things that went well and things that went badly. Learning from the project means a certain amount of mutual intrusion based on the sharing of data, information, and judgments about facts and not people. Again, during closure, the global vision and professionalism are also important. The project experience must in fact be distilled and put into a format that can be reused from a company point of view. The global vision makes it possible to concentrate on matters that count, which the company can mostly reuse, while professionalism adds the right level of terminological and content-based rigor to documents on the lessons learned. Moreover, note that the project closure must also assess the satisfaction level of stakeholders, customers *in primis*. A good level of openness on the part of the PMT makes it possible to gain a deeper understanding and share these evaluations with the stakeholders.

Below is a last case of project followership during project closure. The case refers to openness.

PRIVATE LESSONS LEARNED

In the end the Laby project had a fairly positive closing. The widespread feeling was that some things had been done very well, while others could be greatly improved. For a better understanding of the situation and, above all, to prepare for other projects of similar complexity, the project manager organized a lessons learned meeting, during which participants were asked to explain the good practices adopted and propose improvement actions for critical areas. Knowing that critical areas always create tensions, the project manager decided to start with the strengths and asked a team member who had performed extraordinarily in his tasks to share the working methods used. The response lacked openness: "I'd be crazy to explain how I did it, then everybody would be able to match me. If they want to learn, they should make their own efforts. I struggled hard to acquire the skills that led me to achieve these performance levels, and I don't see why I should share them with others without receiving anything in return."

2.4 CONCLUSIONS

Modern project management practices highlight the importance of the PMT as a center of excellence of project management. The PMT is required to exercise a widespread and consistent project management approach, guided by the wise direction of the project manager. This managerial capacity distributed in the project coordination team takes the name *project followership*. Each member of the PMT is required to provide a twofold contribution: specific expertise in his or her subject area and managerial skill in the key stages of the project. Project followership means proactive participation in all aspects of the project work, both technical and managerial, within an individual's visibility horizon.

There are six distinctive features of project followership: global vision, openness, professionalism, initiative, adaptability, and influence.

Project followership is divided into a series of concrete actions, with reference to the different project management process groups. Project followership actions are nothing more than project management activities for the use and consumption of project team members.

Each member of the PMT is expressly required to endorse the typical actions of project followership and implement them, taking into account the specific project situation he or she is facing.

Project sponsorship actions assume that the project team member knows how to implement the six distinctive features of project followership.

For example, during project initiation, and in particular in kickoff meetings, the project team member must demonstrate a clear global vision.

The importance of each feature varies depending on what stage the project is at. For example, during planning the personal influence that the project follower knows how to exert over the project manager and the other members of the PMT is essential, while during execution personal initiative and adaptability gain precedence.

The systematic implementation of the skills and actions of project followership is a clear measure of the degree of managerial maturity possessed and acted on by individual members of the PMT.

REFERENCES

Bjugstad, R., E.C. Thach, K.J. Thompson, and A. Morris. 2006. A fresh look at followership: A model for matching followership and leadership styles. Institute of Behavioral and Applied Management.

Blanchard, K., and S. Bowles. 1998. *Gung ho! Turn on the people in any organization*. Sydney: HarperCollins.

Chaleff, I. 1995. *The courageous follower: Standing up to and for our leaders*. San Francisco: Berrett-Koehler Publishers.

Crawford, L. 2000. Profiling the competent project manager. Presented at Proceedings of PMI Research Conference: Project Management Research at the Turn of the Millennium.

Belschak, F.D., D.N. Den Hartog, and D. Fay. 2010. Exploring positive, negative and context-dependent aspects of proactive behaviours at work. *Journal of Occupational and Organizational Psychology* 83, 2: 267–273.

Frese, M., and D. Fay. 2001. Personal initiative: An active performance concept for work in the 21st century. In *Research in organizational behavior*, ed. B.M. Staw and R.L. Sutton, 133–187. Vol. 23. Stamford, CT: JAI Press.

Gareis, R. 1991. Management by projects: The management strategy of the 'new' project-oriented company. *International Journal of Project Management* 9, 2: 71–76.

Kelley, R.E. 1988. In praise of followers. *Harvard Business Review* 66, 6: 142–148.

Kelley, R.E. 1992. *The power of followership*. New York: Doubleday.

Marrone, J.A., P.E. Tesluk, and J.B. Carson. 2007. A multilevel investigation of antecedents and consequences of team member boundary-spanning behavior. *Academy of Management Journal* 50, 6:1423–1439.

Murphy, P.R., and S.E. Jackson. 1999. Managing work-role performance: Challenges for 21st century organizations and employees. In *The changing nature of work performance*, ed. D.R. Ilgen and E.D. Pulakos, 325–365. San Francisco: Jossey-Bass.

Pearce, C.L. 2004. The future of leadership: Combining vertical and shared leadership to transform knowledge work. *Academy of Management Executive* 18, 1: 47–57.

Pinto, J.K., and D.P. Slevin. 1988. Project success: Definitions and measurement techniques. *Project Management Journal* 19, 1: 67–72.

Project Management Institute. 2006. *PMI's code of ethics and professional conduct*. Newtown Square, PA: Project Management Institute. http://www.pmi.org/en/About-Us/Ethics/~/media/PDF/Ethics/ap_pmicodeofethics.ashx.

Project Management Institute. 2008. *A guide to the Project Management Body of Knowledge*. 4th ed. Newtown Square, PA: Project Management Institute.

Pulakos, E.D., S. Arad, M.A. Donovan, and K.E. Plamondon. 2000. Adaptability in the workplace: Development of a taxonomy of adaptive performance. *Journal of Applied Psychology* 85, 4: 612–624.

RECOMMENDED READINGS

Conger, J.A., and R.N. Kanungo. 1988. The empowerment process: Integrating theory and practice. *Academy of Management Review* 13, 3: 471–483.

Ford, R.C., and M.D. Fottler. 1995. Empowerment: A matter of degree. *Academy of Management Executive* 9, 3: 21–32.

Kirkman, B.L., and B. Rosen. 1999. Beyond self-management: Antecedents and consequences of team empowerment. *Academy of Management Journal* 42, 1: 58–75.

Manz, C.C., and C.P. Neck. 2004. *Mastering self-leadership: Empowering yourself for personal excellence*. 3rd ed. Englewood Cliffs, NJ: Prentice-Hall.

May, D.R., and B.L. Flannery. 1999. Cutting waste with employee involvement teams. *Business Horizons*, 38: 28–39.

Pearce, C.L., and J.A. Conger, eds. 2003. *Shared leadership: Reframing the hows and whys of leadership*. Thousand Oaks, CA: Sage Publications.

Pearce, C.P., and H.P. Sims Jr. 2002. Vertical versus shared leadership as predictors of the effectiveness of change management teams: An examination of aversive, directive, transactional, transformational, and empowering leader behaviors. *Group Dynamics: Theory, Research, and Practice* 6, 2: 172–197.

Section II

Project Followership during Project Initiation

3

Kickoff Meeting

KEYWORDS

Constraints
Distribution of information
Meeting
Organization of the project
Project charter
Project presentation
Requirements
Sharing

READER'S GUIDE

This chapter is for people who

- Often find the project kickoff meeting is of little use or even a waste of time
- Find themselves working on a project as if they were in a closed box; someone tells them what work needs to be done, but they don't have much interaction with the world around them
- Find it difficult to understand the strategic value of the project in the context of company objectives
- Are plagued by doubts and uncertainties that they cannot dissipate because their position does not allow direct contact with the sponsor or client and no one can stand in for them
- Do not feel they belong to a team and are not sufficiently involved

---

3.1 WHY THE KICKOFF?

What is the best way to start a project? The list, from commitment at the top to the collecting of requirements at the bottom, may be long, but the element that most characterizes a good beginning to a project is the meeting that marks its start. This meeting is generally known as the kickoff meeting.

Ideally, a kickoff meeting is a workshop type meeting in which the principal stakeholders and participants in the project are briefed on the goals and objectives of the project, how it will be organized, etc., and who are then able to contribute to its planning, assignment of responsibilities, target dates, etc. (Wideman 1998–2001).

The kickoff meeting is one the most used project management tools in organizations with both low and high project management maturity (Besner and Hobbs 2004).

One of the main aims of the meeting is to formally notify the stakeholders of the project start-up, and at the same time check that everyone has understood their role and relative responsibilities. It is also likely to be one of the few occasions the stakeholders have the opportunity to meet each other, and this is why team members should take full advantage of it, to get to know the main stakeholders and their expectations and strategies (see Section 2.2 on global vision). Unfortunately, it is not hard to find team members who, not being sufficiently aware, perceive this meeting as an unnecessary element that "steals" time and adds nothing to the management of the project. Team members that have the opportunity of being involved from the outset, being able to play an active part, should recognize the kickoff meeting as a unique occasion that, if managed well, can provide the answers to many questions and help to spread the sense of belonging and involvement.

3.1.1 Kickoff Objectives

Just like the project that must be presented, the meeting must also have its objectives that will serve to measure its success:

- Officially communicate the start of the project.
- Introduce the stakeholders.
- Present the organizational structure of the project so that the hierarchical and functional relationships within it are clear.

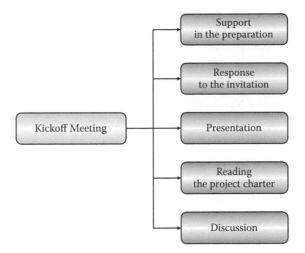

FIGURE 3.1
Structure of a kickoff meeting from a project team member's point of view.

- Present the project objectives and constraints. The main objectives are generally known before the members of the project team have been identified, but the objectives are clarified, completed, and quantified with their collaboration.
- Explain/discuss the most important aspects of the project.
- Involve and obtain the commitment of the major stakeholders, as only through their proper involvement it is possible to dissipate or mitigate many of the elements that undermine the success of the project, such as incomprehension, tensions, and misunderstandings.

Figure 3.1 presents a structure of a kickoff meeting from a team member's point of view. It will be explained in detail throughout the following paragraphs.

3.1.2 Support in Preparing the Kickoff

In general, preparing the kickoff meeting is the project manager's responsibility. In any case, team members can make valid contributions so that the preparatory activities can pave the way for a successful meeting. Contributions can be in the form of

- The collection and distribution of the necessary documentation
- Help in defining the list of people who should be invited to the meeting
- Collaboration to define the agenda

MISSING STAKEHOLDERS

The project manager, having just been hired by the company, set the date of the kickoff for the presentation of the new manufacturing improvement project. After opening the meeting successfully, with a well-defined agenda, he went on to present the project. Having finished the highly linear presentation, the project manager asked to discuss solutions to improve the performance of some pieces of machinery and their speed. This question, however, hit a brick wall, as one project team member pointed out that all the pieces of machinery had been designed and manufactured by outside suppliers, and therefore only they had the knowledge to answer that question. Unfortunately, the project manager was not aware of this and had not bothered to discuss it with anyone before the kickoff meeting. Many of the team members, however, were aware of this information.

- Analysis of the documentation so that comments can be relevant and enable those who did not have a good grasp of the topics to gain a better understanding of the project scope
- Supporting the project manager and the sponsor in the presentation of the project and its organizational aspects

The project manager does not always require help in preparing the kickoff meeting, but when this happens, it is an excellent opportunity to improve one's knowledge of the project and provide useful skills to improve its subsequent management.

3.1.3 Response to the Invitation and Receiving the Information

As in all meetings, much attention must be given to organizational and content-related aspects in order to obtain real benefits; it should therefore be planned well in advance so that all those required to participate will be available. Sometimes the date of the kickoff meeting is so close to when it was called that people already have prior engagements. In this case, it is a good idea for the project team member to clearly inform the project manager that the lack of participation is due to prior engagements that cannot be shifted as there is too little time between when the meeting was called and the kickoff date. Even in the case of possible partial participation, i.e., not for the entire kickoff meeting, it is a good idea to inform the project manager of the situation so that the project manager can change the order of the topics to be discussed so as to enable good participation.

There are no standard rules on the duration of a project kickoff meeting; the project team member may be asked for a commitment of one hour for fairly simple projects up to one or two days for highly complex projects.

To make the kickoff effective, the project documentation must be made available and sent out before the meeting so that everyone has a chance to consult it and express any doubts or uncertainties during the meeting.

All the team members must conduct a detailed analysis of the information they are sent, as they will only be able to ask relevant questions in order to clarify obscure points if they have understood it well. Participants also have the right/duty to ask the project manager for additional information before the kickoff meeting if the invitation does not provide enough information on their role in the meeting, the topics that will be discussed, and the contributions that may be provided.

All the team members are obliged to participate in these meetings because, as we shall see in more detail later, they will acquire information useful to understand the role that they must play within the organization of the project, its requirements, and its structure.

However, poor sensitivity and a lack of strategic vision on the part of companies must be recorded, as these opportunities for sharing are still uncommon, and without such organizational maturity team members will always have difficulty attaining a clear vision of the project.

Not participating in kickoff meetings damages both the project and those involved. Damage to the project comes from missing the opportunity to take in information that might be of interest to the different stakeholders, with the subsequent poor decision making or forming of erroneous expectations. As we saw in Chapter 2, the more decisions or changes are delayed, the more costly they are to implement, and it is therefore important to have valuable information as soon as possible.

Damage to those involved comes from two factors:

- The late communication of important information may create negative reactions in the other stakeholders, such as: "Seeing as you knew all these things, why didn't you bother to inform us of them immediately rather than afterwards?"

- There may be more difficulty in creating good contacts with the other stakeholders, contacts that may be useful as the project progresses. The kickoff meeting, if well managed, is in fact a highly social occasion, and not being there may make it more difficult to integrate into the work team. This aspect is much more important when there are people who do not know each other.

In addition to stressing the importance of attending, also note that it is appropriate to suggest to the project manager the participation of other colleagues who may be able to provide a valid contribution. In fact, it often happens that the project manager, not being completely clear on the terms of the problem, does not invite individuals whose presence would be useful due to a lack of knowledge of their skills.

3.1.4 Presentation of the Stakeholders and the Organization of the Project

In order that a project can be successful, it is important to remember that it is not comprised of a series of individuals, but of a team, and a team that must operate as such.

The project team, the definition of responsibilities, and the planning and control system represent the conceptual triad of project management, which distinguishes project management from other forms of company management.

A very common practice, in projects characterized by team members who do not know each other or collaborate occasionally, is mutual introduction. The introduction is not only a moment of politeness, but it is useful for all stakeholders involved, allowing them to understand each other's characteristics and expectations for the project.

A typical introduction should cover the following points:

- The role held in the company
- Seniority
- Main expertise
- Personal expectations about the project, if the information sent out with the invitation made it possible to understand the project objectives

A project has a greater chance of success if a good team is created. Creating the team is certainly the project manager's job, but it is not just

THE PARTICIPANTS AS THE MAIN CHARACTERS

The company WorldNet decided to launch a new project that entailed the involvement of people from all the offices located on the five continents.

In consideration of the fact that the kickoff is the first time all the stakeholders have the opportunity to meet each other, the project manager decided that in order to avoid future possible conflicts between team members, the best thing was to ask, during the introduction of the participants, for an explanation of the unique characteristics of their cultures so that everyone knew how to behave without offending others.

up to him or her. In fact, it is possible to be a team because there is a desire to be a team. The project manager is an important facilitator, but if the team members do not want to collaborate, it will be an uphill road. A good team also adopts rules and mechanisms that facilitate its cohesion. The right moment to define and share them is during the kickoff meeting.

The project team members' task will be to collaborate with the project manager, so that the team can be formed and is collaborative, through a discussion of and the sharing of general work rules. It must support the project manager in identifying behaviors that differ from what should be expected and collaborate in the management of critical situations that may exist between one or more team members due to work conflicts and differences in character and opinions.

Only through understanding and harmony between the members of the project team it is possible to create team spirit.

3.1.5 Reading the Project Charter

A highly pragmatic and effective way to present and summarize the key information of the project is through the project charter, a preparatory and central aspect of the kickoff meeting. Preparatory because the project could not exist without this document, and central because it contains the essential elements of the project.

Team members who are not familiar with the terminology and project documents thus come into contact with one of the most important documents of the entire project. The project charter formally authorizes the project and gives the project manager the necessary authority to manage it.

So that the project team participant has a good understanding of its characteristics and importance, we shall provide a brief overview of it:

- The project charter is written by the project manager and the sponsor, but is issued under the responsibility of the latter. It is therefore the sponsor who assigns the full powers to manage the project to the project manager.
- It must contain the following information:
  - Requirements expressed by the sponsor and by the first project stakeholders, which must meet their needs, demands, and expectations. It is not uncommon for some information relating to the requirements to derive also from the opinions or ideas expressed by team members.
  - A high-level description of the project, commercial requirements, and reasons the project is being undertaken.
  - Assumptions and constraints of organizational, environmental, or external nature.
  - The main risks the project may face based on an initial analysis conducted by the sponsor and the project manager.
  - The budget available to the project and the date by which it should be accomplished.

3.1.6 Discussion of the Project

While the project manager must explain the project's basic characteristics, team members are required to play a particular role in order that the meeting is successful. They must in fact collect as much information as possible through the questions that arise from the analysis of the documentation previously sent out and from the presentations they took part in. The purpose of these questions is to obtain as much information as possible in order to successfully begin the activities they are responsible for. Typical questions include the following:

- Will the project be part of a more complex program?
- What priority should this project have in my agenda?
- Is the project charter definitive or is there a certain margin of flexibility?

- Has a description of the requirements been obtained from the needs analysis?
- Is the project team final or will there be changes?
- Are there specific project constraints?
- Have solutions already been predefined/imposed by third parties?
- Can the team work in a single location?
- Will part of the work be entrusted to external suppliers?
- Have the external suppliers already been identified?
- Are there privacy or security requirements?

3.2 PROJECT FOLLOWERSHIP ACTIONS FOR THE KICKOFF MEETING

- Contribute to the planning and organization of the kickoff meeting.
- Attend the kickoff meeting.
- Read the documentation sent out.
- Request missing information, if deemed important.
- Provide the information requested.
- Actively participate, proposing solutions and asking questions.
- Contribute to the creation of a positive and collaborative atmosphere.

3.3 CONCLUSIONS

Too many people sometimes consider the kickoff meeting to be a complete waste of time, but it contains all the characteristics for the success of the project, in which the key role is held by the sponsor, the project manager, and the team members.

It is the occasion (and perhaps the only occasion) on which the sponsor describes the project, its limits, and its budget, and it also provides an opportunity to debate its contents in order to clarify and understand them. Without this opportunity to share the project, it may experience heavy delays during the planning phase.

The meeting must be prepared and managed and must see the active participation of team members, who must read the documentation sent out and produce that requested, actively discuss its contents, and contribute to the creation of a harmonious atmosphere so that the project starts with a high probability of success.

See page 250 for the exercise relating to this chapter.

REFERENCES

Besner, C., and B. Hobbs. 2004. An empirical investigation of project management practice: In reality, which tools do practitioners use? Presented at Proceedings of the 3rd PMI Research Conference, London.

Wideman, M. 1998–2001. Comparative glossary of project management terms v3.1. http:// maxwideman.com/pmglossary/.

RECOMMENDED READINGS

Egeland, B. 2013. How to successfully kick-off the project engagement. March 2. http://www. projectsmart.co.uk/how-to-successfully-kick-off-the-project-engagement.html.

Henkel, S. 2007. *Successful meetings: How to plan, prepare, and execute top-notch business meetings.* Ocala, FL: Atlantic Publishing Group.

Lencioni, P. 2004. *Death by meeting: A leadership fable ... about solving the most painful problem in business.* Danvers, MA: Jossey-Bass.

Lent, M.L. 2012. *Meeting for results tool kit: Make your meetings work.* BookBaby.

Pocket Mentors. 2006. *Running meetings: Expert solutions to everyday challenges.* Boston: Harvard Business School Press.

Roth, R. 2010. Why project kick off meetings matter. Presented at the University Health and Safety Lunch and Learn, University of Minnesota, February 12.

Schwalbe, K. 2009. *Introduction to project management,* 92–93. Boston: Course Technology, Cengage Learning.

Sisco, M. 2002. A well-planned kickoff meeting sets the tone for a successful project. TechRepublic. http://www.techrepublic.com/article/a-well-planned-kickoff-meeting-sets-the-tone-for-a-successful-project/1038879 (accessed July 15, 2013).

Young, T.L. 2007. *The handbook of project management: A practical guide to effective policies and procedures,* 88–90. London: Kogan Page.

4

Requirements Analysis

KEYWORDS

Baseline
Requirement
Requirements collection
Requirements traceability matrix
Stakeholder

READER'S GUIDE

This chapter allows you to

- Understand the vital importance that requirements play in the success of the project
- Enhance the ability to navigate in the project environment, interfacing with the different types of stakeholders
- Collect the shareholders' expectations
- Describe and validate the project requirements
- Reconcile irreconcilable expectations

4.1 WHY A REQUIREMENTS ANALYSIS?

One of the first activities to be performed during project planning is the requirements analysis. The requirements analysis is essential for the success of the project, basically for these reasons:

- The project environment is populated by numerous and diverse stake-holders who pile the project with expectations (synonyms: require-ments, needs). The expectations may be stated or implied, consistent or inconsistent with the project objectives, feasible or nonfeasible.
- What cannot be refuted is that stakeholders' expectations are valid as such. In fact, the project is justified to the extent to which it fully or partially meets the stakeholders' expectations. The more complex the project, the more complicated and extensive the system of expec-tations becomes. The expectations actually increase in number and type, highlighting where the stakeholders' interests converge and diverge. The result is a real challenge for the project manager and the project management team. The solution is to convert expectations into project requirements and use them to formulate the project management plan and the project communication system.
- Requirements are the primary input for the project scope defini-tion. Chapter 5 will examine the topic of the project scope. We can reveal in advance that the scope determines what should be accom-plished by the project, with respect to the constraints set in the proj-ect mandate. The scope makes it possible to clarify what is included in the project and what is not—in other words, what the project will address and what the project will not address.
- It is normal for a project to change characteristics as the work pro-gresses. The initial requirements analysis makes it possible to estab-lish a line of reference (called baseline in jargon) that represents the path to follow during execution of the project. Clear, understood, and shared requirements facilitate the definition of the project base-line and the management of change requests to it, which occur as work progresses.

We could stress the centrality of the requirements analysis in the overall economy of the project, highlighting the major problems encountered in the absence of a detailed requirements analysis: disregarded expectations, conflict among stakeholders, ambiguous scope subject to endless disputes, uncontrolled changes as work progresses, increased project costs and times, lower quality of results, confusion and inefficiency in the project team, and contractual disputes with customers and third parties. Better to avoid them, right?

But what exactly do we mean by *project requirement*? The PMI® (Project Management Institute 2008) states: "a condition or capability that must be met or possessed by a system product, service, result or component to satisfy a contract, standard, specification, or other formally imposed document. Requirements include the quantified and documented needs, wants and expectations of the sponsor, customer, and other stakeholders."

In other words, the requirements convert expectations into measurable characteristics of the projects/services that the project must produce.

By nature expectations are subjective, unlimited, and contrasting, in view of the number and diversity of the stakeholders involved.

Requirements, for their part, must instead be objective, limited, and consistent in view of the considerable analysis effort that must be made by the project manager and the project management team.

It goes without saying that the project "competes" on the requirements and not the expectations: the game is in fact played with respect to quantifiable specifications, which are also linked to the project's rewards system. If well formulated, the benefits become an element of integration and motivation for the entire project management team, insofar as they set a challenging but achievable goal toward which to direct each member's skills and energies.

4.2 ROLE OF THE PROJECT TEAM MEMBER IN THE REQUIREMENTS ANALYSIS

The project has been started and has just entered the planning phase. There are many doubts and few certainties. The project environment is crowded with stakeholders who, behind the project title, catch sight of many different things to each other. Each one piles the project with expectations that they consider compatible with the profile of the project, until proved otherwise.

The project management team (PMT) is faced with a huge challenge: in often reduced times and with an equally constrained workload, it must map the stakeholders, collect their expectations, convert them into requirements, and validate them. The PMT is therefore an engine of the requirements analysis.

In such a scenario it is unthinkable that the project manager, even by getting heavily involved in person, could cope with the complexity and workload associated with the requirements analysis. Added to which the requirements analysis requires a certain understanding of the topics covered. The collection of the stakeholders' expectations, through interviews, focus groups, and guided workshops, is likely to be a failure if conducted by people who are not very familiar with the business of the stakeholders consulted. The interviewer is easily influenced by the moods and ideas of the interviewees. The collection of expectations brings everything together and then some, creating the false belief that everything will, in one way or another, be acknowledged and endorsed by the project.

The requirements analysis is a good testing ground for practicing project followership, with particular reference to skills concerning openness, professionalism, and influence.

As part of the requirements analysis, project team members are required to perform the following tasks:

- Act as a point of reference for specific stakeholders, on the strength of their understanding of the contents and familiarity with the organizational context of these stakeholders
- Collect the stakeholders' expectations and convert them into requirements specific to the products/services to be produced
- Use a requirements specification syntax, shared with the project managers and the other members of the project management team
- Guide the requirements validation activities with respect to stakeholders they are responsible for, encouraging the clarification of requirements and the resolution of conflicts over incompatibilities and priorities

4.3 REQUIREMENTS ANALYSIS: STEPS AND TECHNIQUES

4.3.1 General Outline

The project requirements analysis is developed by carrying out the key steps indicated in Figure 4.1.

4.3.2 Classify the Stakeholders

The first step, classify the stakeholders, aims to identify and map the project stakeholders. This step is useful to define the project environment in terms of the numbers and types of stakeholders involved. The stakeholders are

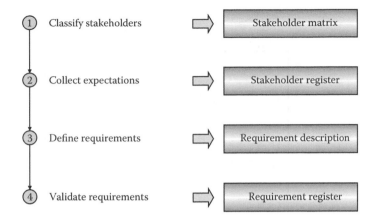

FIGURE 4.1
Key steps of the requirements analysis.

the starting point: in fact, they state the expectations, which in turn are converted into requirements.

Obviously the stakeholders are not all equal, in the sense that some of them exercise greater influence over the project than others, and at the same time, some of them are more affected by the progress and outcome of the project than others. The expectations of stakeholders that are highly involved in the project and have great influence over it carry more weight than the expectations of stakeholders that have little influence over the project and are marginally affected by the project results. In other words, not all expectations assume the same importance: the effort of converting the expectations into requirements must therefore take into consideration the relative weight associated with each expectation.

A useful tool for classifying stakeholders, and consequently for attributing weight to their expectations, is the stakeholder matrix.

A type of stakeholder matrix is shown in Figure 4.2. The two axes of the matrix have the following meanings:

- Interests: the level of influence that the project has on the stakeholder's business area, in terms of objectives, activities, and results. The interest is high if the project substantially affects the stakeholder's situation: the stakeholder therefore has a strong interest in developing the project and it being concluded in a certain way. Vice versa, the interest is low when the project outcome does not result in big changes to the stakeholder's situation: the stakeholder views the project with detachment and experiences it with low intensity.

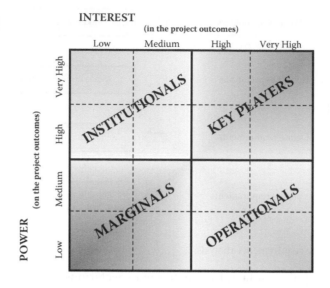

FIGURE 4.2
Project stakeholders matrix. (Adapted from Mendelow, A.L., Stakeholder Mapping, *Proceedings of the Second International Conference on Information Systems*, Cambridge, Massachusetts, 1991.)

- Power: The level of influence that the stakeholder can exercise on the setting up, operation, and results of the project. The power is high if the stakeholder can really affect the project profile through one or more forms of power, such as, for example, hierarchy, technical skills, purchasing power, the performance of rules and laws, and public opinion. The power is low when the stakeholder's radius of action on these forms of power is very limited or even nonexistent.

Crossing the two axes results in four types of stakeholders:

1. Marginal stakeholder. As the word implies, it represents stakeholders on the fringe of the project: these figures experience the project indirectly without being able to significantly affect it. Examples relating to product development projects include external suppliers for whom the project represents a routine job order, other project managers whose projects have limited connections with the project in question, and logistical functions of the company (general services, etc.).

2. Institutional stakeholder. Stakeholders that indirectly participate in the project by providing a contribution of support or control belong to this type. Examples relating to product development projects include purchasing, auditing, legal, and certification bodies.

3. Operational stakeholder. Operational stakeholders are parties significantly involved in the project (solution given, activities performed, organizational choices); at the same time, these parties, while providing tangible guidance and contributions, have little influence on the project decisions. Examples relating to product development projects include parties responsible for selling the product, product managers, product users, and help desk operators who provide product assistance.

4. Key stakeholder. This type is represented by parties that play a central role in the economy of the project insofar as they are directly affected by its results and are capable of significantly influencing project decisions. Examples relating to product development projects include the project management team, the project sponsor, the customer representative, opinion leaders, and suppliers with partnership relations.

The placement of stakeholders in the matrix makes it possible to prioritize the requirements analysis activities. Great attention should be paid to the expectations of the key stakeholders. Significant attention should be paid to the demands of operational stakeholders, which, if intercepted well, can produce a qualitative leap for the project. Formal and rigorous attention should be paid to the needs expressed by institutional stakeholders. And finally, residual attention should be paid to the marginal stakeholders.

For a better understanding of the contribution of project team members in the classification of stakeholders, below is a symbolic example.

THE MISSING STAKEHOLDER

The project to construct a new highway that was to connect two towns was progressing punctually. Some unforeseen issues were cropping up during excavations to construct the tunnels, due to the texture of the rock being different from what was expected. Nevertheless, the project was on schedule. The works, which affected a stretch of 31 miles, had been set up to start at the two ends of the highway: site 1 was working in a southbound direction, while site 2 had started in the south and was working in a northbound direction. The unforeseen issue occurred 6 miles from site 2. On the future stretch of the highway, precisely 6.8 miles ahead, stood a restaurant that was very popular and famous in the area. The highway, which would have become a flyover for that stretch, was designed to pass over the roof of the restaurant at a distance of 32 feet.

In theory, the restaurant did not have to be moved or demolished. In practice, however, the restaurant owner sued the construction company on the grounds that the restaurant, initially in a splendid position on a valley, would have completely lost its attractiveness to customers due to the construction of the highway. The result was that work at the sites was halted for over 6 months and substantial compensation for damages had to be awarded to the restaurant owner. A subsequent inquiry showed how the team member assigned the job of mapping the terrain to be expropriated, and in consultation with the citizens negatively affected by the highway, had completely undervalued the importance of the restaurant owner stakeholder, providing partial information at the same time. He actually told the restaurant owner that the highway would pass nearby, but it would not affect the restaurant's view and attractiveness, offering an amount of around US$260,000 as compensation. When the restaurant owner, seeing the highway construction sites approaching right in the line of collision with the restaurant, understood that what he had been told did not correspond to the truth, he sued the company constructing the highway. This brought the works to a halt and the restaurant owner received compensation of around $2.6 million.

This example shows how a team member's superficial classification of the stakeholders can seriously affect the entire project both in economic terms and as regards execution times. Furthermore, as regards the perception of the project, journalists were quick to write many negative articles.

4.3.3 Collect the Expectations

The second step, collect the expectations, aims to discover the stakeholders' expectations. The term *discover* has been used deliberately, as expectations are not always clearly expressed by stakeholders. At the beginning of the project it is common to come across stakeholders who do not know exactly what they want, beyond the generic statements of intent. Even the language used by stakeholders to express their needs often represents a barrier: each stakeholder uses terms, codes, expressions, and cognitive assumptions that are typical in his or her line of work. The diversity of the languages is one of the reasons why the team member's contribution is essential. Dialog is in fact greatly facilitated by a better understanding of a specific work environment. Added to this is the fact that each stakeholder "takes advantage" of the project to pile it with many expectations, which are not always consistent with each other.

The expectations are therefore brought to the surface and reformulated in close collaboration with the stakeholders themselves. It would be a serious mistake to formalize only expectations provided in writing. It would be like stopping at the tip of the iceberg, and as we know, the submerged part is much larger than the visible part. The expectations should be discovered through refined elicitation activities. *Elicit* means "to bring out, draw out, provoke, extract, obtain."

Elicitation is an approach applied increasingly often in project management, for various purposes. One of the principles is in fact the requirements analysis (other interesting applications are the risks analysis and the formulation of project estimates).

The assumption underlying the elicitation approach is that tacit knowledge is the exclusive and often unconscious property of those who possess it. The challenge is getting the holder of the knowledge to bring it out and make it explicit. The requirements analysis, which we stress will seriously affect the entire project profile, is a challenge of this type.

The project manager and the members of the PMT, in their role as project followers, are required to play a key role in this sense. The challenge should be accepted using a varied set of techniques based on an elicitation approach.

The main analysis techniques are summarized in Table 4.1 (Hass and Hossenlopp 2007, Zowghi and Coulin 2005, Cooke 1994, Goguen and Linde 1993).

The stakeholders' expectations should be appropriately recorded so they can then be converted into specific requirements. The stakeholder register is used for this very purpose. For each project stakeholder, as mapped in the stakeholder matrix, the register lists a description of the relative expectations, together with their level of importance, urgency, reliability, and the methods used to identify these expectations. In the case of projects with strict planning constraints, the recording of expectations in the stakeholders' register may be limited to the key and operational stakeholders—in other words, the stakeholders most affected by the project.

4.3.4 Define the Requirements

The third step, define the requirements, attempts to convert the expectations into requirements. This job may have already been partly done in the previous step, for example, during the focus groups and guided workshops.

TABLE 4.1

Main Techniques of the Expectations Analysis

Technique	Profile
Interview	Direct interviews with the people involved, with a well-defined objective agreed on between the parties. The interviews are usually conducted on a 1:1 basis (interviewer and interviewee), but they can also be conducted using a method that involves more interviewers or interviewees. The degree to which the interview protocol is structured can vary from more guided forms (directive interview) to more open forms (in-depth interviews), including intermediate forms (semistructured interview). The quantity and use of the questions (open/closed, objective/subjective) depend on the type of interview to be conducted. The interview has a considerable intrinsic cost for both the interviewer and the interviewee, in terms of preparation, exchange, reviewing, and the assumption of responsibility. The interviews, as part of the collection of expectations, should therefore be carefully selected and organized.
Focus group	This is a form of group interview. A suitably prepared moderator encourages discussion in a small group of people with expertise on the subject in question. The group is usually comprised of people from the same source (homogeneous groups) in order to encourage dialectic discussion on a theme of common interest, thanks to their experiences and individual points of view.
Guided workshop	A meeting in which stakeholders from different areas participate. It therefore acquires interfunctional value. The length of the meeting varies depending on the number of participants and the amount of topics to cover. In any case, organizing short guided workshops is suggested (lasting a few hours, one day at the most if it is necessary to optimize the transfer costs of participants). Here too, as for the focus groups, it is the moderator's task to encourage and manage the discussion. Given the participants' diversity, different expectations should be brought to the surface and, if possible, reconciled in the same session. The guided workshop, independently from the topic covered and the conclusions reached, should be exploited as an occasion to improve levels of knowledge, communication, trust, and collaboration between the project stakeholders. For instance, think of product development workshops attended by end user representatives, commercial and marketing figures, technical experts, and purchasing. In the context of software development, guided workshops are called joint application development (JAD). Another technical term is quality function deployment (QFD), used in manufacturing. The guided workshop may also include an analysis of different scenarios considered representative of the topic addressed, through an appropriate representation system, such as Unified Modeling Language (UML).

TABLE 4.1 (*Continued*)

Main Techniques of the Expectations Analysis

Technique	Profile
Group creativity techniques	Focus groups and guided workshops become even more productive if synchronous group creativity techniques are used. Some of the group creativity techniques that can be used are brainstorming (the free generation of ideas) in its different forms, mind maps, affinity diagrams, and multivoting techniques. For further details on these techniques see the specialized literature. Divergent techniques can also be applied asynchronously, namely, remotely, and recorded. For example, the Delphi technique is a way of encouraging free exchanges between experts, remotely and guaranteeing anonymity to avoid distorting forms of influence. The Delphi technique uses questionnaires; the answers are then processed by the facilitator and presented to the experts again for further study.
Questionnaires and surveys	These techniques include the collection of expectations based on predefined schemes, organized around different types of written questions. The questions urge the stakeholders to state what they would like. They are used when it is necessary to collect the views of large segments of the population, for example, sales networks, frontline operators, and geographically dispersed technical facilities. There are gains in terms of time, cost savings, and the comparability of the collected data. On the other hand, losses are represented by all the information not sought by the questions/survey, the attitudes and state of mind of the respondents, and direct comparison between them.
Direct observation	This is the most precise and costly analysis technique. It is based on a set of observations of stakeholders' actual working environments, such as the working conditions at the counter in the branches of a bank. The interlocutors are not asked to state their expectations, but they are required to be observed "by an outsider" while they work. The technique, even when shared, in any case influences the behavior of the individuals observed. Nevertheless, this distortion should not have much effect on the reliability and the priorities of the expectations collected.

Nevertheless, it is a good idea to dedicate a specific time and place to restate the requirements described above, and to describe the remaining requirements from scratch. This work can be done with or without the involvement of the stakeholders. There are different requirement classification models. They vary depending on the project market sector. The diagram in Figure 4.3 shows the first two levels of a generalized requirements taxonomy, based on the subject examined (project or product).

The product/service requirements refer to the characteristics of the components of the solution that must be produced by the project, whether it be

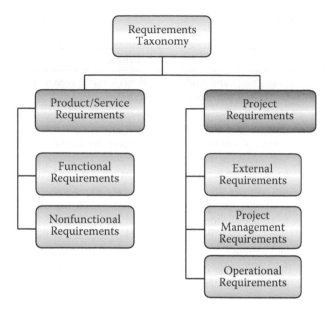

FIGURE 4.3
Requirements taxonomy.

physical products (a new production line) or intangible services (training operators on the use and maintenance of the new production line). These types of requirements can be broken down into functional requirements and nonfunctional requirements.

Functional requirements define what the product/service must do from the end user viewpoint. These requirements answer the question: What should the system do?

CUSTOMER RECORDS APPLICATION REQUIREMENTS

Let us imagine we are developing a simple customer records computer application. Define the requirements by answering these questions:

- Functional requirements: What features should be available to system users (add, edit, delete, print, etc.)? What data should be managed? Are there any specific rules?
- Nonfunctional (system) requirements: What volume of data must the system be able to handle? For example: How many clients in the database? How many add, edit, and delete operations per day? How many operators could gain access at the same time?

Nonfunctional requirements, also called system requirements, instead describe the characteristics (both technical and otherwise) through which the product/service must provide its functionality. These requirements answer the question: How should the system behave?

It should be emphasized that neither of these requirements has anything to do with how the system should do what it must do. The "*how*" in fact depends on the technical analysis activity that comes after the requirements analysis activity. The *how* depends on the *what*, so let us first understand and define the *what*, and then we shall decide the *how*.

An example, taken from an IT project, may be useful to clarify the difference between functional requirements and system requirements.

The project requirements refer to the project characteristics, understood as a means of producing specific products/services. The project requirements are divided into three subtypes:

1. External requirements relating to laws, guidelines, regulations, and codes of conduct with which the project must comply.
2. Project management requirements, which define the methods with which the project must be planned, executed, controlled, and closed. Examples of requirements are the planning and control standards, or the fact that the project must be coordinated by a certified project manager.
3. Requirements, when fully operational, relating to the methods with which the products/services produced by the project must be put into operation. This refers, for example, to having to arrange for a local test of the machinery installed and the need to train local workers to use the new system.

It is worth repeating that requirements are essential in any project, as they help us to define what there is to do. The main reasons that drive us to heavily invest in the requirements analysis are

- The client will only accept the project result if it meets the agreed requirements. Since the ultimate goal of every project is acceptance and use by the customer, every prior effort should be made to understand and agree on how to built a system deemed acceptable by the client. It is no coincidence that, once specified, the requirements form the basis for the technical analysis, but also for the preparation of the system acceptance tests.

- Defining what there is to do (project scope) and the construction of the work breakdown structure (WBS) (see Chapter 5) are based on the product/service requirements. The project, cost, and schedule estimates directly depend on the work that needs to be done, irrespective of the estimate method used. The correct definition of the requirements is the best guarantee we have to formulate reliable estimates, and therefore to properly plan the project in terms of both time and budget.
- The requirements may change as the work progresses, making it necessary to put the brakes on the project, or redo part of the work, or to add things that were not initially planned. All this is physiological for the project, but the essential prerequisite for managing the change effectively is the existence of a base of reference, called the baseline, which tells us with respect to what the changes are being made.

THE IMPORTANCE OF DEFINING THE CUSTOMER RECORDS APPLICATION REQUIREMENTS

If we return to the example of the customer records application, we can try to apply the reasons given above to a more real context, imagining what kind of problems could occur following a failed or incomplete requirements analysis activity:

- System acceptance problem: The record developed clearly does not do what the client expected; its company standards provide for 12-digit codes and the system has been set up to use 6-digit codes. As it stands, the system is unusable.
- Project estimate problem: Whoever estimated the printing activities imagined that each record card could be represented on a single line, but in reality the client wants to manage a lot of data, so one page per card is not sufficient, and from a technical point of view a much more complex database than was initially thought must be designed.
- Change request management problem: The client realizes the layout of the printouts does not correspond to the company standard and is convinced an example was provided before starting. The printouts are in the development phase; it is now necessary to stop, understand the extent of the change, and redo them. How can we understand how many of the client's change

requests are real changes and how many are instead only adjustments caused by an incorrect interpretation of the work on the part of the technician? If we do not have a base of reference that tells us what the initial agreement was, it is impossible to say.

What is the difference between a good requirement and a bad requirement? Table 4.2 lists some "golden rules" for a good definition of the requirements. However, bear in mind that the line between one rule and another can be quite faint. For instance, stating that a requirement must be correct implies that it must be complete. Nevertheless, a good requirement can be defined as one that satisfies the rules indicated in Table 4.2.

4.3.5 Validate the Requirements

The fourth and last step, validate the requirements, aims to make the requirements official in order to activate the subsequent project planning processes.

One or more formal validation points should be provided for the requirements specified in the previous step. The goal is to identify possible problems with the requirements before it is too late, i.e., before the execution of the work begins.

The purpose of the validation cycle is to check that the documented requirements are correct. In this phase any omissions, ambiguities, and conflicts should be revealed. In fact, there will be conflicting requirements whatever method is used to collect the requirements, or there will be conflicts between the requirements and the available resources or the project constraints.

In these cases it would be better to avoid unilateral decisions in an attempt to work to identify mediation solutions that are approved by all the stakeholders. Where the project is governed by a contract, there must be a trace of the negotiations even at the contractual level, to avoid unpleasant discussions afterwards.

Only three verification techniques are used during the validation cycle: reviewers, prototypes, and acceptance tests.

4.3.5.1 Reviewers

The most traditional method is undoubtedly to appoint reviewers from outside the PMT whose responsibility is to reread the requirements searching for errors.

TABLE 4.2

Rules for the Requirements Specification

1. Connected: The method used for the requirements documentation must make it possible to clearly identify the existing links between the different requirements and the way in which the requirements contribute to the creation of the solution that the project must achieve.
2. Complete: Not only must all the requirements be documented, but it is also a good rule of thumb to provide a definition of the glossary used, the acronyms, and to structure the documents so that each requirement is identified unambiguously.
3. Understandable: The drafting and agreement on requirements call for the involvement of all the stakeholders. Whatever method is used to document the requirements, it must be easy for everybody to understand.
4. Congruent: Congruence must be guaranteed on several levels: (a) within the system itself, by ensuring that one requirement is not contradicted by another; (b) with the other systems that must come into contact with the system for which requirements are being defined; and (c) using a language that does not contain terminological conflicts (everything is referred to in just one way, and a name corresponds to just one thing and that thing only).
5. Shared: The requirement must correspond to the stakeholder's request exactly. This is a delicate issue, as it often happens, due to the stakeholder's lack of experience in defining requirements, that the PMT "forces" the requirements in a certain direction (for example, toward a solution that is already available and recyclable, or toward more technically satisfactory solutions). In the requirements definition phase, this type of approach may also go unobserved and the resulting requirements may seem correct, but the risk is that once the solution has been implemented, the stakeholder, for example, the customer, realizes that this was not exactly what was wanted and that the requirements defined were simply wrong.
6. Explicit: It expresses everything there is to say explicitly, even aspects that may be implied.
7. Feasible: Achievable with the available technology and skills.
8. Measurable: If a metric estimation system is used (for example, the function points model in the software development field), the formulation of requirements must also aim to measure them.
9. Alterable: The requirements documentation structure must allow their incremental development and also any subsequent changes. This will affect both the way the requirements are documented (document format, indexes, etc.) and the subdivision of the requirements; for example, if a requirement is "spread" in several places, changing it later and finding all the points in which it appears becomes very difficult.
10. Unambiguous: Requirements must not be subject to interpretation. Above all, the use of natural language lends itself to different interpretations, as opposed to more formalized language. In terms of natural language, sentences should primarily use the future or present imperative, for example, "the system will," "the system must," or "the system must not." Conditional sentences, such as "the system should," are dangerous, as it is not clear whether that aspect is required or not. For that matter, there are special languages for drafting requirements specifications, the specific aim of which is to avoid ambiguities.

TABLE 4.2 (*Continued*)

Rules for the Requirements Specification

11. Prioritized: This is a neologism that we shall allow ourselves in order to understand that the requirements must be classified in order of priority. In general, requirements can be classified as mandatory, highly desirable, and hoped for, i.e., good but not essential. Understanding which category a requirement belongs to helps us in its management. For instance, if there are many requirements and not all are expected to be implemented in a single version, knowing the priority of each requirement can help us to select which should go into one version and which into another.

12. Stable: As far as possible, the requirements must be studied and agreed on, and then, hopefully, they will be less subject to rethinking.

13. Testable: All the requirements must be tested before delivery to the client, and they will probably be retested by the client. Bearing in mind they must be tested while conceiving and documenting them is a good way to ensure they are expressed properly.

14. Traceable: Each requirement must be identified unambiguously (with a unique code, for example), and it must always be possible to reconstruct their origin and history. Moreover, it is vitally important to create a clear and well-documented link between the requirements and subsequent planning documentation, so that it is always possible to trace the reason why certain choices, even technical ones, were made. An approach of this type will, among other things, make it possible for new people joining the project team to quickly understand the project scope, and it will facilitate the handover to whoever inherits the system afterwards.

15. Unique: Each requirement should be specified just once and should not overlap with other requirements.

16. Reusable: Effective formalization of the requirements makes it possible for them to be used as a reference even after the end of the project, if necessary for evolutionary maintenance or support.

The reviewers should be carefully selected, and if they have no previous reviewing experience, it may be useful to provide them with some support tools to guide them in identifying specific errors (inconsistencies, poor readability, etc.). It is important that the team of reviewers contains the right people, namely, that all the stakeholders are represented (for example, if the project is for a customer, all the end users must be represented).

4.3.5.2 Prototypes

A prototype is a first version of the system that can be used for experimental purposes.

The development of prototypes is a highly efficient way to validate the requirements. Prototypes are very useful to define requirements that are not very clear, as they help to contextualize the solution. In fact, it is one thing to read a description of how the system will function and another to try and use a simplified model to see if it really meets one's needs. It is easier to criticize something that exists than to criticize an idea.

It is a clear advantage to verify in the field the degree to which the prototype corresponds with the expectations before launching headlong into the production of the actual products/services, especially if there are significant economic and time factors involved.

Prototypes are a typical example of the gradual development of the project. The approach followed is in fact incremental: in an iterative manner and in close collaboration with the stakeholders involved, validation cycles occur that include the development of the prototype, its testing by users, the formulation of feedback, and the definition of the specifications for the next version of the prototype. Essentially, the prototype poses the following questions to stakeholders: What do you like about the product/service? What is superfluous? What is missing? What must be changed?

Prototypes can be developed from two viewpoints:

- With the subsequent intention of throwing them away, so the sole purpose is to illustrate the requirements
- From a developmental viewpoint, in which the prototype is the first version of the final system, and the requirements upon which the prototype was developed are those confirmed to date

The necessary condition for the use of prototypes is that they can be developed in a fairly early stage of the project, and that the development is not too onerous in terms of time and costs.

4.3.5.3 Acceptance Tests

An essential characteristic of a requirement is that it is possible to verify whether it has been met or not. Requirements that cannot be verified are vague desires. One way to prove the validity of the requirements is the production of acceptance tests. Inconsistencies or imprecisions in the requirement may already arise in the preparation of tests. However, if the preparation is successful, the requirement can be considered acceptable.

All the documentation on requirements should be carefully formalized, in light of the considerable efforts sustained and the heavy implications of continuing the project.

This step must therefore cover the formalization of requirements in a format suitable for the characteristics of the system, project, and its stakeholders. It is necessary to choose from the numerous methods available on the specification of requirements. An example in this respect is the document called software requirements specification (SRS), which was proposed by the Institute of Electrical and Electronics Engineers (IEEE) and has become an American National Standards Institute (ANSI) standard.

Most organizations whose business centers around projects have company standards that indicate which methods should be adopted for the requirements specification. In the case of large jobs (for example, the construction of a new cruise liner), it is the client company that requests to adopt a particular requirements specification method. In Figure 4.1 the output of this step has been generically called the requirements register. This term is intended to emphasize the importance of recording all the information on requirements in a standardized and approved format. This is to unambiguously identify each requirement and trace its development during the course of the project. We are in fact talking about the requirements traceability matrix.

For a better understanding of the contribution that the project team member can make during the requirements validation, it is interesting to examine the example below.

THE MISSING VALIDATION

In a project concerning the development of a company web portal, the user requirements were described in full and were easy to understand. Nevertheless, when the system became operational the users reacted very negatively, refusing to use the system, as it did not correspond with what was required. For their part, the IT consultants who had written the requirements said that the users had requested those features. To confirm this, they showed the records of the interviews conducted, accepted in writing by the users. The users did not deny the correctness of what was written in the report, but they pointed out that it did not contain a high enough level of precision to be able to go ahead, unequivocally, and implement the system. In essence, the IT specialists had converted the interviews into a format that was useful to them for the subsequent system development activities, and they "filled" the information holes by making their own assumptions, which seemed absolutely reasonable to them. In essence, the requirements validation had never been activated on the final version of the document.

This example shows how the team members acted incorrectly, albeit in good faith, contenting themselves with requirements that contained little detail and above all not validating the final version with the users, which would have revealed inconsistencies with what emerged during the interview phase.

4.4 CONCLUSIONS

The requirements analysis is an essential process for the success of the project. The standard principles of project management clearly support it.

The requirements analysis is the arena in which the stakeholders, their interests, their expectations, and their convergences and divergences meet, come up against, and collide with each other.

The results of the requirements analysis, for better or worse, have a significant effect on all the subsequent project planning steps, with particular reference to the scope planning processes.

The requirements analysis, in order to be performed effectively, requires a well-defined sequence: classify the stakeholders, collect the expectations, define the requirements, and validate the requirements.

The classification of the requirements includes the use of the stakeholder matrix in which the project stakeholders are positioned on the basis of their level of interest and power in the project. It results in four major categories of stakeholders: key, operational, institutional, and marginal.

The collection of expectations should be performed applying the concept of elicitation and using specific analysis techniques, such as the interview, focus group, guided workshop, group creativity techniques, questionnaires, surveys, and direct observation. The expectations are brought together in the stakeholders' register.

The definition of requirements is based on a well-defined taxonomy (product/service requirements and project requirements and their subcategories) and on a series of requirements specification criteria, such as completeness, traceability, sharing, consistency, and measurability. Particular attention should be given to the specification of functional requirements and to system requirements.

Once specified, the requirements should be made official through an accurate validation process. The tools to use for this purpose are reviewers, prototypes, and acceptance tests. The validated requirements are brought together in the requirements register or similar documents, such as the requirements traceability matrix.

With the exception of very simple projects, the members of the PMT, and not the project manager, are the engine of the requirements analysis. This activity is a classic example of the application of project followership insofar as it assumes, on the one hand, expertise on the content and familiarity with the stakeholders' context, and on the other, a grasp of project management techniques to manage the project scope.

Each member of the PMT, as a project follower, can and must make a difference in all the steps of the requirements analysis process. The requirements analysis represents an excellent opportunity to gain legitimacy in the eyes of the stakeholders and to acquire more authority within the project coordination team.

See page 251 for the exercise relating to this chapter.

REFERENCES

Cooke, N.J. 1994. Varieties of knowledge elicitation techniques. *International Journal of Human-Computer Studies* 41: 801–849.

Goguen, J.A., and C. Linde. 1993. Techniques for requirements elicitation. In *Proceedings of IEEE Symposium on Requirements Engineering*, 152, 164. San Diego: IEEE.

Hass, K.B., and K. Brennan. 2007. *Getting it right: Business requirement analysis tools and techniques*. Vienna: Management Concepts.

Mendelow, A.L. 1991. Stakeholder mapping. Proceedings of the Second International Conference on Information Systems, Cambridge, MA.

Project Management Institute. 2008. *A guide to the Project Management Body of Knowledge*. 4th ed. Newtown Squire, PA: Project Management Institute.

Zowghi, D., and C. Coulin. 2005. Requirements elicitation: A survey of techniques, approaches and tools. In *Engineering and managing software requirements*, ed. A. Aurum and C. Wohlin, 19–46. Berlin: Springer Verlag.

RECOMMENDED READINGS

Alexander, I., and L. Beus-Dukic. 2009. *Discovering requirements: How to specify products and services*. Chichester: John Wiley & Sons.

Byrd, T.A., K.T. Cossick, and R.W. Zmud. 1992. A synthesis of research on requirements analysis and knowledge acquisition techniques. *MIS Quarterly* 16, 1: 117–138.

Christel, M.G., and K.C. Kang. 1992. *Issues in requirements elicitation.* Technical Report CMU/SEI-92-TR-012. Software Engineering Institute, Carnegie Mellon University.

Hass, K.B., and R. Hossenlopp. 2007. *Unearthing business requirements: Elicitation tools and techniques.* Vienna: Management Concepts.

Podeswa, H. 2008. *The business analyst's handbook.* Boston: Course Technology.

Robertson, S., and J. Robertson. 2012. *Mastering the requirements process: Getting requirements right.* 3rd ed. Upper Saddle River, NJ: Pearson Education.

Sommerville, I., and P. Sawyer. 1997. *Requirements engineering: A good practice guide.* Chichester: John Wiley & Sons.

Section III

Project Followership during Project Planning

5

Planning the Scope

KEYWORDS

Constraint
Decomposition
Deliverables
Gold plating
Product scope
Project scope
Project scope statement
Scope
Scope creep
WBS dictionary
Work breakdown structure (WBS)
Work package

READER'S GUIDE

This chapter allows you to

- Actively participate in the definition of the project scope
- Avoid the traps of a badly defined and poorly controlled project scope
- Construct the supporting structure of the entire project: the WBS
- Document all the information useful to perform the individual elements of the work breakdown structure (WBS), called work packages (WPs)
- Use the scope as a force to unite the people that form the project management team (PMT)

- Enlist, as far as possible, the external suppliers to whom part of the project will be contracted out

---

5.1 WHY MANAGE THE SCOPE?

Every project has implementation constraints. The constraints may concern the timing (the entire project must be completed by September 30, 2013; phase 1 of the project should be completed by March 30, 2013), costs ($250,000 has been allocated for the entire project), resources (only four full-time people have been assigned to the project), regulations/laws (the project must be carried out in compliance with current safety regulations), working methods (the project excludes the use of a specific technology), or the organizational environment (it is essential for the project to use the results produced by another project as its starting point).

The constraints therefore set the boundaries within which the project must be carried out. Once formalized, they are clearly communicated to the stakeholders involved and can only be altered with specific permission. The constraints help to clarify the project; in fact, they highlight the margins for maneuver, the degrees of freedom, and the levels of autonomy in which the project must be able to proceed.

Once the constraints have been clarified, another key aspect remains to be addressed: the scope.

If the constraints establish the conditions under which the project must be carried out, the scope establishes what must be done with respect to these constraints. The scope makes it possible to clarify what is included in the project and what is not—in other words, what the project will address and what the project will not address.

The term *scope* is usually understood to have two distinct and complementary meanings (PMI 2008):

- The first concerns the product scope—in other words, all the products/services that must be created (for example, in a building renovation project, a part of the product scope may be represented by the new wiring system, developed according to certain technical and functional specifications).

• The second concerns the project scope—in other words, all the work that must be done in order to create the expected products/services (for instance, again referring to the building renovation project, part of the project scope is represented by the activities to develop the new wiring system, in compliance with the agreed upon specifications).

It follows that the product scope, once established, in turn determines the project scope.

The relationship between constraints and scope, and between product scope and project scope, is schematized in Figure 5.1.

The scope is usually a highly critical project variable (Baker et al. 1988, Pinto and Slevin 1988, Morris and Hough 1987, Martin 1976). This is due to its strategic value (decisions on what the project will produce and how to produce it are made) and the fact that it is paradoxically one of the least monitored areas (Standish Group 2003), i.e., where "do-it-yourself project management" is the order of the day. The result is projects in which the lack of definition and poor control of the scope prevent the expected objectives from being achieved. This is because the scope (what) is inexorably linked

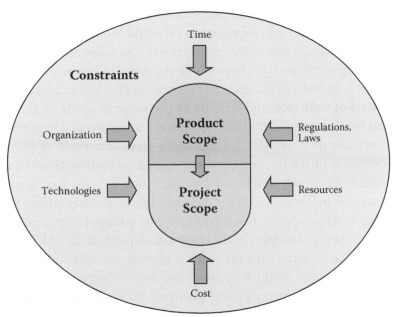

FIGURE 5.1
Constraints and scope.

to the costs (how) and the timing (when) of the project, and more generally, it determines the actual satisfaction of the customer ("Does what I have received meet my needs?").

Accurate definition of the scope makes it possible to assess the real feasibility of the project with respect to implementation constraints (for instance, are the schedule and cost limits compatible with the quantity/quality of the products/services to be created?). Vice versa, an unclear scope inevitably leads to ambiguity in terms of the products/services to be created and compatibility with the project constraints ("we know roughly what we have to achieve but we don't know if we will be able to comply with the set constraints").

5.2 MANAGING THE SCOPE IS NOT EASY

Some projects are characterized by a well-defined scope that remains stable over time, whereas other projects have an unclear scope that is unstable over time. It is clear that the scope will represent a strength for the former type of project and a weakness for the latter. A scope that is clear, understood, and shared actually represents a powerful tool on which to set up the effective management of the entire project. The scope also represents a powerful organizational glue between all the stakeholders involved, in the sense that it channels all the skills and energies in play into a unified vision.

The level of definition and stability of the scope depends on the topic covered by the project. For instance, a project to construct a high-voltage pylon can rely on a well-defined and stable scope, the result of previous experiences acquired in carrying out hundreds of similar projects; conversely, a research and development project for a new drug is by nature characterized by an initial scope defined only in general terms, which gradually becomes specific based on the results achieved over time.

The definition and stability of the scope also depend on the PMT's ability to manage the project. Often the scope is unclear and subject to constant changes due to poor ability to manage the issues concerning the project scope. For instance, during project planning the needs expressed by the customer and the other key stakeholders are collected in a superficial and hasty manner, the requirements arising from these needs are described in an ambiguous and incomplete way, the products/services to be created are not formalized, and therefore the work to be done is not structured.

Similarly, the acceptance criteria of the products/services are not shared by the end users, and even the procedures for handling change requests are unclear.

The PMT should therefore avoid two extremely dangerous situations concerning the scope: the first is scope creep and the second is gold plating. Scope creep means an ongoing requirements increase without corresponding adjustment of approved cost and schedule allowances (Wideman 1998–2001). In other words, changes to the scope that are implemented without having assessed the consequences on the timing, costs, and project resources, and without these changes having actually been agreed upon among the stakeholders involved. In essence, scope creep is the furtive evolution of the project scope: by the time you notice it, the damage has already been done!

Gold plating (Addiso and Vallabh 2002, Ropponen and Lyytine 2000) in the project means needlessly enhancing the expected results, namely, adding characteristics that are costly, not required, and that have low added value with respect to the targets. In other words, giving more with no real justification other than to demonstrate one's own talent. Gold plating is especially interesting for project team members, as it is typical of projects with a marked professional component—in other words, projects that involve specialists with proven experience and extensive professional autonomy. In these environments specialists often see the project as an opportunity to test and enrich their skill sets. There is therefore a strong temptation, in all good faith, to engage in gold plating, namely, to achieve more or higher-quality work that gratifies the professional but does not add value to the client's requests, and at the same time subtracts valuable resources from the project. As they say in the jargon, "The best is the enemy of the good" (Voltaire).

Below are two examples, one relating to scope creep and the other to gold plating.

To summarize, for the project to be successful, it is vitally important to pay a great deal of attention to the initial definition of the scope in order to then supervise, with just as much attention, the development of the scope while the project is being carried out.

Managing the scope well makes it possible to establish: (1) what work needs to be done in the project, (2) what work does not need to be done in the project, (3) how to organize the required work, (4) how to assess and validate the work actually carried out, (5) how to avoid carrying out work that is not required.

THE PHANTOM FORM

A document management project for a big client in the automotive industry is described. It was the second time that a project team comprised of three people had met to discuss how to develop the form that would enable user research preferences to be saved. The questions that had to be answered were: What time frame shall we use for this? Shall we differentiate based on document types? Is the information to be used in push or pull mode? After the meeting had been going on for three hours, the youngest member of the team, who had been hired about a month ago, asked the fateful question: "What does it say about this in the contract?" After about an hour of reading through the contract, the team, almost incredulous, came to the conclusion that the form that was creating so many problems had never been requested or mentioned anywhere or in any document.

THE EXPENSIVE POINTER

In a management dashboard project, the client was expecting a first prototype for the sole purpose of understanding what the possible graphic output of the project would have been. It was estimated that two working days would have been more than enough to present slides with example static images. A specialist, on the other hand, took a good three weeks of work to present a working prototype (the indicators, which in this case were pointers, moved depending on the data introduced). This did not generate any added value, as the indicators metaphor was so commonplace that no one had difficulty in mentally picturing the movement of a pointer, but it created great pressure on the profitability of the project (13 working days more than planned).

5.3 ROLE OF THE PROJECT FOLLOWER IN PLANNING THE PROJECT SCOPE

There are strong links between the scope and specialist expertise.

Knowledge of the project contents is in fact essential in order to plan the scope well: this becomes impossible without experts. At the same time, feeling that one's contribution is essential in order to determine the project contents and directions provides great professional satisfaction in itself (Vroom 1964). Expertise is therefore an indispensable ingredient in planning the scope, and it should be exploited wisely.

Each member of the PMT is required to have mastery of his or her own branch of specialization. Expertise becomes the prerequisite to become part of the project coordination team as the contact person for a specific subject area. Each specialist typically focuses on his or her area of expertise—in other words, on a specific part of the overall scope of the product and the project. The global vision of the scope and the scope planning methods are often considered by the experts to be the exclusive domain of the project manager. This leads to the creation of a separation that is certainly not conducive to project planning.

The effectiveness of scope planning is directly proportional to the capacity of the entire PMT to pool the individuals' specialist skills and share a work plan in order to gradually refine the scope.

The essential contribution that project followers are called on to provide for effective scope planning is exemplified in the following activities, which will then be explained:

- Describe the characteristics of the deliverables related to their subject area, in accordance with the project requirements
- Actively participate in the construction of the WBS, as a founding moment of the PMT
- Apply the WBS construction rules systematically and with conviction
- Socialize knowledge about the work to be carried out with the other members of the PMT
- Write the pages of the WBS dictionary relative to the work packages (WPs) they are responsible for
- Enlist the external suppliers to whom parts of the project will be contracted out on the basis of the information contained in the WBS dictionary page relative to the WPs to be contracted out

All the topics mentioned above will be addressed in the following paragraphs.

5.4 DELIVERABLES: ESSENCE OF THE PROJECT

The project scope is the raison d'être of the entire project. We have mentioned that the product scope is substantiated in a series of products/services to be created. The technical term, in the project management glossary, that defines each of the project's products/services is *deliverable*.

The term stands for any unique and verifiable product, result, or capability to perform a service that must be produced to complete a process, phase, or project (PMI 2008). Deliverables are nothing more than tangible outputs created by the project. The product scope therefore becomes a set of deliverables to be achieved in accordance with the requirements agreed on with the client and to be delivered to the final users upon their explicit acceptance.

In a building renovation project, examples of deliverables are a new wiring system, a new alarm system, a new floor, and new fixtures. In a training project examples of deliverables are the entrance test, the preliminary readings, the participant's manual, the course provided, satisfaction questionnaire statistics, and the report on the level of learning. In an IT project examples of deliverables are new application software, a new database, new central and peripheral hardware, a new data transmission network, user documentation, and technical documentation for operators of the new IT system.

The difference between external deliverables and internal deliverables should be pointed out. External deliverables are products/services to be delivered to the project client and are by nature established by formal agreement. They are the reason for starting the project and represent the consideration received from the client with respect to the cost it is required to incur. The examples above all refer to external deliverables.

Internal deliverables are the results necessary for project performance and management. The project status report, which must be produced and submitted to management on a monthly basis, is an example of an internal deliverable. Another example of an internal deliverable could be represented by technical documents for the achievement of an external deliverable (for example, technical documentation describing the methods for installing a new wiring system). Clearly the project is not started on account of or justified by the internal deliverables that it produces. The internal deliverables in fact support the external deliverables. Nevertheless, they represent an essential condition for the effective achievement of the project.

The external deliverables are not always expressly requested by the client and are not always established by formal agreement from the outset. In this case, it is the team members' responsibility to propose the deliverables, with considerable difficulty. In fact, deliverables do not occur in nature; they cannot be bought, and instead should be formulated wisely so that, on the one hand, they are appreciated by the client and, on the other, they drive the project team to achieve them. The biggest difficulty is creating deliverables that have value for the client, are easy to understand and use, demonstrate real project progress, and prove the supplier is actively working on the project.

Points of view make all the difference: while a technical deliverable may have meaning for a team member, it may have very little meaning for a client. For example, imagine a project to replace a company's IT equipment (PCs, screens, printers, peripheral devices). A deliverable may be a report on the current state of the IT equipment. The efficiency, or lack thereof, of this deliverable for the client would largely depend on how it is presented. If the report said things like "200 PCs with 466 MHz Pentium processors and 512 MB RAM, 300 USB mice, and 50 inkjet printers," a nontechnical company representative would probably be bewildered, if not even irritated, as this information is unclear and would not have any great value. However, the same information can be used to produce a deliverable that is easier to understand, such as "200 PCs, 300 mice, and 50 printers are to be replaced; for details on the reasons see the attached technical data sheet." In this latter case the deliverable is easier to understand and has value for the client, as it clearly communicates the actions to be taken to move forward in the project.

Each deliverable is associated with a specific recipient—in other words, the person that will use the deliverable in response to his or her needs. It is therefore said that the project must be deliverable-oriented. In fact, the project is justified if, and only if, it produces deliverables that meet the requirements. The PMT will therefore be assessed on the basis of its ability to supply deliverables that meet the requirements in compliance with the set constraints. The specialist expertise brought into play by each member of the PMT must therefore contribute to the achievement of the expected deliverables. Specialist activities are only justified, in terms of time and cost, if they contribute to the production of deliverables. Specialist activities are to serve the deliverables to be produced, and not vice versa.

Projects often suffer not from a lack of appropriate specialist expertise, but because that expertise is not properly targeted. You could say that "the ingredients were of the highest quality but the mayonnaise had curdled," the project being the mayonnaise and the ingredients the specialist expertise brought into play by the people involved. Usually, in fact, projects can rely on people with average skills who are motivated, cooperative, and have corporate awareness. While this is a necessary condition, it is not sufficient to ensure the success of the project. The sufficient element is represented by a clear, understood, and shared scope on the basis of which to construct the plan to be carried out.

It is good practice to formalize the characteristics of the deliverables to be produced in a specific document called the project scope statement (PMI 2008). It is interesting to note the concept of *statement* associated with this document; that is, it involves a formal declaration that makes the project scope official among all the stakeholders involved. It is therefore a written declaration that attests, states, and confirms what the project scope consists of, and with which everyone must comply. The following information should be detailed for each deliverable: (1) the product specifications (how the deliverable is made), (2) the requirements (what capacity/features the deliverable must have), (3) the boundaries (what the deliverable does and does not possess, what it does and does not do), (4) the acceptance criteria (how to establish if the deliverable complies with the requirements and is therefore acceptable), and (5) the end users' target (type, number, physical location).

Writing the project scope statement is a very important step in planning the project. The PMT must therefore follow strict rules. A first rule for deciding what to say and what not to say is to consider the need to define the project. Using this logic, it is advisable to indicate how to exclude from the scope all those areas in which it is feared misunderstanding may arise. In essence, we must list as exclusions (out of scope) all the factors the reader (i.e., any one of the project stakeholders, customers *in primis*) may be doubtful about. For example, when describing new accounting software we could say: "The system will manage accounts payable, but not the issuing of orders." This may be an important statement because the two processes are linked, and therefore, in this case, it would be necessary to clarify that the software would only handle the payments and not the orders. At the same time, in this example, it may be excessive to specify that "the system will not log employee attendance." This is actually a company administrative function that is not normally directly linked to the accounts payable.

A second rule is to involve the entire PMT in the definition of the scope. This way we obtain two important results: a more complete description in line with the scope and greater cohesion in the group with regard to the project idea itself. If necessary, other figures from the client's organization as well as its own can be involved through interviews, focus groups, questionnaires, and short presentations.

5.5 WBS: INSTRUCTIONS FOR USE

5.5.1 Meaning of WBS

The previous paragraphs clarified the concept of scope and its vital importance for the success of the project. The meaning of deliverable, as the transformation of the project scope into tangible and deliverable elements, has also been discussed in more depth. The need to state the characteristics of the deliverables in the description of the project scope document has also been reiterated.

What remains to be done to plan the project scope well? The answer is create the WBS.

WBS is the acronym for work breakdown structure. The product scope (deliverable) and, cascading, the project scope (activity) should in fact be structured around a very specific logic that will influence the entire development of the project. The WBS is used for this very purpose.

Figure 5.2 shows an example of the WBS relative to the renovation of an apartment.

The WBS is a powerful communication tool that clearly highlights (1) what and how many deliverables there are to be produced (the branches of the first level of the WBS), (2) the elements each deliverable is comprised of (the so-called second-level deliverables), (3) the activities necessary to produce each deliverable, and (4) details of the actions each activity is divided into.

In jargon it is said that "what's in the WBS exists and what's not in the WBS doesn't exist!" In fact, the ambitious objective of the WBS is to schematize the entire project scope in different levels of detail. If a project element is found in the WBS, it will be possible to plan and control its accomplishment (for example, assign the responsibilities, estimate the cost of achieving it, decide the delivery times, check the state of progress, assess the result's compliance with the requirements, and obtain the client's acceptance). If a project element does not formally appear in the WBS, it will not be possible to plan and control it using methods; instead, an intuitive, approximated, and nondocumented approach will be used with all the resulting negative consequences. Therefore, if a substantial part of the scope is not reflected in the WBS, the PMT will not be able to manage the project or honor the assignment received.

The WBS is based on the principle of decomposition. Decomposition provides for the construction of a hierarchical structure of the work to be

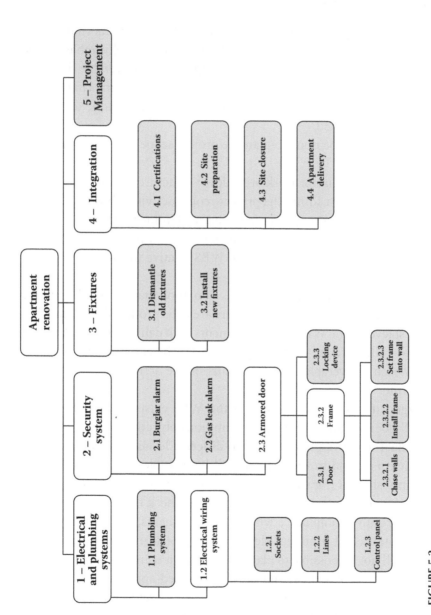

FIGURE 5.2
Example of a WBS.

carried out divided into levels of increasing detail. An element on level N (in the example in Figure 5.2, the armored door) is broken down into several smaller elements on level N + 1 (in the example in Figure 5.2, the frame, the door, and the locking device). The sum of the elements of level N + 1 corresponds precisely with the level N element (the frame, door, and locking device as a whole make up the armored door).

The point of decomposition is therefore to reduce the complexity of managing a result to be achieved, a job to be carried out. In this sense the words of the philosopher and mathematician Cartesio, taken from *Discourse on the Method* (1637), are enlightening: "The second rule is to divide each of the difficulties which I would examine into as many parts as it would be possible, and as might be required to resolve them best. The third rule is to conduct my thoughts in order, beginning with the simplest and easiest objects to know, to rise little by little, as it were by steps, up to the knowledge of the most complex; and assuming even order between those which do not precede each other naturally and vice versa."

The work package (WP) is the atomic element of the WBS. The detail of this element is considered sufficient to clearly assign the responsibility of execution to a specific role. The WP therefore represents the basis of the assignment between the project manager in charge of the entire WBS and the members of the PMT, external supplier, etc. The smaller the WP, the more limited the assignment; the larger the WP, the broader the assignment. The WP may be a detailed action, an activity, or a deliverable. The more detailed the WBS, the more numerous the WPs; the less detailed the WBS, the fewer the WPs. In the WBS in Figure 5.2, the WPs are the 18 elements highlighted in gray.

As deliverables, WPs do not exist in nature; they must be identified, and their intelligent definition heavily influences the project's chance of success.

Here too, sometimes the project team members' technical and specialist vision leads to difficulties that should be highlighted. The biggest pitfall is represented by micromanagement, or rather by too detailed a definition of the WPs, which try to explain all the implementation details from the outset. This mental attitude is decidedly dangerous, as it inevitably leads to a very high level of instability in the WBS and an enormous updating cost.

Just to give a general indication, a WP should last a few days, not hours; it should not contain information with a level of detail such as "remember to call the insulation foam supplier tomorrow." Each team member will manage this information using different media, such as a sheet of paper with memos, Post-it notes, and so on. The WBS is primarily a planning and then also a control tool. It doesn't make sense to plan and control activities that are too small; otherwise, each project would be made up of several thousand activities that would make it unintelligible and, para-doxically, uncontrollable.

5.5.2 Ultimate Purpose of the WBS: To Magnetize the Team

For the project coordination team the WBS represents a founding moment, one of a kind.

The WBS actually represents the first output produced together by the whole team. The WBS is a powerful symbol, produced by the PMT itself, in which it can identify itself. In fact, the following statement applies: "This plan is our interpretation of the project."

In jargon it is said that the ultimate purpose of the WBS is team buy-in. This term literally means "the purchase of the project by the team members." In other words, through the process of building the WBS the PMT "bought the project"; that is, it took full possession of the scope and feels ready to sell it with conviction to the other project stakeholders. The con-struction of the WBS is a key testing ground to measure the PMT's level of mastery of the project. A WBS that no one feels is their own, and that there-fore they do not sell and defend, is a double-negative signal: first because the WBS does not represent the project scope, and second because the people do not feel represented by the WBS, both as individuals and as a group.

In this regard an amusing experiment has been propagated in the project world. The experiment uses the WBS as a litmus test of the extent of team buy-in. It goes like this. Together with all the other members of the PMT, build the WBS of your project and represent it on a large sheet of flip chart paper. Then, when this is done, surprise the other people by asking them to pose for a group photo with the image of the WBS just produced in the center. From the reactions and willingness, or not, to pose for the group photo, but primarily from the facial expressions and poses immortalized in the photo, you will immediately understand the extent to which the team feels the WBS to be its own. Smiling faces, confident expressions, proud attitudes, and hands on the shoulders of others mean that the team is on board and that the WBS is its trademark. If none of this is appar-ent in the photo, measures should be taken immediately: a WBS has been produced for which no one will claim maternity or paternity. Some would even say that the future success (or failure) of the project is already fully contained in this photo!

5.5.3 Rules for Building the WBS

There are some essential rules for building a WBS that is truly representative of the project scope and, at the same time, profoundly shared by the project team (Buchtik 2010, Norman et al. 2008, Miller 2008, PMI 2006, Haugan 2001, Pritchard 1998).

These rules, if followed with care and conviction, lead to the constructive exchange of views within the PMT, which then goes on to produce a WBS in which each member of the team not only feels represented, but also feels he or she provided an essential contribution to its construction. The rules for constructing the WBS are summarized in Table 5.1.

5.6 WBS METAPHORS

An apt metaphor is worth more than a thousand words. Explaining the meaning and value of the WBS through metaphors is not only an exercise in style, but a powerful method of communication. So let's dedicate a few lines to WBS metaphors.

Here are some other WBS metaphors, deliberately not commented on so as not to deprive the reader of the joy of discovery (PMLAB Survey 2010):

- A sheet of music on which to place the notes to play together
- The circulatory system: it goes as far as it is needed

THE ROSETTA STONE

The WBS is metaphorically compared with the Rosetta stone. The Rosetta stone is inscribed, in the dark granite, with a decree issued by Ptolemy from 196 BCE, written in ancient Greek, Demotic script, and hieroglyphics. Discovered in 1799 in the Egyptian city of Rosetta, scholars consider it to be the piece of writing that made it possible to decipher ancient Egyptian hieroglyphs. Similarly, the WBS makes it possible for the different project "languages" to communicate with each other. In fact, numerous and diverse skills and specializations converge in the WBS that find common ground for comparison in the decomposition structure.

- The adventure that awaits us
- The treasure map
- The genetic code of the project
- The Esperanto that prevents the tower of Babel

Incidentally, do you have a metaphor for the WBS?

TABLE 5.1

Rules for the Construction of the WBS

1. Syntax: All the elements of the WBS relating to deliverables must be named with a noun that immediately gives a clear idea of the product/service to "package and release" (with reference to the WBS in Figure 5.2, an example is "frame"). All the elements of the WBS referring to activities must be named with an infinitive verb that immediately gives a clear idea of the action to be carried out (again with reference to the WBS in Figure 5.2, examples are "chase walls," "install frame," and "set frame into wall").

2. Level of detail: The WBS should not necessarily be broken down to the same level of detail as all the branches. In fact, some parts of the project are established practices and may not require further explanations, whereas other parts feature new elements and may have to be broken down further in order to better understand and control the work. It follows that the leaf elements of the WBS (the so-called WPs) may be substantially different from each other: for example, one WP may refer to a deliverable that it has been decided will not be broken down (with reference to the WBS in Figure 5.2, an example is "plumbing system"), while another may refer to an activity to be carried out (again with reference to the WBS in Figure 5.2 an example is "set frame into wall").

3. Branches that are always present: There must always be two branches on the first level, known as integration and project management. The two branches do not add further deliverables other than those specified in the other branches of the WBS. The integration branch encompasses all the work aimed at integrating the deliverables with each other so as to provide a sole solution that works. Examples of items in this branch are designing the system architecture, definition of the system specifications, system test, integration test, interfaces with other systems, test, assembly, pilot installation, regulation, and certifications. The project management branch encompasses all the work necessary for the actual management of the project. Examples of items in this branch are project progress, rescheduling, reporting, PMT meetings, meetings with the project sponsor, meetings with the client, meetings with possible external suppliers, and more generally, all the project coordination work.

4. Coding: Each element of the WBS should be unambiguously identified with numerical coding by hierarchical levels (with reference to the WBS in Figure 5.2, an example of coding is: 2 Security systems; 2.3 Armored door; 2.3.2 Frame; 2.3.2.3 Set frame into wall).

TABLE 5.1 (*Continued*)

Rules for the Construction of the WBS

5. Recurrent activities: While drawing up the WBS you may happen to stumble upon the same type of activities that must be repeated several times. For example, in an IT project, for each function of the software to be developed, the classic activities of analysis, design, programming, and testing must be performed. How should these activities be represented in the WBS? The answer is that these activities must be duplicated under each deliverable because, although they are the same type of activity, they combine to produce different outputs. Moreover, the execution costs/schedule are not necessarily the same.

6. Approaches: The WBS is constructed following two distinct and complementary approaches (the two approaches should be used in combination). The top-down approach is used to identify all the first-level elements of the WBS. It then goes on to detail each branch, gradually descending through each level. This approach is effective when the project is known and similar to other projects that have already been carried out. The PMT can therefore boast of consolidated experience, which allows it to structure the project quickly. If the project features many new elements for which the PMT cannot claim consolidated experience, the top-down approach is not practical except at the first level of the WBS. In these cases a complementary approach to the previous one should be followed, namely, the bottom-up approach, on the basis of which the first thing to do is to freely list all the "things to do," without worrying about putting them in order. Once all the elements have been listed haphazardly (deliverables and activities), they can be organized by deleting duplicates, removing elements that are off-topic, grouping the remaining elements by type, and finally connecting these groupings to already existing branches or, if necessary, creating new branches of the WBS.

7. Grouping criteria: It is suggested that the WBS elements are grouped by deliverables on the first level in order to guide all the work toward the products/services that determine the real value of the project ("What do I get as a tangible return for the price I pay?"). If the project is long-term, the first level can be structured into time phases (for example, analysis, planning, development, production), and within each phase, the second level can be set up for deliverables relative to the phase itself. Constructing the WBS by organizing activities based on the probable sequence in which they will be carried out should be avoided (the WBS should not be a "disguised" flowchart; there are precedence diagramming techniques to determine the sequence of the project). Another mistake that should not be made is grouping the activities based on areas of responsibility, i.e., placing all the work that will be carried out by one department on one branch and all the work that will be carried out by another department on another branch, and so on (there is a specific technique called responsibility assignment matrix (RAM) to define the project areas of responsibility). A WBS constructed to distinguish the areas of responsibility risks becoming a battleground instead of an integration tool for the project team. Tricks such as counting the WPs under one's responsibility from which to derive one's "weight" in the project should be steered clear of at all costs, and this is why WBSs that highlight groupings based on the organizational chart should be avoided.

5.7 WBS DICTIONARY: AN EXTREMELY USEFUL COMPENDIUM

The WBS dictionary is a document organized into pages that detail specific information on the work associated with each element of the WBS. Therefore, each element of the WBS has its own descriptive page inside the dictionary. By *element* we mean both the individual WPs and the higher-level groupings.

The information provided may vary in length, depending on the context and complexity of the project. The dictionary page represents the official source of information for all aspects concerning a specific element of the WBS. The WBS dictionary may add a great deal of value, insofar as (1) it allows more precise control over the project's interim outputs; (2) from a single source it provides each WP owner with a clear picture of what must be done, how it should be done, and how what is done integrates with the outputs of the adjacent project portions; (3) in the presence of external suppliers it makes it possible to isolate their activities, authorize them, and control them independently; (4) it makes it possible to have all the information concerning a single WP in one place, information that would normally be distributed in various points of the project documentation; and (5) the effort of writing the WBS dictionary ensures that the work associated with each deliverable is described in words: often the short descriptions that appear in the WBS item headings are vague and open to interpretation.

However, it is clear that the WBS dictionary has a production cost and an even higher maintenance cost in a context in which the scope is particularly unstable. As always, it involves making an assessment and finding the right balance between the need to clarify things and the need not to "harness" the project too much. The WBS dictionary is only useful if it is kept up-to-date. If necessary, a decision may be taken to produce only the most critical WP pages.

The WBS dictionary is extremely useful for project team members. For each WP under their responsibility project team members can open a specific page in which to record all the relative information. The page represents an official source where everything concerning the WP can be found. Project followers may share their pages with other members of the PMT, specifically those directly involved in accomplishing the WP in question.

WBS dictionary pages are dynamic in the sense that they can be updated at any time with new data and information or with amendments to the existing contents. In its small way it follows the evolution of the WBS as the project progresses.

WBS dictionary pages also represent an excellent tool for enlisting and keeping external suppliers in line. A project team member may actually be responsible for a WP that involves a significant contribution from a third party. In this case, the project team member becomes the project interface with respect to the external supplier. There is nothing better than a WBS dictionary page to clarify the work to be done by the supplier, the ways in which it should be carried out, and the acceptance criteria for goods delivered by the supplier.

A final positive aspect of the WBS dictionary is its use concerning the reuse of knowledge. Some WPs recur in many projects; for instance, think of the obtaining of certain certificates for a final product, or the training plan for final users. The page of a WP, produced for the first time, can be reused in similar situations without it having to be rewritten. The project team member must put the page in a company archive shared by different projects. The archive manager will control the methods of consultation and the updating of the page each time it is used for other projects.

5.8 CONCLUSIONS

The project scope establishes the results that the project must achieve and the work that must be done to achieve them. The scope outlines the boundaries of the project in terms of inclusions and exclusions.

The project scope is a consequence of the requirements analysis. The requirements are in fact transformed into deliverables—in other words, into products or services to be packaged and released. The scope gives rise to all the other planning steps (costs, schedule, risks, etc.).

Planning the scope is one of the more complex tasks in store for the PMT. In many cases, in fact, the scope is difficult to define accurately from the outset, and in any case, it is subject to countless changes during the project. Added to this are undesired effects such as scope creep and gold plating.

Scope planning follows a progressive course: subsequent steps lead to the incremental clarification of the scope. The documents that highlight the project scope are, in order: the project scope statement, the WBS, and the pages of the WBS dictionary.

All these steps require a solid contribution from the entire PMT. Without the experts, in fact, scope planning is impossible. Project followers act as a source of specialist expertise and managerial capacity, essential to determine the project scope.

The WBS is the decomposition structure of the project scope. It specifies each part of the scope at the level of detail considered sufficient to complete the work successfully. The atomic elements of the WBS, in other words, the "leaves of the tree" not broken down further, are known as work packages (WPs). Each WP must have an accountable person who oversees its execution, working on it directly and involving other figures. Very often team members are the WP owners (at times it may be the actual project manager in a limited number of WPs).

The ultimate purpose of the WBS is team buy-in—in other words, the purchase of the project by the PMT. The WBS therefore is a powerful and indispensable organizational glue. The WBS is the founding event of the PMT. Its construction requires following very specific rules aimed at providing it with solidity on the one hand and magnetizing the team with regard to the project objectives on the other.

Using a metaphor, the WBS can be compared to the Rosetta stone. The different languages spoken in the project find a way to communicate with each other through the WBS.

All the information relating to an individual WP is recorded on a special page in the WBS dictionary. The page is updated as the project progresses and is shared by the PMT. When the WP must be accomplished by an external supplier, the page is an excellent tool the project follower can use to enlist the external supplier and guide it through the accomplishment of the work contracted out.

A project's fate, for better or for worse, is often already written in the scope planning.

See page 253 for the exercise relating to this chapter.

REFERENCES

Addison, T., and S. Vallabh. 2002. Controlling software project risks—An empirical study of methods used by experienced project managers. *Proceedings of SAICSIT* 128–140.

Baker, B.N., D.C. Murphy, and D. Fisher. 1988. Factors affecting project success. In *Project management handbook*, ed. D.I. Cleland and W.R. King, 902–909. 2nd ed. New York: Van Nostrand Reinhold.

Buchtik, L. 2010. *Secrets to mastering the WBS in real-world projects: The most practical approach to work breakdown structures.* Newtown Square, PA: Project Management Institute.

Haugan, T.H. 2001. *Effective work breakdown structures.* Vienna: Management Concepts.

Martin, C.C. 1976. *Project management.* New York: Amacom.

Miller, D.P. 2008. *Building a project work breakdown structure: Visualizing objectives, deliverables, activities, and schedules.* Boca Raton, FL: Taylor & Francis Group.

Morris, P.W., and G.H. Hough. 1987. *The anatomy of major projects.* Hoboken, NJ: John Wiley & Sons.

Norman, E., S.A. Brotherton, and R.T. Fried. 2008. *Work breakdown structures: The foundation for project management excellence.* Hoboken, NJ: John Wiley & Sons.

Pinto, J.K., and D.P. Slevin. 1988. Project success: Definitions and measurement techniques. *Project Management Journal* 19, 1: 67–72.

PMLAB. 2010. Metaphors for the WBS. Milan: PMLAB.

Pritchard, C. 1998. *How to build a work breakdown structure: The cornerstone of project management.* Arlington, VA: ESI International.

Project Management Institute. 2006. *Practice standard for work breakdown structure.* 2nd ed. Newtown Square, PA: Project Management Institute.

Project Management Institute. 2008. *A guide to the Project Management Body of Knowledge.* 4th ed. Newtown Square, PA: Project Management Institute.

Ropponen, J., and K. Lyytinen. 2000. Components of software development risk: How to address them? *IEEE Transactions on Software Engineering* 26, 2: 98–111.

Standish Group. 2003. *The chaos report.* Boston: Standish Group.

Vroom, V.H. 1964. *Work and motivation.* New York: John Wiley & Sons.

Wideman, R.M. 1998–2001. Comparative glossary of project management glossary of terms v3.1. http://maxwideman.com/pmglossary/.

6

Project Scheduling

READER'S GUIDE

This chapter is for people who

- Are unfamiliar with the approach and methods used to define the project schedule
- Want to know which techniques make it possible to compress the duration of individual activities and the project as a whole

- Need to understand which activities should be given greatest attention
- Do not feel sufficiently involved in the project scheduling

---

6.1 WHY SCHEDULING?

Time is often the most critical variable for the success of the project. For instance, think of the installation of an energy production plant, with heavy penalties for late delivery.

In contracts that govern project work there is a clause, called "time is of the essence" (West's Encyclopedia of American Law 2008), under which failure to meet a deadline on the part of the supplier automatically invalidates all the obligations undertaken by the customer, for example, the commitment to purchase the work commissioned. In these cases the entire organization of the project revolves around the deadline to be met. More generally, we can state that today project schedules are increasingly compressed and budgets are reduced, while the results to be achieved remain the same or increase.

Close attention should therefore be paid to the time variable throughout the entire life cycle of the project, through a strong ability to schedule that not only involves the project manager but above all the team members.

Scheduling is the process of converting a general or outline plan for a project into a time-based schedule based on available resources and time constraints (Wideman 1995). Scheduling is an important part of the overall management of the project; in fact, it refers to all activities specifically aimed at managing the time variable.

Specifically, during project planning special focus should be placed on scheduling, the purpose of which is to establish the timetable for the project. In this regard the adage attributed to Abraham Lincoln applies: "If I had eight hours to chop down a tree, I'd spend six hours sharpening my ax." Prepare before acting, the thought before the action, the project on paper, and then in the field. Again in relation to presidents of the United States, Dwight Eisenhower used to say, "The plan is nothing, planning is everything." This adage reminds us not to confuse planning capacity with the project plan. The project plan includes the schedule, and it is therefore a set of documents subject to continuous changes as the project progresses. Slavishly following the initial plan, as written and approved, makes it difficult to ensure the objective is achieved. Therefore, the plan in itself does

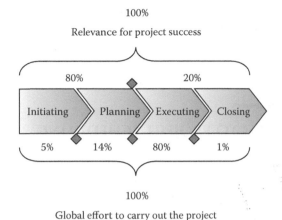

FIGURE 6.1
The importance and cost of planning for the success of the project.

not count for much. Planning, as an organizational skill and even more so as a mental habit, is, on the other hand, essential for developing the project plan through a progressive approach, adapting it to the circumstances without losing sight of the final goal.

It is recognized that the success of the project depends to a large extent on the effectiveness of the planning. At the same time, planning accounts for a small percentage compared to the overall effort required to complete the project. "The ability to influence the final characteristics of the project's product, without significantly impacting cost, is highest at the start of the project and decreases as the project progresses towards completion" (Project Management Institute (PMI) 2012, p. 40). Therefore, the well-known Pareto principle applies, according to which most of the effects (80%) are the result of a limited number of causes (20%). In our case, 80% of the success of the project is determined by 20% of the work—in other words, the work carried out during the project start-up and planning phases, as shown by the diagram in Figure 6.1.

In the absence of a solid project schedule, unfortunately another principle also applies: the first 90% of a job is carried out in 10% of the time, and the remaining 10% of the work in the remaining 90% of the time. This paradoxical observation was made by Arthur Bloch, in the context of the infamous Murphy's law. The project starts off at full tilt, and in a very short time most of the planned activity has been accomplished; it is a pity that the remaining time must be spent redoing, correcting, fixing, changing, replacing, and reviewing the work produced in a hurry at the start of the project. Without a real schedule project progress is only apparent. The project races through all the stages, except for the last one, which is the one that matters!

6.2 APPROACH TO PROJECT SCHEDULING

What does project duration depend on? Good question, which we must know how to answer if our ambition is to beat time to the project and not be beaten by the timing of the project.

The external context and amount of work to carry out (scope) being equal, the duration of a project essentially depends on two factors: the availability of resources (quantity and quality) and the sequence of the work to be carried out. Team members play a key role in both these factors. In the first case, the duration of the activities they are involved in will be influenced by their expertise, their number, and their capacity to work in an integrated and coordinated way, and in the second case, no one is in a better position than the team members to provide useful guidance on what input an activity requires in order to be carried out correctly, and therefore on what connections there should be between the activities.

It should be said immediately that the work sequence is more important than the availability of resources. It is obvious that having greater resources means the project can be completed sooner, but not necessarily. Try adding people to a badly planned project and see what kind of problems you run in to! Nevertheless, in many cases we take the wrong approach and favor resources over organization.

When we have difficulty respecting the project schedule, the first reaction is to ask for more resources in the conviction that the more people there are, the sooner we will finish. In theory it should work like this, but it rarely does in practice. How come? Let us answer with an example.

THE MYTH OF THE F1 PIT STOP

During a Formula 1 Grand Prix, a pit stop is when a vehicle stops in the pits for refueling and to have its four wheels changed. If there are no hitches, just like a magic trick, everything is completed in less than seven seconds! This is a real miracle when compared to the time it takes a normal motorist to change a flat tire: a few minutes pass while the driver curses his or her bad luck, and then a few more minutes are spent desperately searching for the jack and the instruction booklet. Not to mention the time spent attempting to change the tire, holding off on calling roadside assistance due to a sense of pride. Let us return to the Grand Prix: during the fateful seven seconds of the pit stop approximately 20 mechanics work around the F1 racing car. The team of mechanics is faced with a huge challenge: it must complete the job in seven seconds with zero defects. How can the challenge be overcome? Only by having a large number of people available, or by being able to count on a proven and synchronized work plan? Clearly the right answer is the second one. The duration of an activity, and more generally of a project, is inversely proportional to the complexity of the sequence of the work to be performed. The more sophisticated the sequence, the sooner the work is complete. In the case of the F1 pit stop, all the work required to refuel and change the wheels has been broken down into myriad extremely fast parallel micromovements. This breakdown of activities and their parallelization was repeated several times until a work sequence (the so-called network) was found that lasted less than seven seconds on paper. The necessary resources (people and technology) were provided on the basis of this sequence, and many trials were carried out to train people, synchronize the movements, and polish any inefficiencies in the work sequence. This great investment in scheduling made it possible to demonstrate a proven ability to complete the pit stop in seven seconds.

Vice versa, an increase in the resources for a project task where there is no work sequence results in the negative consequences shown in Table 6.1.

In a project there are few activities whose duration is halved if the resources used to perform the activity are doubled. It primarily involves activities where every part, however small, is codified, standardized, regulated, and carried out by personnel who are not particularly professionalized. As soon as an activity's level of complexity rises (decisions to be made, changes to the topic, associated risks, specialist skills in play, people's motivation, etc.), its duration is no longer inversely proportional to the available resources (Putnam 2013, Yang et al. 2005).

The increase in the resources allocated only reduces the duration of the activity if the people are involved in a well-synchronized work plan that

TABLE 6.1

Increase in Resources vs. Lack of Scheduling

The negative consequences arising from an increase in resources, where there is a lack of scheduling

Increased costs to complete the task

Increased incidence of work coordination

Need to align the resources on the work plan to follow

Potential increase in conflict (more people, more points of view)

Lack of homogeneity in the result (different levels of quality in different parts of the final product)

Marginal reduction in the duration of the activity

---

takes into consideration the greater availability of resources (this means that it is not enough to add resources, but the way the work is organized must be adjusted so that the additional resources are used appropriately).

We can summarize the approach to project scheduling by saying that scheduling is organized into

1. A first part called logical scheduling, aimed at defining the schedule network diagram
2. A second part called physical scheduling, aimed at defining the project schedule

Logical scheduling starts with the project work breakdown schedule (WBS) (see Chapter 5) and establishes the logical links between the work packages (WPs). This makes it possible to determine the sequence in which the project work will be carried out. This sequence is called the schedule network diagram. Still in the context of logical scheduling, the durations of the individual elements found in the network are estimated. This makes it possible to determine the total duration of the project. It should be emphasized that logical scheduling reasons on the basis of infinite resources, or better, it assumes the ideal provision of resources to perform the project work. In other words, it does not take into consideration the physical constraints of resources, such as the fact that a resource only has 50% availability (can only work on the project for four hours a day) or is not available in some periods of the year or is involved in several project activities at the same time. Again in the context of logical scheduling, if necessary, network optimization may be done—in other words, the definition of an even more synchronized and therefore time-compressed version of the network. This can be necessary to meet the set project completion deadline.

Physical scheduling starts with the results of logical scheduling (the scheduled and, if necessary, optimized network diagram) and influences it with the real levels of resource availability. Physical scheduling therefore reasons on the basis of finite resources, in the sense that it assigns people who are actually available to carry out the project activities. This is how the project schedule (i.e., bar chart) is obtained, which is then compared with the deadlines (final and interim) imposed as constraints. If necessary, the bar chart can be optimized by moving resources from one activity to another or carefully involving new resources in activities that prove to be bottlenecks in the project. The aim is to fall within the expected deadlines.

6.3 SCHEDULING STEPS AND THE PROJECT FOLLOWER'S CONTRIBUTION

Table 6.2 shows the project scheduling steps. The first three refer to logical scheduling, and the last two to physical scheduling.

The contribution made by project specialists in project scheduling should be pointed out immediately. This contribution is schematized in Figure 6.2.

The importance is highest during logical scheduling and in particular in step 1, the purpose of which is to determine the work sequence and formalize it in a specific project network.

The project team member's contribution becomes less important as the subsequent logical sequencing steps are carried out, namely, estimating the duration of the individual network elements and optimizing the network. The importance decreases further moving from logical to physical

TABLE 6.2

Project Scheduling Steps

	Scheduling Step	Output
Logical Scheduling	1. Determine the project work sequence	Network Diagram
	2. Estimate durations of network elements	Estimated Network diagram (duration of the entire project, critical path, floats)
	3. Shorten the project duration	Optimized network diagram
Physical Scheduling	4. Allocate the available resources	Bar chart (GANTT)
	5. Resource leveling	Optimized bar chart

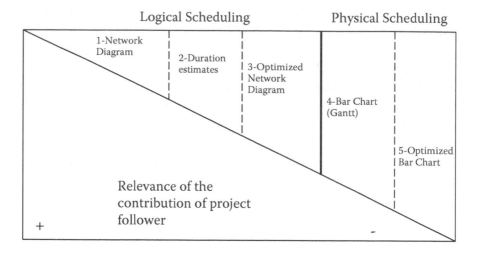

FIGURE 6.2
The contribution of project team members in project scheduling.

scheduling, becoming minimal in the last step in which resource allocations are optimized and, if necessary, other resources are included in order to meet the final deadline of the project.

It is very clear that project followers are critical in the initial scheduling steps.

Later in the chapter, the various contributions that project team members can and must provide for successful scheduling will be explored in further detail. Before, however, let us examine the individual scheduling steps in terms of principles to follow and techniques to use.

6.4 IN-DEPTH STUDY OF THE PROJECT SCHEDULING STEPS

6.4.1 Step 1: Determine the Project Work Sequence

This first step in project scheduling aims to identify and formalize the logical relationships between the different parts of the project. The logical relationships, also called dependencies, specify if and how a project element is connected to other elements, for example, in a building renovation project the fact that the "lay the parquet" activity can only start after the "construct the concrete floor base on which to lay the parquet" activity has been completed.

Again with reference to a building renovation project, we can give other examples of logical relationships:

- The "plaster the walls" activity must be carried out before the "painting" activity, as otherwise the painting serves no purpose.
- The "design the plumbing system" activity may be parallel to the "design the electrical wiring system" activity, because in principle the two systems have no points of contact. Nevertheless, some firms prefer to work on the plumbing system first and then the electrical wiring system.
- The "design the electrical wiring system" activity must precede the "install the electrical junction boxes" activity, because if the design has not been done, no one will know where to install the boxes.
- The "replace the armored door" activity can be carried out fairly freely, as by nature it does not depend on the state of progress of the other activities.

The schedule network diagram summarizes the set of logical relationships between the project elements and determines the sequence of the work to be carried out (Figure 6.3).

In the example in Figure 6.4 activities A and B are connected by a dependency. B is influenced by A. Activity A is called the predecessor and activity B the successor. A network element may act as a predecessor for several successor activities (A with respect to B, C, and D). At the same time, a successor may have several predecessors at the same time (C and D are both predecessors to F).

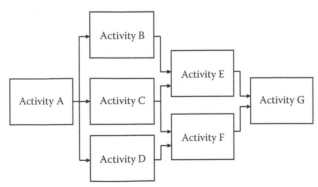

FIGURE 6.3
Schedule network diagram.

Type of dependency	SS – Start-to-Start
Layout	
Meaning	Activity B can only start once activity A has started (in practice the two activities can be carried out in parallel, but one of them must start first).
Example	In a job to asphalt a road, activity B "Level the asphalt" must start a short time after activity A "Spread the asphalt" has started, but not too long afterwards otherwise the asphalt will cool. This constraint often creates near parallels between the two activities with the caveat that in any case activity A "leads the dance." In fact, in our example, if the start of the asphalting is delayed, the leveling will also be delayed.

FIGURE 6.4
Start-to-start dependency.

The logical relationship that we intuitively assume exists between two network elements is finish to start. This means that successor activity B cannot start if predecessor activity A has not been completed. The finish-to-start relationship is the clearest and most restrictive. Clear because it does not give rise to misinterpretations. The rule is very precise and unequivocal: in a relay race the athlete running the second stretch cannot leave, without being disqualified, until the athlete running the first stretch has passed him or her the baton. It is restrictive because it heavily influences the entire project schedule. The finish-to-start dependency profile is summarized in Figure 6.5. However, there are other types of dependencies, described in Figures 6.6 and 6.7.

The definitions and examples show how the other three types of dependencies are not as clear as the classic finish-to-start dependency, and therefore they are more difficult to apply and understand. They are obviously very useful for formalizing specific logical relationships that characterize the specific project. They also contribute, on the one hand, to ensure the expected quality level (see the asphalt example described in Figure 6.7) and, on the other, to define the best project schedule.

Type of dependency	FS – Finish-to-Start
Layout	
Meaning	Activity B (successor) can only start after activity A (predecessor) has finished (in practice the two activities must be performed in succession).
Example	Activity B "Deliver the second day of the training course" may only be carried out if activity A "Deliver the first day of the training course" has been completed.

FIGURE 6.5
Finish-to-start dependency.

Type of dependency	SF – Start-to-Finish
Layout	
Meaning	Activity A can only finish after activity B has started (it is a sort of logical inversion of the FS relationship; in fact, whereas before activity A led the dance, allowing the subsequent activity to start, now the subsequent activity leads the dance; in fact, its start determines the end of the previous activity).
Example	In the renewal of an industrial plant the old production plant can only be brought to a halt once the new one has started to operate.

FIGURE 6.6
Start-to-finish dependency.

The presence of many dependencies in the schedule network diagram other than the classic finish-to-start relationship makes the project more difficult to control. In fact, the work sequence becomes more complex and sophisticated. The aim is to reduce the project schedule by acting on all the possible logical relationships. The ambition to finish early, however, is at odds with the greater complexity in coordinating the work.

Type of dependency	FF – Finish-to-Finish
Layout	
Meaning	Activity B can only finish after activity A has finished (in practice, irrespective of when they started, in order to finish one activity the other must already be finished).
Example	If there are two activities: A "Perform wiring" and B "Perform electrical inspection," the inspection cannot finish until the wiring is finished.

FIGURE 6.7
Finish-to-finish dependency.

At the beginning, it is suggested that only the finish-to-start dependency is used and other types of logical relationships are applied later at specific stages of the initial network, carefully assessing the relative pros and cons.

THE IMPERFECT DEPENDENCY

During a meeting with the project team on the renovation of a residential building, the project manager asked the team members to propose some ideas to reduce the project duration, given that some problems in the initial phases had eroded any safety margin. While the team members were doing their utmost to come up with ideas and solutions, one of them said that his job to move furniture and materials could not be compressed due to the confined spaces for maneuver: even having two more people would have almost caused more chaos than benefits. The project manager noted how many activities were connected by the finish-to-start dependency, and were thus in perfect seriality. The project manager then asked, "Wouldn't it be possible to start moving the apartment furniture into the rooms that have already been painted instead of waiting for the renovation of the entire apartment to be completed?" "You're right, it would be possible to introduce a start-to-start dependency with a small time delay. I hadn't thought of it. That way we would save at least a week on the overall job," replied the team member in charge of this task.

The dependencies can be determined by various reasons. As a consequence, a logical relationship can be classified as (PMI 2008):

- Mandatory: A mandatory dependency is a logical relationship that cannot be overlooked, for example, the fact that a product must be designed before it can be produced. Infringing a mandatory dependency may jeopardize the quality of the project result, or the very sense of the project.
- Discretionary: A discretionary dependency is a logical relationship resulting from a project team preference with regard to the methods used to accomplish the project. For example, many building firms, irrespective of mandatory dependencies, have preferences about how to carry out the work, and therefore they choose, for convenience, to carry out all the demolition work first and then start the reconstructions. In theory they could even proceed room by room, demolishing and reconstructing the individual parts.
- External: An external dependency is a logical dependency between a project activity and an entity external to the project. For example, in an engineering project it is necessary to wait for the availability of a piece of equipment that must be produced by another company project being carried out in parallel to the one in question.

This distinction shows that some dependencies are stronger than others. This will be important later on, when we might find ourselves having to call them into question in order to shorten the project schedule.

A network contains different paths. A path is a chain of elements that connects the start with the end of the project.

The network in Figure 6.3 shows four paths:

- Path 1: A-B-E-G
- Path 2: A-C-E-G
- Path 3: A-C-F-G
- Path 4: A-D-F-G

The paths, as we will see later, make it possible to calculate the project duration. It should be emphasized that the paths are not alternative. In order to complete the project, all the elements of the schedule network diagram must be carried out, and not only those of a particular path.

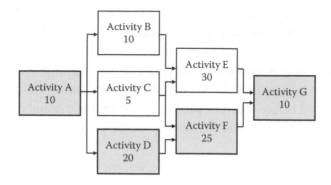

FIGURE 6.8
Estimated schedule network diagram.

6.4.2 Step 2: Estimate the Duration of the Network Elements

This second scheduling step aims to determine the timing of the schedule network diagram—in other words, to assign an estimated duration to each element in the network (i.e., activities), in order to then calculate the overall duration of the entire project.

Let us go back to the network in Figure 6.3, this time estimated in Figure 6.8.

For each activity a duration in working days has been estimated. For instance, activity D has a duration of 20 working days (equal to 28 calendar days), assuming 5 working days for each calendar week. We will see how to formulate these estimates later.

Based on the duration of the individual activities and on the basis of the dependencies of the network, it is possible to calculate the overall duration of the entire project, which comes to 65 working days.

For very simple networks, the overall project duration can be calculated intuitively ("if there are parallel activities, always take the one with the longer duration"). For more complex networks these commonsense rules are not enough and specific calculation algorithms should be used. These algorithms are beyond the scope of this book, not only because they are supported by special project management software that does the calculations for us, but also because these calculations are the project manager's responsibility.

To calculate the overall duration of the project, the paths identified in scheduling step 1 come to our aid. First, we calculate the duration of each path by adding up the durations of each activity in the path, assuming that all the dependencies are finish to start. The calculations are set out in Table 6.3.

TABLE 6.3

Duration of the Network Paths in Figure 6.8

Path	Duration (in working days)
Path 1: A-B-E-G	10 + 30 + 10 + 10 = 60
Path 2: A-C-E-G	10 + 5 + 30 + 10 = 55
Path 3: A-C-F-G	10 + 5 + 25 + 10 = 50
Path 4: A-D-F-G	10 + 20 + 25 + 10 = 65 (critical path)

The path with the maximum duration should then be identified (in the example path 4, with a duration of 65 days). This path determines the project duration.

It is called the critical path insofar as it influences the duration of the entire project. The activities on the critical path cannot be delayed if the project's final deadline is to be met. Each day of delay for an activity on the critical path delays the entire project by one day.

Vice versa, activities that are not on the critical path can last a little longer without delaying the project's final deadline. For instance, activity C can last nine days more than planned, or it can start nine days after the planned start date, without delaying the entire project. Similarly, activity B can take it easy for four days. This "lung" of time that an activity can take, without delaying the entire project, is called float or slack. The higher the float, the more leeway there is in starting, performing, and completing the activity. It goes without saying that activities on the critical path have a total float of zero.

Here too, the calculations can be made intuitively for simple networks (see the example in Figure 6.8), while the application of specific algorithms is required for more complex networks.

As can be imagined, the concepts of the critical path and float are very important in order to respect the project schedule, but the most important aspect is that they represent an excellent basis for comparison between the members of the project team. Having a shared schedule network diagram makes it possible for the project team to have a constructive discussion on issues concerning the project scheduling. For example: "What will happen to our project if I start my task a week late?" "Given that our two tasks are on the critical path, we must stay in close contact and always be aligned on how things are proceeding," "Be aware that some activities have short durations, but if they are not completed, they will prevent the start of activities with longer durations."

THE FUTILE RACE

In a project to open a new shop it became clear that it would be difficult to meet the promised deadline unless a way of reducing the duration of some activities was found. After a discussion with the team members, a first shared action was to contact the furniture supplier and put pressure on him. The team member responsible for this job immediately picked up the phone and, after an intense negotiation, managed to obtain a promise that the furniture would be installed ten days ahead of the planned date. At this point all the problems seemed to be resolved, except that another team member made the following observation: "Forgive me, but even if the furniture arrives early, you do realize that in any case we won't be able to bring the opening forward because the electrical wiring system won't be finished?"

There are another two factors that can influence the duration of the activities: lag and lead.

A lag allows a change to a dependency, providing for the delayed start of the successor activity. An example of a lag is the laying of parquet in a house. Imagining that the laying requires two days, the technical nature of the work in any case requires a settling time of at least ten days before the planing and varnishing can be carried out. In this case, we would have a finish-to-start dependency between the laying and the varnishing activities with a ten-day delay—in other words, the varnishing must be done at least ten days after the laying has been completed.

A lead allows a change to a dependency, allowing the successor activity to start early. An example of a lead, in a project that requires the intervention of a consultancy company, could be to place the task of sending the order to the supplier the week before the actual consultancy activity should start (therefore, a start-to-start relationship with five days of lead time). This ensures the contract can be signed before the work begins, but only when we are certain that the work must actually start—therefore once the project has started.

Lags and leads are therefore combined with logical relationships and slightly change the meaning as they bring forward or postpone the effect. For these issues the specialist contribution of team members is essential, as it is only through in-depth knowledge of the problems that sensible lags or leads can be proposed.

We've come to the last aspect relative to this scheduling step: the criteria for duration estimates. "On what basis can I estimate an activity will last 30 working days?"

The answer is that for each type of activity requiring a duration estimate the standard conditions for its performance should be stated. The standard conditions of performance of the activity indeed represent the best scenario that can be envisaged in relation to the project environment. The reasoning involves establishing the ideal provision of resources that should make it possible to complete the task in the shortest time possible. A further increase in resources beyond the ideal provision stated in the standard conditions does not result in significant time saving. For instance, even if the number of programmers on a software development project is raised from 10 to 50, the application release times cannot be reduced. What's more, it makes the project practically impossible to manage, as 50 developers all together create confusion, and the result is only an increase in costs.

The standard conditions do not consider the physical period of the year in which the activity will fall, the physical people that will perform the job, or their actual availability in that period of the year. These contingent constraints will be taken into consideration later on during the physical scheduling of the project. The resulting duration is usually expressed in working days (or working hours or weeks) and represents the time required to complete the activity assuming the standard conditions of performance to be true.

In other words, it involves clarifying not so much the absolute optimum, but rather the relative optimum (Table 6.4). The absolute optimum places

TABLE 6.4

Absolute Optimum vs. Relative Optimum

Absolute Optimum Purely ideal situations (to avoid)	Relative Optimum Standard conditions of performance (to pursue)
Availability of technologies that are not present and can be implemented in a short time in the company	Optimum functioning of the existing technologies Skilled resources available full-time in the number usually allocated for activities of this type (standard work group)
Unlimited resources (no quantity or quality problems)	Perfect initial definition of the user specifications and no changes during the project
Absolute power over external suppliers	Document sources for understanding application requirements are accessible, complete, and updated
Compliance with contractual conditions on the part of suppliers	

the activity in a purely ideal situation, completely disconnected from the actual reality in which the project originates and develops. The relative optimum, on the other hand, positions the activity in the best situation that the project environment would be capable of ensuring if everything was functioning as well as possible.

6.4.3 Step 3: Compress the Project Duration

This third step in project scheduling aims to reduce the project time frame in cases where the estimated duration of the entire project exceeds the final deadline set as a constraint by the customer.

In other words, it involves rethinking the schedule network diagram to meet the set deadlines. For this purpose schedule compression techniques are used.

The diagram in Table 6.5 sets out the main ones. Let us examine the individual techniques in detail.

6.4.3.1 Fast Tracking

This technique compresses the schedule network diagram acting on the previously defined dependencies. In fact, the purpose of this technique is to find increasingly fast synchronizations between activities. Note that this technique should not be applied indiscriminately to the entire

TABLE 6.5

The Main Schedule Compression Techniques

Technique	Positive Effect	Negative Effect
Fast tracking	Time saving	Increased level of difficulty in performing the schedule network diagram in a more compressed form. Possible reduction of quality when activity execution times are compressed.
Crashing	Time saving	Possible increase in costs due to probable increase in resources.
Quality reduction	Possible time and cost savings	Probable impact on customer satisfaction due to the result not complying with the original requests.
Scope reduction	Possible time and cost savings	Probable impact on customer satisfaction due to the result not complying with the original requests.

Source: Project Management Institute, *A Guide to the Project Management Body of Knowledge*, 4th ed., PMI, Newtown Square, Pennsylvania, 2008; Feather, M. S. et al., Descoping, in *Proceedings of the 27th IEEE/NASA Software Engineering Workshop*, IEEE Computer Society, Greenbelt, Maryland, 2002.

network, but instead it should be applied to the limited number of points on the network where the redefinition of dependencies should generate substantial time savings with respect to the project's final deadline. The technique is therefore applied starting with activities on the critical path.

Here are some possible applications of this technique:

- Breaking down an activity into subactivities and putting them in parallel, working on the internal synchronisms
- Making the successor activity depend only on a part of the predecessor activity, which should first be broken down into subactivities
- Reducing the expected lag between the end of the predecessor activity and the start of the successor activity
- Changing the current type of dependency between two activities by transforming it from finish to start (the most restrictive) into one of the other types of less restrictive dependencies
- Eliminating a dependency between two activities

In theory the compression of activities should not result in an increase in costs; however, in practice the risk of having to redo the work increases significantly, with the relative cost-related consequences. In fact, it is supposed that if two activities were originally placed in sequence in the network, this was done because the content of one depended on the result produced by the other.

For instance, if in the schedule network diagram production must follow design, it is likely that in order to produce the product, the project created by the previous activity will be used. Modifying of this logical

AN EXAMPLE OF FAST TRACKING

When preparing parquet, the main actions of laying, planning, and varnishing should be carried out in sequence. In a hypothesis where the schedule must be compressed in order to deliver the apartment on the agreed date, one solution can be to use the fast tracking technique. The waiting time between laying and planing can be reduced. Doing so, however, creates the need to assess the risk of planing a floor that has not yet settled, with the consequent probability of having a floor where the boards move, which will be followed by the need to lay the floor again.

relationship, namely, parallelization (even partial) between the design and production activities, will result in the production being based, at least initially, on a draft design instead of the definitive version. The risk is that the draft design will be altered (as is natural) during the completion of the design, and that the production must "go back" to keep track of the project changes as they occur.

This technique is certainly convenient in terms of the schedule, but it will probably have repercussions on the costs and perhaps also on the quality.

Another important aspect that should be considered when applying fast tracking fully and unconditionally is the managerial complexity of the network obtained by compression. Let us return to the F1 pit stop example: the pit stop network is compressed to the excess in order to fall within the fateful seven seconds. However, it is then necessary to be capable of executing it with a tight-knit team and the appropriate technologies. We must therefore ask ourselves if the organization called on to produce a project has the skills to perform compressed networks without any kind of float. If the answer is no, less compressed and more manageable networks should be adopted. It's like saying a person buys a Ferrari but is not capable of driving it. The alternatives are to keep it in the garage and show it to friends, always drive it in first gear and burn out the engine, or pretend I know how to drive it and crash it at the first corner!

In fast tracking, a team member's contribution of knowledge is essential. In fact, to an inexperienced eye the creation of parallelisms between activities may seem painless, while in practice it may have significant, if not even catastrophic, impacts.

6.4.3.2 Crashing

This technique involves reducing the duration of activities by increasing the resources assigned to them.

Experience tells us that this is a good technique to adopt only if the activities in question permit it. Not all activities permit the simultaneous work of several people, just as not all durations depend on the number of people involved in an activity (for instance, in a theater project an actor's memorizing of the lines cannot be delegated!).

In any case, even for activities that permit it, schedule compression must be done carefully. Schedule compression, carried out only after having analyzed possible solutions that may have low impact on the project, may occur by compressing the schedule for project activities on the critical

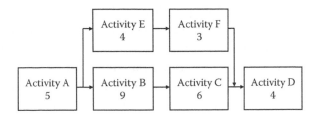

The critical path, represented by activities A, B, C, and D, has a duration of 24. If the aim is to compress the execution time down to a duration of 20, the resources can be increased with the consequent financial impact, or resources can be taken from E and/or F, but only up to a number that will not undermine the new scheduling.

FIGURE 6.9
Example of crashing.

path. It is necessary, however, to assess the increased costs that may result from this, as reduced execution times are generally obtained by increasing the resources assigned to the project.

In order not to incur an excessive cost increase, it is possible to use resources assigned to other activities that are not on the critical path and whose possible delay would not compromise the project scheduling. An example of crashing is shown in Figure 6.9.

The role of team members in assessing the possibilities of crashing is key. In fact, through specific expertise in the activities to be carried out, it is possible to evaluate if, how, and by how much an increase in the assigned resources would result in reduced execution times.

6.4.3.3 Quality Reduction

Another time compression technique is lowering the quality. Lowering the quality may mean reducing project support activities, such as control, testing, production, and support documentation activities. This technique, however, involves risks, as not controlling the execution correctly will increase the probability of something being produced incorrectly. This "sacrifice" is very often favored by the project team, as it allows them to concentrate more on the execution of the activities directly related to the production of a deliverable. However, it is necessary to be aware that very often activities deemed sacrificable do not allow the quality of the project as a whole to be ensured, and therefore what seems like a time-saving measure can subsequently actually increase the time required (change requests, nonacceptance of deliverables). Very often those who are very technically minded have difficulty in understanding which aspects the customer may accept a reduction in quality without this compromising the opinion of the entire project, and for this reason it is a good idea for the project team, and not individuals, to discuss and agree on where to reduce quality.

6.4.3.4 Scope Reduction

The techniques listed in the previous points mainly act on the tip of the triple constraint triangle relative to the project schedule. As the three tips of the triangle are connected to each other, if there is a need to compress the project schedule without increasing the costs, then it may be a good idea to act on the scope tip in order to produce effects on the other two tips (or on just one of them). For example:

- Coming up with a different and quicker way to perform a task, such as purchasing the finished product from the outside instead of producing it in-house, is an example of taking action on the scope.
- Reducing or completely eliminating the planned additional activities of the WBS specifically to manage a project risk factor is another example of reducing the schedule by reducing the scope.
- Reducing or completely eliminating the WBS activities necessary for the production of a deliverable that can be deferred in the economy of the project is the strongest action. In this way a reduced version of the project is produced, but in any case it must still be a significant part of the project ("I'll deliver the essential things within the agreed time, and then I'll deliver the rest"). Obviously scope reduction must be agreed to by the client.

Scope reduction requires active contribution from team members and also great organizational maturity. Active contribution derives from a typical request made by the project manager: "How can we reduce the project scope without visibly damaging the value of the final result?" On this aspect, the specialist contributions of team members may be decisive, providing indications of which parts or services related to the activities under their responsibility can be reduced without the client noticing a reduction of the scope, or in any case providing the project manager with detailed information so that he or she can make an informed decision. Organizational maturity derives from proactively offering to contribute to the scope reduction, sacrificing a part of one's activities or accepting scope reductions with good grace, and therefore without being obstructive.

After the different techniques have been examined, it should be clear that schedule compression rarely occurs without drawbacks. Each of the actions listed above may in itself bring about side effects, some more serious than others. It is important to have a good understanding of what these side effects are and, if possible, formally quantify them in order to discuss them, if necessary, with the client.

Moreover, different approaches can be taken in order to compress the schedule, and it is therefore necessary to equip oneself to make an informed choice. It involves carrying out a possibly quantified analysis of the consequences created by applying one compression approach rather than another. Saving time may result in higher costs, lower quality, and an increase in the complexity of the project (think how difficult it is to coordinate several activities if they are being carried out in parallel).

It is a good idea to remember that the purpose of compression techniques is not to find the "best ever" project plan, but instead to find the optimized project plan, which best combines the time, cost, and scope constraints established by the project. Therefore, a project plan that is realistic with respect to the imposed constraints should be created, and that makes it possible to request more resources, where there is a need to, in a circumstantial and justified way.

6.4.4 Step 4: Allocating the Available Resources

The logical scheduling of the project concludes with the estimated, and if necessary optimized, schedule network diagram. We have put down on paper a network that we consider to be the best compromise between the deadlines to respect, the costs to be incurred, and the organizational capacity to carry out the work in the sequence indicated in the network.

But we have done the math without the host: the actual availability of resources.

This fourth step in project scheduling is therefore aimed at allocating resources to the activities on the network and recalculating, as a consequence of this, the overall duration of the project, and if necessary, noting the changes to the critical path.

The task of allocating resources is not as simple as it may at first seem, as it involves intense negotiation work between the project manager and the department managers (direct managers of the resources used in the projects). When allocating resources, requests from other project managers and the priorities associated with the individual projects must be evaluated. The priorities associated with the projects and their change over time may require the project to be rescheduled. Downgrading may mean valuable resources are released to work on new projects, resulting in the need to find new resources whose level of productivity may be different. At this point it will be necessary to replan the project, or the remaining activities based on the new levels of productivity.

These changes of direction during the project are often experienced negatively by team members, who may feel themselves "tossed here and there" like bargaining chips. Except in cases of clear incompetence on the part of the project manager and department managers, the reasons may be rational insofar as a more important project than the current one requires the collaboration of certain resources over others. Team members must therefore come into syntony with the project as soon as possible so they can immediately provide the maximum contribution. However, they must remember that assignment to a project may be temporary and that, to make a comparison with the medical world, "another patient may require their treatment."

For team members, therefore, the project they are assigned to will represent their work environment for the entire duration necessary. Their performances may influence the course of the project, and they will be assessed on their work. The secret to obtaining good results from both points of view may be searching for personal objectives to pursue in the project (personal growth, professional growth, improved relations, corporate visibility, etc.).

For the effective allocation of resources on different project activities the following inputs must be used:

- Project calendar. The project calendar records the project start date (day, month, year), the dates on which it is known no project work will be carried out (for example, days the company is closed or periods of inactivity), work shifts, the number of hours per day, the length of the working week, holidays, etc.
- Resource calendar. The resource calendar is usually individual and is very different from the general project calendar insofar as it specifies

how and when the physical resource is actually available (e.g., Mary Whiteman is available from January to April for a maximum of four hours/day and from May to July for a maximum of eight hours/day). This calendar should therefore take into consideration the resources' planned holidays, commitments on other nonproject activities, etc.

- Milestone. Milestone means a significant event in the project scheduling, for example, an event that influences future work or determines the completion of a deliverable of primary importance. By nature, milestones must be few in number and recognizable. If this was not the case, all project events would become significant, and it would be difficult to establish if the event had actually occurred in its full reach. Milestones are typically externally imposed deadlines, such as: "We need to submit a first draft by the date law XYZ comes into effect" and even "The contract provides for the first delivery and billing at the end of March."
- The schedule network diagram, finally, and obviously, as a key output of logical scheduling.

The allocation of available resources on the network produces the final project schedule—in other words, an operating plan that states the start and finish dates of each activity in calendar dates, for example, the fact that activity D was scheduled to start on January 15, 2013, and be completed by February 19, 2013.

Usually operative scheduling is represented with the Gantt chart (bar chart). The Gantt chart, named after engineer Henry Laurence Gantt, who invented it in 1917, is perhaps one of the most well-known project management tools. It makes it possible to represent the calendar of activities and the relative states of progress on a Cartesian plan where the x-axis shows the project execution time, divided into time spans (days, weeks, months), and the ordinates, the activities forming the project. The activities are the result of the breakdown of the WPs of the WBS.

In the bar chart horizontal bars that vary in length represent the duration and time span of each activity. While the project is being carried out, these bars can be placed alongside (or overlapped by) others of different colors, indicating the progress of the activities. Activities represented in this way can also be associated with other information relating to the executors of the work and the anticipated cost.

The value of the Gantt chart is that it provides a clear and immediate view of the schedule according to which the project will be carried out, and also clearly shows the distribution of the different activities on the time axes, immediately highlighting which and how many activities are active on a certain date.

It is very likely that project duration would increase, moving from the schedule network diagram to the Gantt chart. In fact, the network reasons on the basis of the ideal but plausible provision of resources. For example, it assumes that two people are available full-time to perform an activity and that this provision, after due consideration, is plausible in the organizational context in which the project will be carried out. It does not take into account whether the two physical people that will be allocated to the activity are available only 50% of the time, or if in the same calendar day they are also allocated to other project activities. In the final analysis, the network does not take into account the physical constraints of the resources, which the Gantt chart, on the other hand, does. Therefore, it could happen that the same activity, estimated in the network to have a duration of 10 working days, in the Gantt chart has a duration not of 14 calendar days (10 working days correspond to 14 calendar days), but 26 calendar days due to the following contributory factors: (1) two mid-week public holidays, and therefore the duration increases from 14 to 16 calendar days, and (2) the availability of the two allocated resources only 50% of the time, and therefore the duration increases from 16 to 26 calendar days.

The theoretical duration in the schedule network diagram and the actual duration calculated in the Gantt chart represent the time range of the project.

Figure 6.10 reproposes the Gantt chart relative to the schedule network diagram in Figure 6.8. On paper the project should last 91 calendar days, equal to 65 working days, but it actually lasts 140 calendar days, due to the actual resource availability levels. As a result of this, some project activities have extended durations.

Figure 6.10 shows the project progress on the date the check was made: it was planned that activities A, B, C, and D would be finished by this date and activities E and F would have started. The situation is very different: activity C, for a number of reasons, has not been started, and as a result, activities E and F could not be started.

6.4.5 Step 5: Optimize the Allocation of Resources and Include New Resources if Necessary

If the Gantt chart shows a schedule that extends beyond the project end date required by the customer, this operative scheduling step must be

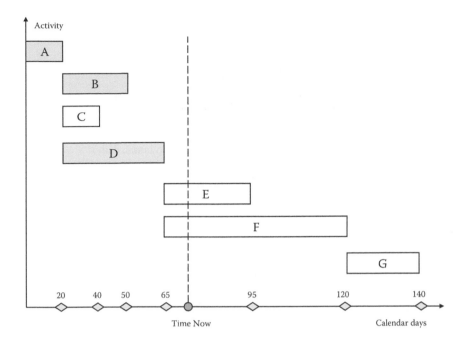

FIGURE 6.10
Example of bar chart (Gantt).

taken. In the example in Figure 6.10, the planned end date is 140 calendar days after the start of the project, while the customer may have requested the project to end after 100 calendar days.

It is therefore a question of moving the already allocated resources in an attempt to reduce the project duration. In particular, the allocation of underutilized resources must be optimized (for example, perhaps one person has some free days that could be used to help perform other activities).

At the same time, conflicts arising from the overallocation of some resources must be resolved.

Resource histograms are used for this purpose. Figure 6.11 gives an example. The x-axis shows the project calendar days, the ordinates show the effort required of a resource for each day, and dark gray indicates the workloads exceeding the daily maximum availability for the project declared by the resource.

As you can see, resource X has given a maximum daily availability of 75%, equal to six out of eight total hours of work. Nevertheless, on days 4, 5, 6, 9, and 10 the project scheduling provides a workload for resource X of over the maximum daily availability, even requiring 125% availability on days 5 and 10.

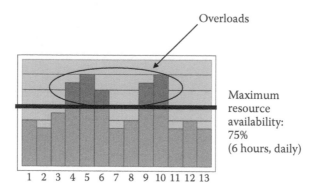

FIGURE 6.11
Resource histogram of resource X.

We are therefore talking about leveling the project resources through the use of specific scheduling heuristics. These heuristics are beyond the scope of this book, and therefore they will not be discussed. Resource leveling is the responsibility of the project manager, who can use project management tools to make simulations and find the best combination of allocating the available resources with respect to the project schedule and costs.

Clearly resource leveling does not always resolve all the scheduling problems: if there is a lot of work to be done and there are few partially allocated resources, it will be difficult for the scheduling heuristics to produce a schedule that respects the project end date required by the customer.

In these cases the resource histograms are still useful: the project manager identifies the resources representing the "bottleneck" and negotiates with the customer to increase the resources (greater daily availability of the resource already allocated; further resources with the same profile to be allocated to the activity that is slowing the project schedule).

6.5 PROFILE OF THE PROJECT FOLLOWER IN PROJECT SCHEDULING

As we mentioned earlier in this chapter, a project team member's contribution is critical for the effectiveness of project scheduling, particularly in logical scheduling—in other words, in the most noble part of the scheduling.

Let us now examine the project follower's contribution in detail, for each step of the scheduling.

6.5.1 Step 1: Determine the Project Work Sequence

Project specialist and logical relationships are strictly linked to each other.

The schedule network diagram lives off the expertise of the people sitting around the table. A network without experts has a short life; in fact, it complicates everyone's life.

The project team member may have a strong influence on the construction of the schedule network diagram by identifying the dependencies, describing the type of dependency, and defining, together with the other members of the project team, the schedule network diagram that makes the best use of the experience of the resources it intends to involve.

There are many ways to arrive at the same solution, so it is good to construct the network by integrating working methods that have proven successful for those involved. In the case of innovative projects, the construction of the network is an ideal opportunity for team building, as it favors the exchange of data and information deriving from the respective specializations in order to design the overall work plan, previously unknown in its entirety.

Therefore, the schedule network diagram is a stimulating meeting ground and an arena for discussions with other members of the project management team (PMT). It should be emphasized how the network becomes the starting track that influences all the subsequent scheduling steps. In this step the project follower takes the lion's share.

6.5.2 Step 2: Estimate the Duration of the Network Elements

The project specialist also leads the game in this step of logical scheduling. In fact, duration estimates should be provided for the activities in the schedule network diagram, based on a solid foundation of expertise.

In this step project team members have a great deal of autonomy, which they must know how to use well for the good of the project and to increase their professional and personal visibility.

All this becomes very interesting, as resource constraints are not considered in this step. Project specialists therefore can and must give free rein to their capacity to propose original solutions that optimize the network. That is, they can "fly high" without having to worry if a resource is not available and should be shared with other activities. The project manager expects this from project followers: breathe life into the project and improve the project scheduling.

Even lags and leads can be exploited to the full by project specialists in searching for faster quality solutions that can be implemented.

The critical path and floats become an important ground for reflection for the entire PMT. The critical path, and even more so the contemporaneity of several critical paths, provides the PMT with a common challenge: "Can we do it?" "Will we succeed in testing ourselves on the network with these timing and dependencies?" "Which of us is on the critical path and will in any case be supported by the others?" "How can we achieve critical mass, given that we are on many activities of the critical path?"

6.5.3 Step 3: Compress the Project Duration

Another great opportunity for project followers: there is nothing more enjoyable than returning to the schedule network diagram in search of ever more original, ambitious, and incisive solutions for scheduling the project.

It is already difficult to construct the network without experts; compressing it becomes impossible if the active and widespread participation of the entire PMT cannot be counted on.

Even the drawbacks arising from compression actions (fast tracking *in primis*) are elective territory for project team members: with one foot they accelerate the project, and with the other they put the brakes on after due consideration. It is this very balancing act between opposite driving forces that produces the estimated and optimized schedule network diagram.

A project follower's failure to contribute in step 1 of constructing the network can be fully remedied during its compression. There is usually no shortage of ideas—it just takes a bit of courage to think outside the box!

Clearly the project manager cannot help but find every way to reward the courage demonstrated by project followers seeking to "square the circle" of scheduling.

6.5.4 Step 4: Allocate the Available Resources

At the end of the logical scheduling the games are over, as regards the project scheduling framework. If the PMT has worked well together, and each member has actively contributed, a consistent, complete, and shared network should have been produced. The PMT can therefore present itself in top form for any negotiations on the resources to allocate to the project. In fact, it must have prepared solid arguments to demonstrate the cost/benefit of the resources allocated, to benefit project scheduling.

In this specific phase, project team members contribute by assisting the project manager upon request in allocating resources, for example, supporting the project manager with the request for resources and encouraging the inclusion of resources in activities they are responsible for.

6.5.5 Step 5: Optimize the Allocation of Resources and Include New Resources if Necessary

The same contribution provided in the previous step should also be provided in this last step of project scheduling. Project specialists can in fact identify possible solutions to resolve conflicts concerning the overallocation of resources, especially those assigned to activities they are responsible for.

Similarly, they can provide the project manager with reasons to request new people to allocate to the project, demonstrating the time savings arising from these additions.

It should be pointed out that this contribution concerns both the quantitative (amount of resources) and qualitative (skills) aspects of the critical resources. The resources are first and foremost people, and project specialists are called upon, as well as working in the first person, to assess the people assigned.

6.6 CONCLUSIONS

One problem that often crops up in projects is that the scheduling does not reflect the real methods of carrying out the work, nor is it based on reliable schedules for carrying out the individual activities. The reason behind this problem should be sought in top-down scheduling, or rather, decided by people who do not have the expertise to understand if what has been proposed is actually achievable. In order to reduce the gap between scheduling on paper and its actual implementation, the contribution of people who understand the operating issues is essential, and therefore team members must be the key players in scheduling the project.

See page 255 for the exercise relating to this chapter.

REFERENCES

Feather, M.S., S.L. Comford, and K.A. Hicks. 2002. Descoping. In *Proceedings of the 27th IEEE/NASA Software Engineering Workshop*. Greenbelt, MD: IEEE Computer Society.

Project Management Institute. 2008. *A guide to the Project Management Body of Knowledge*. 4th ed. Newtown Square, PA: Project Management Institute.

Project Management Institute. 2012. *A guide to the Project Management Body of Knowledge*. 5th ed. Newtown Square, PA: Project Management Institute.

Putnam, D. 2013. Haste makes waste when you over-staff to achieve schedule compression. QSD. http://www.qsm.com/risk_02.html.

Wideman, R.M. 1995. *Cost control of capital projects*. Richmond, BC: BiTech Publishers Ltd.

Yang, Y., Z. Chen, R. Valerdi, and B. Boehm. 2005. *Effect of schedule compression on project effort*. Center for Software Engineering, University of Southern California (USC-CSE). http://csse.usc.edu/csse/TECHRPTS/2005/usccse2005-520/usccse2005-520.pdf.

7

Formulation of Estimates

READER'S GUIDE

This chapter is for people who

- Do not understand why the estimates produced are unreliable
- Use a single method to generate an estimate
- Have noticed that, even with sophisticated approaches, estimates are still misleading
- Are uncertain whether it is best to provide an optimistic or a pessimistic estimate

7.1 WHY IS ESTIMATING SO IMPORTANT?

The topic of estimates is absolutely central in project management. We may have defined the objectives down to the last detail, developed an excellent WBS, and correctly assigned the project roles and responsibilities, but if the estimates concerning the costs, schedule, and use of resources are wrong, we risk embarking on a project that has very little chance of achieving the set objectives.

The estimation process is therefore very important, and project team members play a central role in this regard.

7.2 ESTIMATION TECHNIQUES

In the previous chapter we introduced some issues relating to estimation techniques. In this chapter we will examine the subject more closely.

Estimation methods can be very different in project management. Without going into details beyond the scope of this book, here is an overview of the most common estimation techniques.

7.2.1 Bottom-Up

With the bottom-up estimates overall estimates for the project are built up from the detailed level and aggregated to give totals for the project as a whole (Projectnet Glossary 1997).

A project manager who asks team members to provide estimates for their activities in order to obtain estimates for the entire project is using the bottom-up method. For a project manager the bottom is represented by individual activities or the work packages; for team members the bottom can take into consideration more detailed aspects that may not be visible to the project manager.

For instance, in a residential building project for the project manager the most detailed aspect useful for project planning and control may be "install the fixtures"; the team member responsible for this activity may break it down further into subactivities (unload the fixtures from the truck, transfer the fixtures to the floors, remove the packaging, mount the fixtures, etc.) in order to provide the project manager with a more reliable estimate.

Sharing the bottom-up estimation process with the project manager and colleagues may be useful as activities that no one had thought of, or that conflict or are redundant alongside others, may emerge. In the previous example it may have emerged that the transporters would have unloaded the fixtures from the truck and not the personnel in charge of mounting. Knowing these things in advance is useful not only for providing more accurate estimates, but also for improving project activity coordination.

However, the bottom-up method also has its drawbacks. In fact, starting with the detail in order to reconstruct more complex activities may cause one to lose sight of the global vision, and therefore the actual characteristics of the project. In addition, dealing with many very small activities increases the planning and control effort. In this regard here is an example on which to meditate.

THE COMPLICATED MOBILE PHONE TEST

A participant on a project management course, at the end of one of the training days, asked the teacher for advice: "Excuse me, I dedicate around two hours each day to updating my activity plan, which was developed with professional planning software. I honestly do my best to plan everything as well as possible, but the planning is very unstable; every day I have to review everything and update the plan with new deadlines and new estimates on the durations of the next activities. Just so you can understand the complexity, the plan has 84 activities." In the teacher's mind, based on his experience, 84 activities would represent a project of around three to five months carried out by a small team of collaborators, perhaps three or four people. If this was the case, two hours a day for project management was in fact a little excessive, but otherwise not yet pathological. However, before answering, it was necessary to inquire further. Then came the fateful question: "Sorry, but what project are we talking about? How many people are working on it? How long does it last?"

The response was unexpected: "My job is to test the functionality of mobile phones and compile the report card. I work alone and on average I take a week to complete the project."

The teacher didn't know what to say: on the one hand, the person had demonstrated his passion for project management and had an excellent understanding of how to use the planning software, but on the other hand, how do you explain that breaking down a one-week activity into 84 subactivities was madness?

This example shows the typical case of an exasperating bottom-up approach that didn't deliver value to anyone. An excessive breakdown results in loss of the global vision, as well as being highly unstable: even an unexpected phone call of just ten minutes would have sorely tested the links between the 84 activities, probably requiring the plan to be updated, which would have wasted more time than the event itself (the phone call).

7.2.2 Top-Down

The top-down estimation method starts with the idea of considering the project as a whole, namely, considering it as a system with interconnected elements, and therefore studying an individual element may not allow you to detect the actual interaction between the elements.

Top-down estimates start with the assumption that the person generating the estimate has already dealt with similar projects (Wideman 1995, Rosenau 1988) and is therefore comfortable estimating the whole rather than the individual parts. For instance, those who are used to writing books know that it is more complicated to write a book with others than it is to write one alone. Therefore, if in the past an author took three months to write a 200-page book, the answer to the question how long would it take to write a 200-page book with the contribution of four authors would certainly be longer than three months. The top-down method is not the exclusive domain of the project manager. In fact, team members may also be responsible for relevant groups of activities in which a top-down approach may be applied.

7.2.3 The Experts' Judgment

Various research shows how in most cases companies use an estimation method based on the so-called experts' judgment (Kitchenham et al. 2002, Paynter 1996, Hihn and Habib-Agahi 1991)—in other words, asking team members to provide estimates for activities in which they have expertise.

Being called upon as experts in the estimations does not also mean they will perform the activities covered by the estimate: often this is the case, but not necessarily. This aspect is important and will be addressed later in this chapter (see Section 7.3.2).

7.2.4 Analogy

In some respects this method is a systematic form of expert judgment since experts often search for analogous situations so as to inform their opinion.

The technique involves characterizing the project for which an estimate is required. This characterization then forms the basis for finding similar or analogous projects that have been completed for which effort (or other variables that have to be estimated) is known. These values are then used, possibly with adjustment, to generate the predicted value (Shepperd et al. 1996).

The analogy estimation can be used for both the top-down and bottom-up methods: in the first case projects or groups of activities are compared, and in the second case individual activities are compared directly. Naturally, the more similar the activities, the more meaningful the comparison. The analogy technique makes it possible to provide an initial estimate quickly; this does not prevent team members from using other methods to develop the estimate further, if necessary. When there are plenty of data available on projects, the analogy estimation technique can be more structured by using the historic series.

7.2.5 Historic Series

The underlying principle on which historic series is based is very clear: use data from past performances to estimate future performances. The historic series system can be very complex, requiring advanced skills in statistics. Very often, however, very useful data to estimate the project can be obtained without performing particularly complex analyses.

THE SAME AVERAGE BUT...

Below are the historic series for the time taken to install a specific textile machine at clients in China and Vietnam.

China: 32 32 28 30 26 25 25 23 24 23 22 23 21 20 20 18 18 19 17
        18 18 19 17

Vietnam: 22 23 22 21 24 23 22 22 23 24 25 22 23 21 23 22 22 23 21
          23 22 22 23

The average of both historic series is identical (22.5), but even without applying sophisticated statistical analyses it becomes apparent how the two series are very different. In the case of China the mounting time reduced over time, with a probable stabilization of the duration values around 17–19, while in Vietnam the situation did not show any specific developments.

In theory, the historic series makes it possible to lower the subjectivity and uncertainty of estimates, as they are calculated based on the history of similar activities carried out in the past.

However, it is precisely in attributing similarities that the greatest mistakes are made (Abdel-Hamid 1990). In fact, even when activities have the same name, numerous variables may influence the complexity and characteristics and, consequently, the duration. If these variables are not taken into consideration in the estimation model based on historic series, there is a risk of making decisions based on presumed similarity that is not actually the case. For instance, if new machines were available, this change may make the previous surveys virtually unusable or, in any case, not very meaningful. Therefore, if the history of the variables that have a strong impact on the activities surveyed is not traced, the historic series may lead to poor results.

Finally, a historic series must also be challenged, in the sense that to be competitive, past performances must be surpassed by future ones. An incorrect use of the historic series instead leads to the replication of past behaviors, and therefore a lack of innovation. Project team members may use the historical analysis of the duration of past activities as a basis for future estimates, but they must be careful to assess whether there are truly comparable activities within the historic series, and they must try and find a way to improve on past performances.

7.2.6 Models

When team members often carry out activities that are very similar to each other they may attempt to build forecasting models that support the estimation process.

For instance, if a team member discovers that a recent graduate takes 30% longer to carry out an activity than someone who has been working at the company for over a year, he or she could use these data as the parameters for a model that takes into consideration collaborators' experience in order to obtain the activity duration estimates. Naturally the models may also be highly complex compared to the brief example given, but the logic is the same: incorporating the variables and parameters into a project activities estimation model.

The effectiveness of the model depends on its capacity to incorporate the variables and parameters that actually determine the characteristics of the activity (Kemerer 1987). A model can also take account of 100 variables, but if the one with the most impact is not detected, its practical value can be severely limited.

In general, models can represent valid supports under stable conditions, while they may not be very reliable in conditions where sudden change occurs (Kemerer 1987). In fact, a model grows and is perfected based on the experiences of those who created it, and therefore it is unlikely that unexpected events will already be part of the model being used.

The choice between different estimation methods is not only based on rational elements, such as the actual similarities between projects, which may lean toward a more automated and stable system of producing estimates. Cultural elements also come into play. Some companies start with the assumption that no model can replace human skill; others think that humans are too unreliable to produce consistent estimates, and that the estimates may be distorted to create personal gain.

7.3 PITFALLS IN THE ESTIMATION PROCESS

Some points of the estimation process must be taken into careful consideration by the team member who provides the estimates during project planning.

7.3.1 Different Degrees of Tolerable Approximation

A first point that very often creates difficulties, if not even embarrassment, is the fact that all projects are based on estimates and not accurate data, and that the approximation and uncertainty of these estimates may even vary within the same project.

This aspect becomes more important the more the level of approximation required in the estimation process moves away from the level of approximation (or certainty) that the team member is used to in performing the nonproject work activities (Sampietro 2010).

For instance, those working in fields where the margin of error or accepted approximation is very low (think of mathematics, accounting, measuring with high-precision tools) may find it very difficult to have to provide estimates with very high approximation margins and perhaps in a very short time, insofar as it requires a different mindset. On the contrary, those who are used to approximation (those who work on advertising campaigns, creative types in general, teachers, strategists, etc.) may be uneasy working on projects that require highly detailed estimates. Moreover, even within the same project there may be times when a high level of detail is required (the planning of schedules in projects with penalties linked to significant delays), and others where approximation can be tolerated (the first budget simulation to understand whether the project makes economic sense).

Below is an example highlighting the degree of approximation within projects.

ARE THEY RIPPING US OFF?

During a planning meeting for the construction of a new industrial plant, the secretary handed the managing director of a company that produces steel coils an offer sent by fax for the construction of a machine nearly identical to one that the same supplier had built four years ago. The offer was two pages long and therefore, as it was short, the managing director decided to read it immediately. Everything went smoothly as he read the first page, but when he read the timing and costs his expression suddenly changed. He shook his head vigorously and said: "They're crazy! Who do they think they're dealing with, inexperienced people?"

The problem quickly identified by the managing director was this: four years ago the same supplier had built the same machine and the cost required was 450,000 euros in a time frame of 12 months. The managing director therefore expected a slightly higher cost (inflation and the cost of raw materials) and lower times, based on the consideration that the second time the same project is carried out, fewer errors should occur, and so it should take less time. Instead, the situation set out in the quote before his eyes was completely contrary to common sense: 16 months for delivery time at a cost of 800,000 euros. The manager of the technical office, who had designed the machine both four years before and this time, making small changes, was also present at the planning table. The managing director, to get a general idea of what a reasonable price increase might be and what, on the other hand, should be considered absolutely unreasonable, started to make some calculations: "Okay, let's try and understand, in broad terms, how much material and how much labor goes into this machine.

We know that the cost of labor has increased by around 3% per year, so over four years that's around 12–15%; therefore, I'd be willing to acknowledge this percentage, even if I expected a compensatory effect due to fewer person-hours being used, as this would be the second time they have built the machine. In terms of raw materials, how much of an increase has there been in the last four years?" the managing director asked the technical office manager.

"I don't know, I'd have to go through the project folders and see how much we paid four years ago and how much we paid recently for the same type of steel. If you want, I can go to the office and give you an answer within about half an hour."

"No, I'm not interested in accurate figures right now. I want to understand, more or less, how much steel has increased in the last four years. So?" asked the managing director.

"I'd have to check; off the top of my head I could make a mistake."

"Okay, but seeing as you deal with these issues, I wanted to know if you could give me a quick estimate. In any case forget it, from memory it's around 100–120%. Tell me instead, more or less, how much steel is there in our machine?"

"I don't know, I'd have to go to the computer and check the amount of steel-only components used from the technical drawings. I should be able to tell you in around two hours."

"Listen, you don't seem to have understood. I'm not interested in knowing the exact weight. I want to understand, in broad terms, how much the supplier is asking for in excess. Then, if need be, we'll do the detailed calculations later. So very broadly speaking, therefore, does this machine contain 1, 5, or 10 tons of steel?"

"I don't know, I'd have to see the calculations, from memory. I might be wrong."

"I repeat, I'm interested in an order of magnitude. I know the machine weighs around 10 tons and I know they are not all of steel. I wanted to understand the proportion or the weight, but really very roughly."

"Yes, but from memory I might make a mistake, I'd have to see the calculations…."

The managing director got even more irritated and in the end, thanks to answers provided by other collaborators less experienced than the technical office manager, but with more mental flexibility, it took a few minutes to arrive at the estimate that an increase in price of around 20% would have been tolerable. Later, in order to refute the quote received, the managing director asked the managers of the technical office and the human resources office to accurately calculate the weight of the different components subdivided by material, the increase in the prices of the different types of materials over the last four years, and the increase in labor, again over the last four years.

This is an example of how a team member did not adapt to the degree of approximation useful in that situation. An answer of 3 to 6 tons would have been absolutely plausible, but this answer never came, creating strong tension in addition to that caused by an unreasonable quote. Subsequently, to respond in kind to the quote sent by the supplier, it was necessary to provide more precise calculations, at which time the team member was much more at ease.

7.3.2 Optimistic Estimates

Some people, when faced with a request to provide estimates, tend to give answers that are too optimistic or that underestimate the use of resources, the time required to perform a project activity, or the cost associated with it. It may seem strange, but what may appear reasonable, namely, that an expert is capable of providing more reliable estimates than a nonexpert, is not always the case (Jørgensen 2002). Experts, and therefore many team members, who precisely, on account of their experience, are called upon to collaborate in projects, very often tend to provide highly optimistic estimates.

Among the causes of optimistic estimates we can list:

- Temporal distance of the activities to be performed. This aspect will be examined in more depth later in the chapter (see Section 7.3.4).
- Focusing on technical aspects (Moløkken and Jørgensen 2005). Some people, especially those with very technical courses of study and professions, base their estimates focusing only on technical problems without considering the influence that other people or other activities may have in the performance of the activity in question.
- Underestimating the actual time available. This aspect will be examined in more depth later in the chapter (see Section 7.3.4).

In any case, generating optimistic estimates does not automatically mean not being capable of honoring them. Given that people may well change their productivity based on restrictions and external stimuli (Barseghyan 2009), self-produced optimistic estimates tend to stimulate people to higher levels of performance, thus increasing the probability of honoring the estimate. This dual relationship between estimate and performance (the expected performance influences the estimate, but the estimate also influences performance) goes by the name of self-fulfilling prophecy (Merton 1968). In general, self-fulfilling prophecies are those predictions whereby the person making the prediction is also capable of influencing its coming about; if there is a high expectation that the prophecy will occur, the individual will behave so that it does.

7.3.3 Pessimistic Estimates

While some people tend to provide optimistic estimates, others tend to do the opposite, namely, provide pessimistic estimates.

Besides personality traits, such as being a pessimist and therefore assessing the activity as more complex than it actually is, pessimistic estimates are a kind of protection against company practices such as (Goldratt 1997) the following:

- Heavy reprimand if estimates are overshot. If an organization is in the habit of heavily penalizing the overshooting of estimates, collaborators will tend to encourage very cautious estimates in order to reduce the likelihood that they are not respected.
- The constant game of negotiation. If, when a team member provides an estimate, the other party systematically responds with a request for its reduction by a certain percentage (20% is typical), collaborators will tend to steer toward pessimistic estimates so that any "discounts" do not have a negative impact on the execution of activities.

7.3.4 Temporal Distance of the Activities to Be Performed

Very often it is necessary to estimate quantities for activities that must be carried out in the relatively near future (a few months time). It has been noticed that people react differently when an activity is still a long way off (Roy et al. 2005, Loewenstein and Schkade 1999, Mischel et al. 1989).

In a project environment people:

- Fail to take into account future problems that might interfere with the project's completion date (Buehler et al. 1994). A lot of people, in addition to collaborating in more than one project, must also perform other continuous work activities. An activity that has to be performed a long way in the future is unlikely to compete with other activities in the agenda. There is therefore a perception that more time can be dedicated to performing the activity. Gradually, as time passes, however, it is highly likely that other commitments will compete with the previously planned activity, thus reducing the actual time available, and therefore making the estimate too optimistic. In the absence of reliable information that makes it possible to realistically estimate the time available for a future activity, a good method is to use actual workloads or those of the same reference period as a basis for the estimate (if the workloads depend on specific time-based events such as seasonal sales, harvest periods in agriculture, university classes for teachers, etc.).
- Simplify the characteristics of the activity and therefore its level of complexity. This attitude derives from the difficulty of representing the events that may occur; future activities are seen as not very real and are represented in a simplified manner (Liberman and Trope 1998). Simplification of the activity's characteristics therefore leads to estimates that are too optimistic.
- Overestimate the complexity of the activity. Instead, some people tend to overestimate the complexity of future activities, as the future is seen as highly uncertain and therefore highly risky (Norem and Cantor 1986, Showers and Cantor 1984). In this case pessimistic estimates will be obtained. Both overestimating and underestimating the complexity can be counteracted by using contextual information, if available, so as to better visualize the future situation, or by using analogy in the case of similar project activities, so as to use past performances as a basis for the forecasts.

7.3.5 Parkinson's Law

Cyril Northcote Parkinson was a British naval historian who wrote around 60 books. In one of these, *Parkinson's Law*, he explained some mechanisms of the British public administration, which were certainly not virtuous.

The book was a great success, and consequently his fame as a historian was replaced by that of an expert in public administration. His claims were based on direct observations, and some of them are even commonly accepted from a scientific point of view.

In 1955 Parkinson wrote in the *Economist*: "Work expands so as to fill the time available for its completion," an observation that is now known as Parkinson's law. The original Parkinson's law explained this result with career and status mechanisms (for a detailed dissertation on Parkinson's law see Parkinson 1955). Nowadays, many people, including us, use the term *Parkinson's law* to represent a different concept. Essentially, people tend to self-regulate their productivity in order to use all the time available for the completion of a task.

The reasons for this behavior can be summarized as follows (Goldratt 1997):

- Finishing a task early does not generate free time, as in an organization there is always a tendency to saturate the resources, so people are discouraged from not appearing busy.
- Finishing early may also indicate that the estimates were too pessimistic, so in the future they will be proportionally reduced; this is therefore an incentive not to demonstrate that the estimates were too cautious.

Parkinson's law can be interpreted like this: it is the time available that determines the duration of the activity to be performed, and not the characteristics of the activity to be performed that determines the time required to complete the activity. Naturally this is true within certain limits; we cannot claim that an activity normally requiring ten calendar days to be carried out can be dealt with in one day, but it is probably possible in less than ten days. Essentially, humans are flexible and capable of adapting to the context (in this case, the context is determined by the time assigned). This flexibility varies from person to person and from activity to activity. For instance, an activity heavily based around manual work has lower flexibility than a mental activity, due to obvious physical restrictions.

How does Parkinson's law relate to the topic of estimates? Very often too rational an approach is used in searching for the perfect date for activities that can be heavily influenced by Parkinson's law, and that are therefore very flexible in terms of completion time. This approach does not generate better estimates; rather, it simply erodes time given that a wide range of choices would have been capable of leading to similar results.

For instance, think of the activity of creating a new company logo. If we look at the physical time it takes to produce a draft, we are talking about a few hours (or even minutes), but if we are talking about the creative phase before, how much time is actually necessary? An almost philosophical answer is that these activities cannot be planned: the logo sees the light when the creative genius decides to emerge. Thinking of a more concrete answer, this is a typical activity where the compression but also the expansion of time has no direct relation to the quality provided (up to a certain limit).

7.3.6 Student Syndrome

Student syndrome, which is often stated together with Parkinson's law, refers to the phenomenon that many students will begin to engage themselves in a task just before a deadline (Ariely and Wertenbroch 2002, Goldratt 1997).

The name of this syndrome derives from the observation of students' behavior during exam and thesis preparation. Many of them, in fact, leave it to the last two or three fateful days to reach an adequate level of preparation, irrespective of the time they had available to study the material. Student syndrome is a form of procrastination. Without getting into a discussion on the reasons behind procrastination on a task, which are often psychological, it is important to assess the effects on a project.

Student syndrome cancels out the benefit of any extra time allocated during the planning phase. In fact, if an activity that could be carried out in 8 calendar days under normal conditions is allocated 13 days, taking into account the possibility of an unfavorable event, the most likely outcome is that the person assigned to the task would start it on the sixth day, therefore canceling out the benefits of a buffer of 5 extra days. Unfortunately, what often happens is that the extra time allocated is not used to counteract uncertainty, and thus as an antidote to the occurrence of unfavorable events, but it is used as nonproductive time at the start of the activity. If an unfavorable event then occurs, it is not absorbed by the extra time allocated, as this has already been used, so it turns into a delay. This is another reason why projects have a natural tendency not to respect the assigned deadlines, rather than being completed in advance or on time.

Project team members who must propose the timing of an activity, for themselves or for others, must be aware of the high probability that creating buffers to counteract any risks associated with the activity may not translate into benefits of any kind due to the very widespread way of working that leads people only to perform the activity close to its deadline.

7.3.7 Main Activity

It may seem obvious to state that the duration of an activity depends on the tasks it involves. The duration of each specific task being equal, an activity that contains 20 tasks will require more time than an activity that contains 5 (the resources used being equal). Based on this truism, let us reconnect to how activities are very often communicated, described, and correlated in order to understand if this may have an impact on the production of estimates.

Below is an example.

Why were the estimates for this project so wrong? First, estimates are provided for an activity based on its description, which inevitably is very often simplified, when in actual fact other support activities are carried out in addition to the stated activity. In this specific case, contacting the users to define the interview schedule, preparing a record of the interviews, and organizing the results of the interviews are all support activities to the main one (collecting the user requirements), which, however, were not included in the estimate.

Essentially, we tend to plan the activity as we perceive it from the standpoint of the tasks included, but there may be a discrepancy between what is perceived and what is actually required (Rossi 2012). In order to provide correct estimates, project team members must therefore:

- Ask the project manager what actual tasks are included in an activity
- Communicate back to the project manager what tasks are necessary in their opinion to carry out a certain activity, in order to check if the same name means similar things to them

WHAT DOES THE ACTIVITY ACTUALLY CONSIST OF?

A company was embarking on a new project for the development of software to support the commercial department. As part of the project, the commercial director, with the role of project leader, asked the IT specialist to provide an estimate of the time necessary to conduct a user requirements analysis involving his ten collaborators. The specialist, on the basis of his experience, replied that five calendar days would be sufficient. When the project went into implementation phase, the activity in question required ten days, double the time estimated. This naturally angered the commercial director.

- Ask the project manager, or in any case check during the planning, who the recipients are of the output of the activity in question and what are the incoming inputs, in order to understand if activities to make these handovers more fluid (output in input) are required

7.3.8 Measuring Time

Different units of measurement for the duration of an activity can be used: we can speak of hours, days, weeks, months, and even years. It has been noted that the unit of measurement used to produce time estimates has a significant impact on the estimate itself (Dunning et al. 2005).

This example, which shows the findings of some research and surveys in the field, tells us how the unit of measurement influences the estimate itself.

In general, an estimate of the duration in days is more reliable than an estimate given in weeks, months, or years. This is because the measurement unit of a day is related to the nature of people, namely, the wake-sleep cycle. As this cycle has, for several millennia and to a large extent even today, marked the alternation between working time and nonworking time, our brain finds it easier to allocate activities on a daily basis rather than using other units of measurement that do not have a direct link with our vital mechanisms. For example, one month, a completely arbitrary unit of measurement, is experienced by our brain as a very long interval of time during which many activities can be carried out. The simple conversion of the month unit into working days instead makes it easier for us to understand the actual length of a month time unit, and therefore to check that a month is not such a long horizontal time period, as it is only comprised of 20 to 22 working days. A year represents an even more extreme situation; it is such a long time span that it can almost seem infinite.

DOES 1 MONTH EQUAL 42 DAYS?

"How many months will it take to move the machines from one location to another?" the project manager asked the team member. "Well ... I'd say one month is enough," replied the team member.

"Perfect, so I'll tell the team responsible for calibrating the machinery to start work in 21 days," said the project manager. "No, no, just a minute, I think two months is a more reasonable time frame," concluded the team member.

It is better for team members who are usually involved in shorter activities to reason in terms of short time measurement units, such as a day; otherwise, there is a risk they will underestimate the duration of the activity. Our natural inclination to allocate work on a daily basis is, however, moderated by the habit of reasoning and dealing with other measurement units. If, for example, the company standard time measurement for projects is a week, with experience we will become accustomed to reasoning in these terms. However, the fact remains that this method of estimating is less natural and requires additional practice.

7.3.9 Availability of Information

It is normal that, when asked to provide a quick estimate, we base our answer on experience. Unfortunately, many tasks' duration, cost, and risks can be heavily influenced by variables that we have never experienced or we are not so used to experiencing. Asking additional information is fundamental in order to evaluate if we are still able to provide reliable estimates or adjust the estimates based on the new setting. This is especially true when the variability of the outcome can be very high. Let us consider the example below.

MILAN–GENOA

Estimate request in the planning phase: "So, for a whole week during the project half our team will work in Genoa. It won't be possible to stay overnight, so 30 people will have to go back and forth between Milan and Genoa each day. How long will it take?" asked the project manager. "Look, it normally takes me an hour and a half," answered a team member.

What happened during the execution phase: "This is a disaster, you told me it took about an hour and a half each way, so three hours a day, and instead it took eight. This made the transfer to Genoa a bloodbath in economic terms, as the parent company, as per company policy, considers travel time working time, and we made a really bad impression with the client as we arrived two hours late on the first day. And to think that I asked you for an estimate because you've been making that journey for years and I considered you an expert."

Let us analyze what happened.

The response to the question of how long it takes to get from Milan to Genoa on the highway during the week was almost immediate and was based on assumptions that are true in most cases:

- We'll go by car.
- The car will be able to travel continuously at the maximum cruise speed stated in the highway code.
- The volume of traffic will be the same as it normally is on working days.

However, in this particular case the 30 collaborators traveled in a company bus, so the cruise speed was lower, and in addition, the transfer coincided with the international boat show in Genoa. This is why context makes a difference and has a direct effect on estimates. Having information on the activity and the context makes it possible to exit the trap of producing an estimate that may be correct on average but rarely in the details.

7.3.10 Actual Time Available for the Project

In projects the time variable can be measured in three ways: the duration in calendar days (called elapsed time in jargon), the time in working days (called duration in jargon), and the commitment in days/person (called effort in jargon).

While the first two are very common measurements even in daily life, effort is a measurement typical of project environments. The effort is the measure of how long the project would last if it was carried out by one person working full-time. So saying that a project is 100 person-days means that one person alone would take 100 working days to complete the project (with the formula of 8 working hours per day). Similarly, 100 person-days is equal to 800 person-hours. Adopting a slightly simplified approach, if two people work at the same time on the same project, the estimated effort in person-days would be the same, while the duration in calendar days or working days would be lower. In our simple example, assuming that two people manage to carry out the project work in parallel, the project would last 50 working days, with the effort being equal (100 person-days).

Some people find it easy to reason in terms of calendar days or working days, while others prefer to reason in terms of effort. In theory the correct logical step would be to calculate the required effort for a new activity independently from the available resources, and then match the calculated effort with the actual availability of resources (how many people can work on the activity and with what level of availability, for example, full-time or part-time), and consequently obtain the duration of the activity in calendar days. If the result is not satisfactory, the available resources being equal, it is necessary to assess if other activities could be postponed or more diluted in order to allocate more hours per day to performing the activity in question and therefore reduce its duration.

It should be pointed out that an activity's duration and effort are not necessarily proportional to each other. Obtaining a building permit, an essential condition to start a house restructuring project, is an example of an activity that may last several weeks and requires limited effort (a few working days from the surveyor spread here and there over time). Vice versa, the activity "provide a training course for the sales network," as part of a project to launch a new product, is an example of an activity that lasts a short time (for example, 2 working days) but requires much effort (for example, 22 person-days in the case of ten sellers attending a course held by one teacher). So be careful not to equate doubling the resources with halving the time. With reference to the previous examples, the time required to obtain the building permit does not reduce even if there is an army of surveyors physically occupying the municipal office, just as the duration of the training course would not increase if there were more participants. What this means is that many project activities require separate estimates for duration and effort. The project activities estimate is a great way to increase the value of a project team member's contribution.

One problem often found is that during planning too many hours of availability are foreseen, then during the execution of the works agendas are much fuller, thus delaying the completion of a specific activity (this topic has already been introduced in Section 7.3.4). The explanation for this phenomenon is that people, when planning and therefore scheduling the future, tend to adopt a simplified view. When planning an activity that must be carried out in three months' time, they see their agenda is free, but this does not guarantee that it will remain so even close to the date of performing the activity; other activities and urgencies may compete in the same period. Essentially, it is rare that 100% working time means 100% of the time available for a specific project activity. If this is not taken into consideration, there is a risk of providing optimistic estimates that then cannot actually be maintained. In this case the study of the historic series may be very useful. For instance, if we notice that around 40% of the working time is dedicated to urgencies, it would be wrong to say that we can dedicate ourselves to the project full-time.

7.3.11 Forecasts for Others

Sometimes a project team member might be required to provide estimates for colleagues dealing with similar issues.

This request is mainly made of project team members considered experts in their field. At first glance, the basic idea can be shared: an expert is familiar with the activities to be performed to a higher level of detail and experience than the others, and is therefore the most suitable person to provide reliable estimates.

Unfortunately, the actual situation is different (Hinds 1999); in fact, it has been noted that experts can provide good estimates for themselves and other experts (see Section 7.3.2 for a discussion on estimates provided by experts), but they are not capable of providing estimates for people with lower skills than them. In particular, their estimates tend to be optimistic, thus making it improbable that colleagues will be capable of performing the activities within the time frames set by the expert. The explanation for this phenomenon is that the expert, now having fully metabolized the activity, loses the capacity to imagine the problems that a collaborator with less experience may encounter in performing the tasks; moreover, even if the expert could imagine the problems, he or she would be able to resolve them more quickly than a less experienced collaborator.

7.3.12 Closeness of Temporal Phenomena

When the historic series is not formalized and analyzed, experience is relied on. Nevertheless, an expert is a person that, in a particular field, has accumulated much knowledge and often experienced situations similar to those to be tackled. Here we wish to bring attention to a problem that nonformalized experience can create. Humans unconsciously tend to give more weight to events that are closer in time (Hillson and Hulett 2004).

The below example applies.

The explanation was that the anomalous data of a duration of 20 days was obtained by Andrew a long time before, and by Lucy recently. Lucy therefore provided a highly pessimistic estimate, as she was influenced by negative data obtained recently.

EQUAL BUT DIFFERENT HISTORICAL SERIES

Two specialists, Andrew and Lucy, were working on similar projects and activities. In a planning meeting the project manager asked them to provide duration estimates for the "review of project documents" activity; Andrew replied that the estimated duration was 11 working days, and Lucy, 18. Given the considerable discrepancy in the estimates, the project manager got angry, but both Andrew and Lucy said that these estimates were obtained from their historical series. The project manager asked to see the historic duration data. This request caught both Andrew and Lucy off guard, who replied that they did not need written data as they remembered the durations from memory. The project manager then asked them to write down, from memory, the durations of the "review of project documents" activity for the last 20 projects. The result was as follows:

Andrew: 20 12 10 13 11 12 10 10 12 11 13 11 10 12 10 12 11 11 10 13
Lucy: 13 10 11 11 12 10 12 10 11 13 11 12 10 10 12 11 13 10 12 20

The project manager pointed out that the average of the two historical series was the same, namely, 11.5 days, and that even as a trend there was no particular phenomena to report. So why did Andrew and Lucy provide such different estimates?

7.4 PROJECT FOLLOWERSHIP ACTIONS TO IMPROVE ESTIMATES

The contribution that a project team member can offer the project in terms of estimates can be summarized as follows:

- Assess whether the estimation technique chosen generates good results or should be improved
- Assess whether other estimation techniques can be used with respect to those normally used
- Assess whether the estimates have accounted for elements of the context these activities come under
- Check if the estimates have been influenced by psychological factors

- Correct the estimates if errors are identified in the formulation process
- Use estimates as a stimulus for improvement and not with cautionary logic

---

7.5 CONCLUSIONS

The formulation of estimates with a good level of reliability is a highly critical process, as errors in the estimates can influence project performance. Errors in the planning of schedules and costs, and in the calculation of the absorption of resources, may lead to situations that, depending on the cases, can vary from unpleasant to dramatic.

A central role in the process of formulating estimates is played by project team members who, based on their experiences, should provide reliable information. Unfortunately, this does not always happen and the "blame" cannot be attributed to a lack of experience, but rather to a lack of knowledge of estimation techniques and the "traps" connected with them.

See page 255 for the exercise relating to this chapter.

REFERENCES

Abdel-Hamid, T.K. 1990. On the utility of historical project statistics for cost and schedule estimation: Results from a simulation-based case study. *Journal of Systems and Software* 13, 1: 71–82.

Ariely, D., and K. Wertenbroch. 2002. Procrastination, deadlines, and performance: Self-control by precommitment. *Psychological Science* 13, 3: 219–224.

Barseghyan, P. 2009. Human effort dynamics and schedule risk analysis. PM World Today 11, 3. http://www.pmforum.org/library/papers/2009/PDFs/mar/Human-Effort-Dynamics-and-Schedule-Risk-Analysis.pdf.

Buehler, R. et al. 1994. Exploring the 'planning fallacy': Why people underestimate their task completion times. *Journal of Personal and Social Psychology* 67: 366–381.

Dunning, D., C. Heath, and J.M. Suls. 2005. Picture imperfect. *Scientific American Mind* 16, 4: 20–27.

Goldratt, E.M. 1997. *Critical chain*. Great Barrington, MA: North River Press.

Hihn, J., and H. Habib-Agahi. 1991. Cost estimation of software intensive projects: A survey of current practices. In *International Conference on Software Engineering*, 276–287. Los Alamitos, CA: IEEE Computer Society.

Hillson, D.T., and D.A. Hulett. 2004. Assessing risk probability: Alternative approaches. Presented at PMI Global Congress Proceedings, Prague, Czech Republic.

Hinds, P.J. 1999. The curse of expertise: The effects of expertise and debiasing methods on predictions of novice performance. *Journal of Experimental Psychology: Applied* 5, 2: 205–221.

Jørgensen, M. 2002. A review of studies on expert estimation of software development effort. *Journal of Systems and Software* 70, 1–2: 37–60.

Kemerer, C.F. 1987. An empirical validation of software cost estimation models. *Communications of the ACM* 30, 5: 416–429.

Kitchenham, B., S.L. Pfleeger, B. McColl, and S. Eagan. 2002. A case study of maintenance estimation accuracy. *Journal of Systems and Software* 64, 1: 57–77.

Liberman, N., and Y. Trope. 1998. The role of feasibility and desirability considerations in near and distant future decisions: A test of temporal construal theory. *Journal of Personal and Social Psychology* 75: 5–18.

Loewenstein, G., and D. Schkade. 1999. Wouldn't it be nice? Predicting future feelings. In *Well-being: The foundations of hedonic psychology*, ed. D. Kahneman, E. Diener, and N. Schwarz, 85–105. New York: Russell Sage Foundation.

Merton, R.K. 1968. *Social theory and social structure*. New York: Free Press.

Mischel, W., Y. Shoda, and M.L. Rodriguez. 1989. Delay of gratification in children. *Science* 244: 933–938.

Moløkken, K., and M. Jørgensen. 2005. Estimation of web-development projects: Are software professionals in technical roles more optimistic than those in non-technical roles? *Empirical Software Engineering* 10: 7–29.

Norem, J.K., and N. Cantor. 1986. Anticipatory and post hoc cushioning strategies: Optimism and defensive pessimism in "risky" situations. *Cognitive Therapy and Research* 10, 3: 347–362.

Parkinson, C.N. 1955. Parkinson's law. *The Economist*, November 19, pp. 635–637.

Paynter, J. 1996. Project estimation using screenflow engineering. In *International Conference on Software Engineering: Education and Practice*, Dunedin, New Zealand, 150–159. Los Alamitos, CA: IEEE Computer Society Press.

ProjectNet Glossary. 1997. *Project Manager Today*. http://www.pmtoday.co.uk.

Rosenau, M.D. 1988. *Software project management*. Los Angeles: Lewin Associates.

Rossi, G. 2012. I processi di stima nel Project Management: analisi sulla variabilità della risorsa tempo in funzione delle tecniche di pianificazione. M.Sc. thesis, Bocconi University.

Roy, M.M., N.J.S. Christenfeld, and C.R.M. McKenzie. 2005. Underestimating the duration of future events: Memory incorrectly used or memory bias? *Psychological Bulletin* 131, 5: 738 –756.

Sampietro, M. 2010. Issues in project estimates. Unpublished document, SDA Bocconi School of Management.

Shepperd, J.A., J.A. Ouellette, and J.K. Fernandez. 1996. Abandoning unrealistic optimism: Performance estimates and the temporal proximity of self-relevant feedback. *Journal of Personality and Social Psychology* 70, 4: 844–855.

Showers, C., and N. Cantor. 1984. Optimism and defensive pessimism: Cognitive strategies for risky situations. Unpublished manuscript, University of Michigan.

West's Encyclopedia of American Law. 2008. Independence: The Gale Group.

Wideman, R.M. 1995. *Cost control of capital projects*. Richmond, BC: BiTech Publishers Ltd.

RECOMMENDED READINGS

Armstrong, J.S. 2001. *Principles of forecasting: A handbook for researchers and practitioners.* Norwell, MA: Kluwer Academic Publishers.

Beswick, G., E.D. Rothblum, and L. Mann. 1988. Psychological antecedents of student procrastination. *Australian Psychologist* 23, 2: 207–217.

Connoly, T., and D. Dean. 1997. Decomposed versus holistic estimates of effort required for software writing tasks. *Management Science* 43, 7: 1029–1045.

Deese, J., and R.A. Kaufman. 1957. Serial effects in recall of unorganized and sequentially organized verbal material. *Journal of Experimental Psychology* 54, 3: 180–187.

Josephs, R.A., and E.D. Hahn. 1995. Bias and accuracy in estimates of task duration. *Organizational Behavior and Human Decision Processes* 61, 2: 202–213.

Levine, L.J., V. Prohaska, S.L. Burgess, J.A. Rice, and T.M. Laulhere. 2001. Remembering past emotions: The role of current appraisals. *Cognition and Emotion* 15: 393–417.

Sannal, L.J., and N. Schwarz. 2004. Integrating temporal biases. The interplay of focal thoughts and accessibility experiences. *Psychological Science* 15, 7: 474–481.

8

Project Risk Management

KEYWORDS

Acceptance
Contingency plan
Impact
Investigate
Mitigation
Observe
Opportunity
Probability
Remove
Risk
Risk analysis
Risk identification
Risk management
Risk owner
Risk response
Transfer
Uncertainty

READER'S GUIDE

This chapter is for people who

- Have noted that many of a project's negative occurrences could have been managed in advance and even resolved if only someone had thought about it beforehand

- Have noticed that a project is in a continuous state of emergency
- Have unfortunately found that the occurrence of continuous emergencies has negative impacts on people as well as the project performance

8.1 WHY PROJECT RISK SHOULD BE MANAGED

Risk and projects are in an inescapable combination. Projects are undertaken by organizations so they can seize market opportunities or improve the company's internal efficiency. Projects, as we have stressed several times, are complex and innovative activities. Innovation brings a certain level of uncertainty, or rather, imperfect knowledge of events that will occur during the project. Each project is therefore physiologically risky. It becomes pathologically risky if the uncertainty linked to it is not addressed and managed methodically and with conviction.

A project risk is defined as "an uncertainty that matters" (Hillson 2009). "Uncertainty" insofar as it refers to a potential event, "that matters" insofar as the occurrence of the event affects the project. The risk is such if it affects the project objective. "It could rain tomorrow" is without doubt an uncertainty. It becomes a risk to the extent to which it prevents the project objective being achieved, for example, an open-air theatrical performance. It does not represent a risk if our objective is to stay comfortably at home and read a book.

Uncertainty can also generate positive impacts. In this case we talk about opportunity, which if identified and managed proactively can bring benefits to the project. Not managing the risks (as both threats and opportunities) means not taking into consideration the innovative aspect of projects—in other words, the essential element that differentiates them from operational or recurrent activities.

Within the context of project management, planning activities provide us with the course to take; risk management first tries to remove disturbances that tend to take us off course. For the purposes of this book, we shall concentrate on risk as a threat.

The figure of the team member is essential in risk management, as it is really the specialists, with their in-depth knowledge, who will be able to identify the risks with certain activities and propose the best strategies for responding to them.

8.2 PROJECT RISK MANAGEMENT PROCESS

An initial aspect that must be clear to participants in a project team is that risk management is not a one-off activity, but an ongoing way of thinking and behaving, which at times is of particular importance in the so-called project risk management meetings.

Two keywords within this approach are *systematicity* (Project Management Institute (PMI) 2004) and *proactivity* (Smith and Merritt 2002, Chapman and Ward 2007):

- Systematicity refers to following an organized and professional approach in risk management as well as attributing importance to the continuity of its management.
- Proactivity means developing an attitude and way of working that lead to the identification and management of risks before they occur, without requiring the ability to see into the future—something that is not required of any team member.

Project risk management can be schematized through the five logical phases model shown in Figure 8.1.

FIGURE 8.1
Project risk management processes. (Adapted from Mulcahy, R., *Risk Management: Tricks of the Trade® for Project Managers*, RMC Publications, Minneapolis, Minnesota, 2003.)

Project team members participate, with different levels of commitment, in all the risk management phases. They are

1. Planning the risk management process, which involves determining the operating method for executing the management process and identifying the people involved and the procedures to follow
2. Identification of the risks, which involves identifying the specific project risks through the involvement of the different available sources of information
3. Risk analysis, which involves studying and qualitatively or quantitatively assessing the risks identified in the previous phase and deciding which require special attention
4. Planning the risk response, which involves determining which actions to take in order to manage the project risk
5. Monitoring and controlling the risks, which involves implementing the risk response plan as soon as they occur or exceed a certain threshold of attention and collecting useful information for the future

The risk management process should not be seen as an isolated activity. Risk management should instead be periodic: in fact, it is only as the project progresses that new risks can emerge (or some that are already present may cancel each other out) and new information useful for analysis and planning may be collected.

8.3 PLANNING THE RISK MANAGEMENT PROCESS

The main objective of this phase is to provide guidelines for risk management activities, structuring the chosen approach and making it comprehensible. This phase is normally monitored by the project manager and can even be standardized to a large extent for homogeneous project teams or at the structural-organizational level (information systems, research and development, design, etc.).

Of the contributions that a team member can and must provide in this phase we can mention:

- Support in assessing the most appropriate sources of information to use to detect risks (historical data, knowledge of the people, past project documentation, external sources, etc.)

- Help in determining the most appropriate risk identification techniques (interviews, brainstorming, questionnaires, etc.)

In this initial phase team members must wait for the project manager to provide information that will make it possible to act in an organized and efficient manner throughout the course of the project.

Specifically, information of interest to team members includes

- The commitment required, in terms of the frequency and duration of formal meetings aimed at risk identification and analysis, or in terms of the amount and frequency of the documentation to fill in
- Clarification of the roles and responsibilities in risk management
- Communication of the measurement scales to be used in the risk analysis
- The stakeholders' level of tolerance to the risk

Below are a couple of examples that refer to the last two points.

THE INCONSISTENT SCALES

EXAMPLE 1

"I don't get it. You're trying to drive me crazy with this! In the project carried out six months ago the risk probability was classified on a scale of:

low–medium low–medium–medium high–high–very high

The project carried out three months ago used the scale:

0.2–0.4–0.5–0.6–0.8–0.9

The scale used for the current project is:

unlikely–quite likely–likely–very likely

Can't you create a single scale once and for all?"

EXAMPLE 2

"You're incapable. Now we're late thanks to you! You didn't manage a risk classified as medium, and now we have to take measures! Sorry, but in the previous project medium risks weren't even taken into consideration!"

WHAT DO THE STAKEHOLDERS WANT?

During a project risk management session a team member noticed that his area, which was highly innovative, was subject to numerous risks. To set some priorities, the team member asked the project manager, "Excuse me, Joanna, but as there are more risks to manage than there is time available, we should give them priorities. Essentially, is it better to focus on the risks that affect the quality, the schedules, or the costs? If I knew this, I would be able to act much more effectively." The project manager answered, "My feeling is that in this project the cost variable is dominant, but it's only my feeling; it never occurred to me to ask the project sponsor. Maybe I'll put it on my list of things to do."

8.4 RISK IDENTIFICATION

The risk identification phase plays a crucial role, as partial identification of the risks may lead to the real complexity of the project being underestimated. Identifying the risks means:

- Generating a list of risks that may affect the project
- Describing the risks, so that the other team members and the stakeholders in general are able to understand their real meaning
- Understanding the causes that generate the risks

The role of team members in this phase is key. It is, in fact, team members who have the expertise to assess which risks may occur during specific activities. The professional aspect of having a well-defined area of knowledge makes it possible to perform an in-depth identification contextualized around a specific project. Project managers can and must know how to facilitate risk identification activities, but they must not replace the team members who possess specific expertise.

One of the problems that team members face in the risk identification phase is discrimination between a project risk and a process risk. Let us look at the following example: a project team meets to discuss the risks concerning the development of a new bottling machine. In the risk

TABLE 8.1

Example of a Risk Description

Cause	Risk	Effect
Given that the provider has supply issues	There is a risk that the delivery of electrical engines may be delayed	Resulting in the project schedule being delayed by at least one month

Source: Adapted from Hillson, D. A., *Managing Risk in Projects*, Gower Publishing, Burlington, Vermont, 2009.

identification brainstorming session the plant engineer mentions the fact that the electricity may be cut off, thus causing a halt in the production line, and also that some caps may be faulty due to the poor quality of the raw materials. These, however, are not project risks, but process risks, namely, risks that may occur when the machine built as a result of the project is fully operational. This is not to deny the existence of contacts between these types of risks and project risks. The connection lies in whether there is acceptance, within the project requirements, of the fact that the machine is able to proceed even without electricity (and therefore ensure the provision of an uninterruptible power supply) or that it is able to analyze the quality of the inbound raw materials (and therefore not produce waste caps due to the defective nature of the inbound raw materials).

In order that they are understandable and do not become the source of misunderstandings, the risks identified must be accompanied by short descriptions. The description should be divided into three parts: cause, risk, and effect, as indicated in Table 8.1.

To clarify, the cause is the event that triggers the risk, but what we consider to be a cause may be an effect for others. How thorough the investigation into the causes is depends on the resources available and the control we have over the events. The cause "given that the provider has supply problems" may actually be determined by other events, such as upstream suppliers experiencing a financial crisis, which may be the result of other causes, and so on. These other causes may be unknown to us. It would only be constructive to trace the real causes if the people involved in the project were able to take action. In the previous example, knowing that the supply problem is a result of difficulties in obtaining the raw materials used for electric engine winding adds little to our analysis, as we do not have the power to remedy it.

> ### INCOMPLETE DESCRIPTIONS
>
> "I opened the file you sent me but I need to clarify a few points. For example, there are three risks all referred to in the same way, i.e., as 'supplier risk.' Is this a mistake or is there a difference? Another small problem, there is a risk referred to as 'see above.' The problem is that this is the first risk, so there is nothing above. Is this because you reordered the data according to a certain logic, and therefore the references have been lost? Was it too much trouble to describe the risk clearly, instead of wasting time finding the missing or unclear information?"

The risk description, despite its conceptual simplicity, is in practice often a problem for team members. This is because drafting descriptions so they can be understood by other team members, who may have very different expertise than our own, is no simple task. What happens is that when describing the effect there is a tendency to suggest technical effects on the activity and not effects that occur at the project level, which typically affect variables such as time, cost, and quality. For example, when faced with a problem concerning the quality of the raw materials, stating that the effect will be a low-quality component is not a good description insofar as it does not provide information at the project level.

8.5 ANALYSIS OF RISKS

The identification phase provides a list of risks that alone is of little use to project management. In fact, a long list of risks may create more confusion than benefits, as the attempt to manage all of them would most likely result in their multiplication (the risk of doing too many things together).

It is therefore necessary to take another step, which consists of analyzing the risks in order to understand their characteristics and focusing attention on the priority ones. The threshold of attention that leads to risk management depends on each individual company and sometimes on each individual project. This issue must be managed by the project manager, who has the information to be able to understand how many and which risks can realistically be managed.

During the analysis phase each risk should be associated with the following variables (Mulcahy 2003, Sampietro and Poli 2004):

- The probability of occurrence
- The timing of the event
- The frequency of the event, if the risk can be repeated
- Identification of the project activities impacted
- Identification of the impact on the individual activities and the project as a whole, relative to the schedules, costs, quality, and any other significant performance dimension for the project (legal impacts, security, reputation, etc.)

It should be emphasized how this information cannot be provided by the project manager alone, but similarly to the identification phase, the involvement of people who are more closely aware of the risks and their characteristics is required. In the example of the risk described in Figure 8.2, it would most likely be the purchasing department that would provide useful information.

Impact Probability	1 Marginal	3 Limited	5 Relevant	7 Critical	9 Vital
9 > 75%	9 R1	27	45	63 R3	81
7 50% – 74%	7	21 R10	35	49	63
5 25% – 49%	5	15	25 R4; R7	35	45 R8
3 5% – 24%	3	9 R2; R9	15	21 R5	27
1 < 5%	1	3	5	7	9 R6

FIGURE 8.2
Example of a probability–impact matrix.

The risk analysis can be both qualitative and quantitative. In this text we will focus on the qualitative analysis, which is by far the most widespread.

The qualitative analysis of the risk is based on assigning values to the variables concerning the risk and can sometimes be based on subjective assumptions, especially where it is impossible to obtain further information or obtaining it is too expensive compared to the importance of the risk. A good qualitative risk analysis is based more on the concept of consistency than on precision. In other words, if we have three risks, with impacts respectively estimated to be 9, 7, and 5 on a scale of 1 to 10, the consistency requirement does not so much require the first risk to have an actual value of 9 (if it does, all the better; it means the estimate is reliable), but rather that it really does have a bigger impact than the others.

Scales, which can have different forms, are normally used when assigning values to the variables used in the risk analysis. Tables 8.2 and 8.3 suggest scales for probability and impact, respectively.

TABLE 8.2

Example of a Scale to Assess the Probability of a Risk Occurring

Scale	Probability	Frequency	Description
5	>75%	>¾	Very high
4	50–74%	½–¾	High
3	25–49%	¼–½	Medium
2	5–24%	1/20–¼	Low
1	<5%	<1/20	Very low

TABLE 8.3

Example of a Scale to Assess the Impact of a Risk

Scale Project Objective	1—Marginal Effects	2—Limited Effects	3—Relevant Effects	4—Critical Effects	5—Vital Effects
Cost	<5%	5–15%	15–25%	25–35%	>35%
Time	<5%	5–15%	15–25%	25–35%	>35%
Quality	Almost invisible	Visible but still within the limits of acceptability	Over the tolerance but easily repairable	Over the tolerance and requires much reworking	Over the tolerance and requires total revision
Other objective	...	...	...	...	...

In the risk analysis, team members may encounter difficulties and be subject to certain distortions. In fact, we can state that

- Predominantly those with strong technical expertise are reluctant to provide estimates on the variables that describe the risks if not supported by certain data, historic series, and analyses. For some it seems almost offensive to have to provide, perhaps in a few minutes, numerical assessments based on personal feelings. Yet the qualitative analysis works that way and is effective. As previously mentioned, it is important to manage the consistency between the risks more than obtain perfect estimates (Sampietro 2010).
- There is a tendency to expand, which can even create tension among colleagues, and elaborate on whether the impact of a risk is 6 or 7 when the focus should be on creating an ordered list (a requirement of the consistency mentioned above) rather than on providing perfect estimates (Sampietro 2010).
- There is a tendency to confuse the impact of the risk on an individual activity with the impact on the project. For example, a risk that may delay an activity by 80% may be seen as having a high impact when in reality the impact on the project may be less than 1% (Sampietro 2010).
- Colleagues are not always interested in knowing the most minute technical detail of why a risk is truly a risk and the scientific reasons why they have been attributed certain values. If everyone was like this, a risk analysis meeting could go on for days (Sampietro 2010).
- A risk that may happen in the near future or that recently occurred is overestimated in its probability of occurrence (Chandran and Menon 2004, Hillson and Hulett 2004, Trope and Liberman 2003).
- A risk that touches us directly is normally overestimated in its probability and impact (Sjöberg 2000).
- A risk that we have already successfully addressed in the past, or to which we think we know how to react, tends to be underestimated in its probability and impact (Langer 1975, Langer and Roth 1975, Lefcourt 1973).
- The risk may be used as an organizational tool. For example, there may be a temptation to hide the risks to make it seem like we have the situation under control or overestimate the risks so we can then pose as heroes able to manage situations that were highly complex on paper. These situations are part of the so-called motivational bias (Hillson and Hulett 2004).

Being aware of these limits helps us to provide more realistic estimates.

A classic but effective way of representing the risk analysis is by using the probability–impact matrix. Due to the limited nature of resources, it is clear that not all risks can be managed with the same attention. Risks must therefore be divided into homogeneous groups so that different measures can be applied. The majority of the resources should be dedicated to responding to priority risks.

The priority of a risk is usually calculated by multiplying its probability and impact values. Using the assessment scales indicated in Tables 8.3 and 8.4, the priority range is from 1 (probability 1 × impact 1) to 25 (probability 5 × impact 5). The minimum priority value is 1; the maximum priority value is 25.

The probability–impact matrix sets out all the previously identified project risks, highlighting the priority associated with each risk, as shown in the example in Figure 8.2.

Ten risks are taken into consideration, and they are coded R1, R2, R3, and so on.

It is customary to subdivide the matrix into zones. Each zone identifies a priority level. In the matrix in Figure 8.2 three zones are highlighted, from the top right-hand light gray one, in which the highest-priority risks are placed, to the bottom left-hand dark gray one, in which the lowest-priority risks are placed. Medium-priority risks are placed in the white central zone.

Note that the matrix is arranged on the assumption of risk aversion, namely, the assumption that a high-impact but low-probability risk is considered more dangerous than a high-probability but low-impact risk. It follows that the simple multiplication of probability and impact may result in a few "devastating but remote" risks not being taken care of (those that fall into the bottom right-hand zone of the matrix, such as risk 6). These risks should instead be taken into great consideration and carefully monitored: they may, in fact, suddenly jump across into the light gray zone.

Below are two examples that caution us with regard to the analysis of project risks.

THE USELESS DETAIL

"I don't mean to be argumentative, but we've been discussing whether a risk has a 75 or 80% probability for 20 minutes now. I'd understand if the doubt was between 10 and 90%, then the meaning would change radically, but here we have a risk with a high probability irrespective of the exact numerical value, so the operative message is very clear and providing a perfect estimate does not add much."

THE DANGEROUS CALCULATION

"I wanted to remind you not to do what one of your colleagues did who, in ordering the risks according to dangerousness criteria, used the simple multiplication of the probability and impact. This means that risks with a catastrophic impact but low probability can be considered less important than risks that would not prejudice the outcome of the project even if they occurred. I remember that one month ago we had to stop a project precisely because a catastrophic risk with low probability occurred. What's worse is that the risk had been correctly identified, but because it had been incorrectly classified, it was then forgotten about and priority was given to risks that in practice were less dangerous."

8.6 PLANNING THE RISK RESPONSE

The risk analysis provides information useful for identifying the priority risks and focusing on the relative response actions.

In jargon priority risks are known as the vital few. This means that, for better or for worse, a limited subset of risks (20%) influences the greater part of the project outcome (80%), by virtue of the well-known Pareto's law. Conversely, and again in jargon, all other project risks are known as the trivial many. It is the job of the project manager and the members of the project coordination team to bring the vital few to the attention of the stakeholders, at the same time avoiding that each project stakeholder concentrates their attention on the closest risk. This would create a paradoxical situation in which all the project stakeholders channel their energies into managing the risks but the project goes into fibrillation: large-scale uncoordinated movement by all those involved without a real response to the priority risks.

The objective of this phase is therefore to define the actions to take in order to reduce the overall risk to the project, thus reducing the probability of occurrence or the impacts of the priority risks.

The project team members' contribution is also decisive in this phase, as they can use their expertise to suggest and assess successful actions relative to the risks under their areas of responsibility.

Team members must think of prevention responses (actions to take to manage the risks or the impacts before they occur) and remedial responses (actions to take when the risks have occurred).

Prevention actions imply immediately using additional resources, finding alternative ways of reaching the same objectives, or reducing the project scope, without being certain that the risk will actually occur. They therefore represent a preventive investment in order to avoid a loss of greater magnitude later. The remedial actions come into play when the prevention actions did not work or when it has been decided to not use additional resources immediately, starting with the assumption that it is not possible to affect the risk beforehand, or that it could be done but it is not convenient (the cost is not worth the effort). A rational decision is made to wait for the risk to happen before taking action. The advantage is that no preventive investments are made without knowing if the risk could actually occur. The disadvantage is that there are fewer response options and that some impacts are no longer remediable.

There are essentially four types of risk responses that can be implemented both as prevention and remedial actions (PMI 2008):

- Avoid: Avoid the risk by not performing the activity it concerns (and therefore making changes to the WBS). Deciding to transport the guest speakers in a car with a driver instead of by taxi is a removal action relative to the risk "there may not be any taxis available due to unannounced strikes."
- Transfer: Transfer the risk; namely, assign the risk to better-equipped parties (this is typical in insurance). Contracting out the organization of an event to a specialized external company is a transfer action relative to the risk "the project team may not have all the skills necessary to organize the event independently."
- Mitigation: Performing additional activities aimed at reducing its probability or impact. This may mean acting on both the risks and, preferably, the causes. Being more specific in the definition of the supply specifications list, meeting the supplier more often, and agreeing on the intermediate deliveries being closer in time are mitigation

actions relative to the risk "the current supplier may not deliver the component outsourced to it on time."

- Acceptance: This strategy indicates that the project team has decided not to change the project management plan to deal with a risk, or is unable to identify any other suitable response. Acceptance can be active or passive. The most common active acceptance strategy is to establish a contingency reserve, including amounts of time, money, or resources to handle the risks. Passive acceptance requires no action except to document the strategy, leaving the project team to deal with the risks as they occur.

All these actions may have an effect on the project structure, and therefore the project plan may require changes.

Two other response strategies are applied when there is not enough information available to make an operational decision (Sampietro and Poli 2004):

- Observation, which consists of monitoring the risk development
- Investigation, which consists of searching for information in order to be able to form a more reliable opinion on the risk

The two above-mentioned response strategies must be considered temporary; in fact, they are not able to alter the risk profile of the project.

When actions must be put into practice, the team member who provided the risk identification and analysis information will not necessarily also be the manager (the so-called risk owner) or executor of these actions. The risk owner, in fact, must have the power and autonomy necessary to be able to perform this task, and team members do not always have the organizational leverage to be able to act successfully.

Below are a couple of important situations.

THE UNCONVINCING STRATEGY

"I might not be an expert in project risk management, but it seems very strange to me that for two months the only management strategy has been passive acceptance. Are they not capable of providing concrete responses?"

THE FACTOTUM PROJECT MANAGER

"I'd like to remind everyone that the risk owner does not always have to be the project manager. It's true that the project manager has over-all responsibility for the project, but things work if we all collaborate and if those who have the power to shift some situations take responsibility for doing so. If the project manager has to get involved in every aspect of the project, there would not be enough hours in the day. So, guys, everyone take care of their own responsibilities."

8.7 RISK MONITORING AND CONTROLLING

The main objective of monitoring is to assess whether the actions taken on risks have had the desired outcome, while controlling involves implementing the changes necessary for the correct management of the project.

During this phase both positive events, such as risks that cease to be such, and unexpected negative events, such as the emergence of risks that were not previously identified, can occur. In this case rapid corrective actions must be taken.

On closer inspection this phase relaunches the risk management process, as an assessment of the effectiveness of the response actions taken up until that point provides the information to decide on the new courses of action.

The role of the team members in this phase is to promptly provide the project manager with truthful information so that he or she can acquire a realistic vision of what is happening and can update the risk management plan, avoiding situations such as those below.

AND THEN?

You can never understand how it turned out from reading the project documents. They contain many great ideas, but then it's impossible to understand if they were implemented and what the outcome was.

THE USUAL UNKNOWN SUSPECTS

"I suspect we're not learning from our mistakes. I've noticed that very often the causes of the problems are the same. Maybe it wouldn't be such a bad idea to share the risk control phase and make it more effective."

8.8 PROJECT FOLLOWERSHIP ACTIONS FOR PROJECT RISK MANAGEMENT

Project risk management, before being a set of methods and techniques, is above all a habit. Project team members are required to view things from the proper perspective and endorse the following principles:

- Firmly believe that risk is an element inherent to the nature of projects, and it should therefore be considered and managed
- Feel they have a key role to play in defining the "rules of the game" for managing project risks
- Feel they are authorized to request information that best defines their field of action, the time commitment required, the level of formality, and the means to use in managing risks
- Make an effort to identify risks, *in primis* those concerning their area of responsibility, and describe them so they are comprehensible to everyone
- Avoid being influenced by subjective elements during the risk analysis, for instance, in the probability and impact estimates
- Assess the impacts at the project level, and therefore not confuse project with activity
- Suggest feasible actions, not unattainable desires
- Keep track of what has been done and the results of the risk management actions

8.9 CONCLUSIONS

A project that is not risky is a project that is dead at the outset, as low risk means low innovation and therefore a low probability that the market will reward the project.

On the other hand, care should be taken not to unnecessarily increase the rate of risk through reckless actions that are far from organic. In this chapter we have presented some ideas and methods that all team members should know.

It is important to understand that project risk management is not only a set of techniques, but primarily a way of thinking and acting. Limiting risk management to predefined moments is not enough and is not effective.

Risk can only be managed correctly through the implementation of everyday behaviors.

See page 257 for the exercise relating to this chapter.

REFERENCES

Chandran, S., and G. Menon. 2004. When a day means more than a year: Effects of temporal framing on judgments of health risk. *Journal of Consumer Research* 31: 375–389.

Chapman, C., and S. Ward. 2007. *Project risk management: Processes, techniques and insights.* Chichester: John Wiley & Sons.

Hillson, D.A. 2009. *Managing risk in projects.* Burlington, VT: Gower Publishing.

Hillson, D.A., and D.T. Hulett. 2004. Assessing risk probability: Alternative approaches. Presented at PMI Global Congress Proceedings, Prague, Czech Republic.

Langer, E. 1975. The illusion of control. *Journal of Personality and Social Psychology* 32: 311–328.

Langer, E.J., and J. Roth. 1975. Heads I win, tails it's chance: The illusion of control as a function of the sequence of outcomes in a purely chance task. *Journal of Personality and Social Psychology* 32, 6: 951–955.

Lefcourt, H. 1973. The function of the illusion of control and freedom. *American Psychologist*, 28: 417–425.

Mulcahy, R. 2003. *Risk management. Tricks of the Trade® for project managers.* Minneapolis: RMC Publications.

Project Management Institute. 2004. *A guide to the Project Management Body of Knowledge.* 3rd ed. Newton Square, PA: Project Management Institute.

Project Management Institute. 2008. *A guide to the Project Management Body of Knowledge.* 4th ed. Newton Square, PA: Project Management Institute.

Sampietro, M. 2010. Issues in project risk management meetings. Unpublished document, SDA Bocconi School of Management.

Sampietro, M., and M. Poli. 2004. Project risk management. In *Organizzare e gestire progetti. Competenze per il project management*, ed. V. Baglieri, A. Biffi, E. Coffetti, C. Ondoli, M. Pilati, N. Pecchiari, M. Poli, and M. Sampietro. Milano: ETAS.

Sjöberg, L. 2000. Factors in risk perception. *Risk Analysis* 20, 1: 1–11.

Smith, P.G., and G.M. Merritt. 2002. *Proactive risk management. Controlling uncertainty in product development.* New York: Productivity Press.

Trope, Y., and N. Liberman. 2003. Temporal construal. *Psychological Review* 110, 3: 403–421.

RECOMMENDED READINGS

Cooper, D., S. Grey, G. Raymond, and P. Walker. 2005. *Project risk management guidelines. Managing risk in large projects and complex procurements.* Chichester: John Wiley & Sons.

Grey, S. 1995. *Practical risk assessment for project management.* Chichester: John Wiley & Sons.

Kendrick, T. 2009. *Identifying and managing project risks.* 2nd ed. New York: AMACOM.

Rosenberg, L., T. Hammer, and R. Gallo. 1999. Continuous risk management at NASA. Presented at Applied Software Measurement Conference, San Jose, CA.

Wideman, R.M. 1992. *Project and program risk management. A guide to managing project risks and opportunities.* Newton Square, PA: Project Management Institute.

Section IV

Project Followership during Project Execution and Control

9

Change as a Natural Factor in Projects

KEYWORDS

Change
Change costs
Change management
Life cycle
Opportunity
Uncertainty

READER'S GUIDE

This chapter is for people who

- Have seen cases of positive change and cases of negative change
- Have noticed that change is a natural part of projects
- Have seen many particularly turbulent projects and few relatively stable projects
- Would like a better understanding of how to manage change in projects

9.1 WHY ARE PROJECTS CONSTANTLY CHANGING?

Those who do not frequently participate in project activities or, due to the responsibilities assigned to them, do not require a global vision of the project very often feel that projects are a chaotic, disorganized environment where the company, more than providing support, almost seems to be rowing against the current.

It is rare during a project that what is planned is then carried out without undergoing changes: revisions to schedules, budgets, and the objective are very common and plagued by ubiquitous urgencies.

Let us clear up any misunderstandings: it is true, some projects are turbulent due to a real inability to manage them or even because those who should manage them actually make the environment even more turbulent and instead of "putting out the flames, throw fuel onto the fire." However, many other times the project manager and the company in general do a good job, but despite this, the projects are still unstable: the decisions made are called into question and work plans are frequently updated. Why does this happen? How should a project team member interpret this continuous shuffling of the cards? And finally, how can a project team member help to stabilize a project?

One characteristic that all projects have in common is the attribute of innovation: uniqueness. Similar projects exist, but there are no identical projects. This characteristic translates into another element: uncertainty. Given that there are many variables at play in a project, and given that these variables can change from project to project, by nature projects become uncertain and unstable environments.

The situation can be depicted by the diagram in Figure 9.1, which represents the so-called cone of uncertainty.

The diagram can be interpreted as follows: the horizontal axis represents time, while the vertical axis represents the estimate errors referred to the

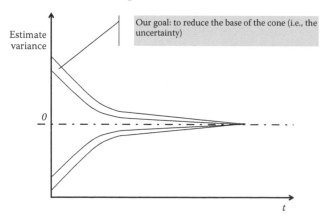

FIGURE 9.1
The cone of uncertainty. (Adapted from Boehm, B., *Software Engineering Economics*, Prentice Hall, Upper Saddle River, New Jersey, 1981; McConnell, S., *Software Project Survival Guide*, Microsoft Press, Redmond, Washington, 1997.)

typical project variables (time, cost, use of resources), compared to the real values of the project (the horizontal line with the number 0). As we can see, the worst time to make forecasts is at the start of the project, as that is when the uncertainty is greatest. Logically, uncertainty in the estimates is reset to zero at the end of the project, as by that stage the values have been calculated (in reality, in some situations even the final calculations are uncertain, but this is a discussion that touches on project control systems).

Unfortunately, in reality, the first time estimates are typically required, which are essential for producing the budget, calculating its future profitability, and proposing an acceptable delivery date to the client, coincides with the estimates' highest point of uncertainty. This is why some changes during the course of the projects cannot be explained by their poor management, but rather by the fact that they are inherent to the nature of the project, linked to the estimation process. The challenge is to understand to what degree the error rate is physiological and to what degree it is instead pathological.

It would be utopian to think of removing uncertainty, whereas it is realistic to try to reduce it.

Project team members have great responsibilities concerning this aspect, as they very often collaborate in estimation processes, and therefore are partly responsible for the subsequent instability of the project. In complex projects, then, the high number of activities makes estimation errors even more macroscopic: many badly planned activities, in fact, result in a project that contains even highly significant errors.

So how can project team members help to reduce the cone of uncertainty? Part of the answer has already been provided in Chapter 7: the most suitable estimation techniques for a specific situation must be chosen, and attempts must be made to counteract physiological errors that are introduced even unconsciously.

Besides this, however, another way to reduce the cone of uncertainty is to lower the innovation rate, and thus the uncertainty of individual activities. Note that lowering the innovation rate of individual activities does not mean carrying out a project lacking in innovation. Real innovation actually exists, which leads to benefits in the product or service developed, but fake innovation also exists, which consists of creating products or services from scratch that are actually already available on the market, thus rejecting the already existing external knowledge. This attitude is called not invented here (NIH) and consists of rejecting or considering any idea, product, or service from outside, which has therefore not been invented by us or our team, to be of inferior quality (Clagett 1967, Katz and Allen 1982, Lichtenthaler and Ernst 2006).

The problem is then defining the boundaries between what is considered in-group and what is considered out-group since the in-group does not want to share or collect information from the out-group. The concept of in-group is not linked to the legal entity (the company), but it can be found at different organizational levels: departments, projects, teams, and individuals. It may happen that certain departments dismiss the ideas of others or do not use semifinished products or services for the simple fact that they come from another area of the company. It is thus apparent how project team members are key players in promoting, accepting, or rejecting the NIH syndrome, and therefore how their decisions can help to make the project more or less stable.

9.2 PARTIAL VISION OF THE PROJECT AS A CONTRIBUTION TO ITS PERCEIVED INSTABILITY

From a project team member's point of view, the project may seem unjustifiably turbulent. Let us take the following case as an example, which occurred in an important financial institution.

AN INCAPABLE PROJECT MANAGER, QUITE THE OPPOSITE IN FACT

"I think our project manager is incapable: this is the sixth time he has postponed the execution of the two activities I'm responsible for. We're talking about ten working days, nothing complex, so how is it possible that he can't plan it correctly?"

"I have the same problem," added a colleague. "This is the fourth time he has shifted a small two-day job. I think our project manager needs to attend a good intensive course because this is just unacceptable. He obviously didn't get the position on his own merits."

Indeed, the project manager did have some gaps in his specialist knowledge, but in any case he was a valid and competent person. What had happened was, in good faith, with the idea of simplifying the work of his collaborators, he had only informed them of the activities that they had to perform and not contextualized them within the broader project concept. The activities were actually part of a much broader project plan: around 500 activities and a two-year time frame. Following the advice of a project management expert, the project manager called a meeting where the entire project was presented to the collaborators. The following sentence summarized the team members' new awareness of the situation: "Now I understand why you kept shifting my activities: you have to manage such a chaos that I have no idea how you even found the time to inform me of the postponement."

This case shows how failure to communicate the real characteristics of the project did not allow the team members to understand its complexity, creating useless tensions and negative opinions about the project manager's actions. Project team members therefore not only have the right but also the duty to ask for information that gives them a better understanding of the context in which their activities are included. This is the global vision introduced in Chapter 2. This allows team members to be more rational in their judgments, as they will be more aware of the complexity in which they are operating.

But there is also another reason, related to efficiency and effectiveness, why the project team member should ask for contextual information. For a better understanding of this point, let us examine another short case study.

THE BOARD OF DIRECTORS

"So, Philip, how was your day?"

"Look, it was a disaster. As the sales manager often asks me, I extracted the half-year sales figures from the management system, put them in Excel, and created charts with short comments. This task takes around two days and I finished it just yesterday. Today the sales manager came into the office shouting, saying that I was incapable and that I should have worked on the report all night to make it presentable. I rechecked the work I had sent, and it had been done the same way as the last times and the feedback had always been positive. I can't understand why the project manager reacted like that."

The following day the sales manager returned to the office saying that he had had great difficulty altering the report to present it to the board of directors. The collaborator was amazed: "Sorry, but if I'd known the report was for the board of directors I would have created it using a completely different logic. Until yesterday you were the only one that read the report and you usually told me, so as not to waste time, not to concern myself with formality and to concentrate on the contents. If I had known, I would have made the graphics more engaging and included more comments."

As the case shows, failure to communicate a contextual element, which was innovative compared to the past, resulted in the work being less effective and also caused inefficiencies, so much so that the work was redone, increasing both the execution time and costs. In this case openness and professionalism (Chapter 2) are the project followership characteristics that should be used.

9.3 CONTRIBUTING TO THE REDUCTION OF CHANGES

Changes to projects may come from various sources: they may be encouraged by clients, they may imposed by regulatory changes, they may result from unexpected moves by the competition, and they may come from within.

Changes belonging to the last group include those supported by project team members. Project team members, in performing the activities they are responsible for, may in fact request different types of changes: the renegotiation of schedules or the budget for the activity, a change to the activity's expected output, a change to the input necessary to carry it out, a change of processes or the instrumental means supporting it, and a change in the other collaborators involved in the activity.

Contributing team members should ask themselves two questions: "Do the changes I am requesting really support the project objectives?" and "Are the changes really necessary?" Let us start with the second question in order to then tackle the first.

Similarly to what was stated in Chapter 7 with regard to estimates, humans experience some distortions in the interpretation of events, distortions that can have an impact on various aspects, one of which is the request for changes that, depending on the point of view, may be considered necessary to a greater or lesser extent.

Let us examine some of these situations.

9.3.1 Proximity of Temporal Phenomena

Let's take a situation where a team member is responsible for an activity in which other colleagues are involved. Let's imagine that the activity managers and the project manager meet every 15 days to take stock of the situation, discuss any problems, and then support their resolution. If a colleague involved in an activity makes a serious mistake ten minutes before the meeting, it is very likely that this problem will be mentioned during the meeting. There will be talk of dissatisfaction with regard to the collaborator and perhaps of replacing him or her, thus making a change request. If the meeting had taken place three days later, it is very likely the dynamic would have been different and the problem would not have even been mentioned. This is because problems that are closer in time are experienced more intensely than more distant problems. This dynamic is linked not so much to memory, but the time necessary to rationalize and analyze the situation better and, if necessary, reestablish calm.

9.3.2 Pressure over Results

When people are under pressure they tend to see problems that they would not have otherwise noticed. A trivial example: a printer that jams in the middle of printing documents that will be needed in a few hours is an event experienced much less negatively than if a jam occurs when we are about to print documents that our boss is waiting for on his or her desk. The example shows how very often changes are requested only because the problem occurs at a critical moment and not because of the problem itself, which might not be so unusual.

9.3.3 A Project Environment That Is Very Different from How Operational Activities Are Carried Out

Sometimes a project manager adopts a different management style to the one prevalent in the company. For instance, when dealing with a very hierarchical and bureaucratic company culture, the project manager may adopt a more participatory style focused on listening. This difference in style may lead to the emergence of an excessive number of changes with respect to the actual needs, as the project is perceived as a rare occasion to have one's voice heard, a sort of place of compensation for one's own discomforts and frustrations. So a team member with a contributory approach should

> ### FREE SOFTWARE
>
> A project management consultancy company also offered training services. Clients typically requested a two-day course, and to provide a more practical edge, the consultancy company included a two-hour exercise on project management software. The profitability of the courses fell over time, and so the consultancy company started to be very selective even in the teaching material provided, in order to contain costs. The team member responsible for the software exercise proposed replacing the software with the new version, which would require a considerable outlay. The project manager pointed out that, while on the one hand the new version had numerous improvements, on the other, these improvements could only be appreciated with continued use; during the two-hour exercise it is only possible to demonstrate the basic functions, for which even free software would do the job.

therefore take these physiological phenomena into consideration in order to limit change requests that have no deep rational roots.

Let us now comment on the theme of aligning the changes with the project objectives. Starting with the consideration that a change request is aimed at improving a situation, team members must assess if the improvement is in tune with the project objectives or if it opposes them. For a better understanding of this point, let us refer to a case study.

The example shows how a request that could have at the most had a slight impact on the quality perceived by the client would have essentially threatened an increasingly important performance dimension such as cost. In general, a change could also generate improvements, but it is necessary to assess whether it would support the project performance dimensions deemed to be priorities or whether, to improve a secondary dimension, the priorities would be affected.

9.4 HOW TO EFFECTIVELY COMMUNICATE CHANGES

While on the one hand some changes are not capable of benefiting the project, and should therefore be limited, on the other hand sometimes team members complain that project managers or project sponsors do not take their change requests into consideration. Sometimes this is down to project management attitudes that are hard to share, but other times there is a different reason: team members do not communicate their requests effectively.

The problem is well known and occurs each time one party with certain skills must dialog with another party with different skills (Eppler 2007, Kushlan 1995). To simplify, a common situation is where the project team member has highly developed specialist skills while the other party has more managerial or specialist skills in another area. The team member, to support the reasons for change, tends to describe the situation by going into operating details, which, from his or her point of view, are the real justifications. Unfortunately, there is a risk of the other party not understanding these details, and therefore the creation of additional tension. The problem is therefore that the two parties are speaking different languages: the team member speaks in detail about technical problems, maybe using acronyms, and the project manager or project sponsor speaks of benefits and the impact on costs and productivity. Thinking that the project manager or sponsor will acquire the skills necessary to fully understand the technical problem is utopian; it is the team members who must make an effort to convey their requests in other terms.

Another aspect is the way changes are requested. All too often the oral method is used, especially in teams or companies that are small, perhaps in an impromptu fashion at the earliest opportunity. There are a few reasons why this may not be very effective:

- A request expressed at any time, therefore without requesting an appointment or at a specific time, may be perceived as impromptu, not well thought out, and therefore based on irrational reasons (Maltz 2000).
- A request expressed only orally may be badly interpreted, only remembered in part, and badly communicated to others (Robbins and Judge 2009).
- A request expressed only orally cannot be filed, and therefore does not become part of the important project documents to be analyzed.

To conclude, Table 9.1 shows an example of a useful document for formalizing change requests used in a company that constructs transmission belts.

TABLE 9.1

Example of a Document for Formalizing Change Requests

Name and surname of applicant	Role
Project code	Project title
Change request name	
Description of the change	
Product performance dimensions affected by the change and quantification	
Length (km)	
Noise (db)	
Production cost (euros)	
Impact on the activity	
Execution time (days)	
Cost (euros)	
Skills required (description)	
Equipment required (description)	

As it can be noticed, not only the technical features of the change request are asked, but also the impact on the activity the change request is linked to, thus permitting the project manager to better evaluate the request in management terms.

9.5 WHEN CHANGE IS BENEFICIAL AND WHEN IT IS NEGATIVE

Change cannot be defined as positive or negative from the outset.

Change obviously means having to rethink, update documents, and inform colleagues of the new state of affairs, and therefore it is an activity that always requires a financial and time commitment. From an organizational point of view, then, change means questioning one's expectations and plans; in summary, it is more difficult to change than not to change. It could be said that all change originates in a slightly unfriendly environment because there is a tendency to seek stability, whenever possible. Therefore, while change requires a higher outlay of energy from an individual's point of view, it is also true that change can be very beneficial, as it makes it possible to increase the probability of a project succeeding. In a dynamic context, the rigorous execution of a plan can transform into high performances in terms of time and costs, but poor performances in terms of the acceptance of the product/service on the market and client satisfaction.

The problem is that while the impact on times and costs is relatively easy to calculate, the benefits in qualitative terms are more difficult to appreciate. Therefore, without expecting to have objective and numerical answers on all dimensions of project performance, one way to assess the effectiveness of a change is to ask the following question: How does this change help to improve the project?

This question, which may even appear obvious, is in fact not always answered because, as we saw earlier, changes can result from irrational motivations that are not related to the project success dimensions. It may seem strange, but the positive nature of the change depends on when it is proposed. To explain this concept better, let us use the diagram in Figure 9.2.

The figure shows a classic diagram referred to as the life cycle of the project, broken down into time phases. Besides that of the life cycle, two other curves are represented. The first is called the "cost of modifying curve," and it describes the fact that the cost associated with a change to

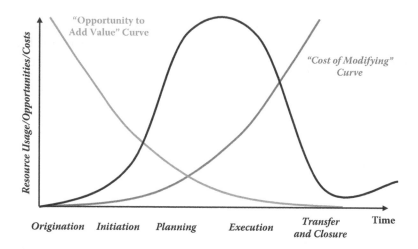

FIGURE 9.2
Project life cycle and the cost of the change. (Adapted from Wideman, R.M., *A Framework for Project and Program Management Integration*, Project Management Institute, Newton Square, Pennsylvania, 1991.)

the project varies depending on the progress of the project. Specifically, the closer one is to the end of the project, the more costly it is to implement the changes. For instance, when a house is almost complete, adding a window means knocking down walls, rebuilding a part of them, adding reinforcements, etc. The same alteration during the design phase would have been easy to implement. The second curve is called the "opportunities to add value curve," and it communicates that a change can significantly increase the value of the project (intended as performance improvement), above all if it was promoted in the initial phases; the same change then gradually loses value as the project progresses. This downward curve depends on the existence of the cost to modify curve, which on the other hand grows as the project progresses. In summary, a potentially positive change ceases to be such when the cost associated with its implementation surpasses the benefits.

The existence of these two curves is very important, as it provides project team members with behavioral guidelines: it is useful to state their opinion, express their doubts, and make proposals above all in the initial phases of the project; the technique of waiting, working in isolation in the hope that in the end all the pieces of the puzzle will fall into place can be very dangerous, as it delays the emergence of problems and therefore of changes, making them more costly and more traumatic. In view of these considerations, project progress meetings and discussions on the deliverables must not be seen as moments of judgment, but instead, they should become valued moments for throwing light on critical situations and lowering the negative impact of the performances through changes.

9.6 PROJECT FOLLOWERSHIP ACTIONS FOR CHANGE MANAGEMENT

Changes are an integral part of the project and must be faced with an open and constructive attitude. This attitude translates into the following actions to be carried out by project team members:

- Do not introduce useless complexities, and therefore possible instability, through the reasoned rejection of solutions proposed by others.
- Try to understand whether, when faced with the idea to propose change, the reasons are rational or irrational.
- Do not wait to suggest changes; their postponement may be more difficult and costly.
- When communicating changes, use language that can be easily understood by those involved.
- Express change requests formally.

9.7 CONCLUSIONS

From the point of view of team members, the ideal situation would be to have maximum stability in the activities that fall under their responsibility. Unfortunately, however, project environments can be very turbulent. A part of this turbulence comes from external factors, but a large part of it also comes from internal factors. Given that change requires energy and resources, a good rule is to only try and implement changes that have a positive impact on project performance, and to anticipate them as much as possible, so as to reduce the cost of their implementation.

Team members play a key role in these dynamics, as they are both the recipients and the proposers of change. Through this dual role they can contribute to both greater stability and greater turbulence, and they can try to both anticipate the phenomena and address them when there are no more alternatives. In short, many virtuous or vicious project dynamics depend on team members. The correct state of mind with which a team member should address changes is therefore sound rationality, whereby changes are not labeled from the outset, but they are put forward for discussion and analyzed to assess the benefit of implementing them.

A project that is highly unstable in the initial phases may become more stable in subsequent phases through an in-depth comparison of the different possibilities of action; the initial stability of a project is not in turn a guarantee of success if decisions are postponed and addressed too late, prejudicing the outcomes.

See page 257 for the exercise relating to this chapter.

REFERENCES

Boehm, B. 1981. *Software engineering economics*. Upper Saddle River, NJ: Prentice-Hall.

Clagett, R.P. 1967. Receptivity to innovation—Overcoming. NIH paper submitted as partial fulfillment of the requirements for the master of science degree at the Massachusetts Institute of Technology. http://dspace.mit.edu/bitstream/handle/1721.1/42453/23987857.pdf?sequence = 1.

Eppler, M. 2007. Knowledge communication problems between experts and decision makers: An overview and classification. *Electronic Journal of Knowledge Management* 5, 3: 291–300.

Katz, R., and T.J. Allen. 1982. Investigating the not-invented-here (NIH) syndrome: A look at the performance, tenure and communication patterns of 50 R&D Project Groups. *R&D Management* 12, 1: 7–20.

Kushlan, J.A. 1995. Use and abuse of abbreviations in technical communication. *Journal of Child Neurology* 10, 1: 1–3.

Lichtenthaler, U., and H. Ernst. 2006. Attitudes to externally organizing knowledge management tasks: A review, reconsideration and extension of the NIH syndrome. *R&D Management* 36, 4: 367–386.

Maltz, E. 2000. Is all communication created equal? An investigation into the effects of communication mode on perceived information quality. *Journal of Product Innovation Management* 17, 2: 110–127.

McConnell, S. 1997. *Software project survival guide*. Redmond, WA: Microsoft Press.

Robbins, S., and T. Judge. 2009. *Organizational behavior*. 13th ed. Upper Saddle River, NJ: Prentice Hall.

Wideman, R.M. 1991. *A framework for project and program management integration*. Newton Square, PA: Project Management Institute.

RECOMMENDED READINGS

Hall, P. 2005. Interprofessional teamwork: Professional cultures as barriers. *Journal of Interprofessional Care Supplement* 1: 188–196.

Wastyn, A., K.U. Leuven, and K. Hussinger. 2011. In search for the not-invented-here syndrome: The role of knowledge sources and firm success. http://ssrn.com/abstract = 1892749.

10

Controlling the Project

KEYWORDS

Acceptance
Assessment
Control
Corrective action
Measuring
Project status report
Reporting

READER'S GUIDE

This chapter is for people who

- Wish to understand the mechanisms for determining how far the project has progressed
- Wish to know their role and the contribution they can provide in order for project progress to be assessed correctly
- Wish to understand which tools are available to bring a challenged project back on track

10.1 PROJECTS AND CONTROL

Project control is an ambivalent topic: everyone recognizes its importance but few apply it effectively. Unfortunately, the consequences for projects are clear to see.

All aspects of a project should be controlled: the solution created by the project must comply with the contractual requirements, the project must be completed on schedule, there is a budget to respect, there is an economic margin to achieve, the end users must be able to see for themselves the advantages offered by the new solution, customer satisfaction should be assured in all cases, and the people working on the project must benefit personally.

Not a day goes by without someone demanding very specific control activities. In fact, each stakeholder has a valid reason for the project to be controlled and pushes for this to happen. The project environment is crowded by stakeholders sensitive to the topic of control.

The ambivalence lies in the fact that this "thirst for control" rarely corresponds to the ability to control the project in a structured and shared way. It is like trying to quench one's thirst with seawater. The thirst increases with dramatic consequences. Likewise, it occurs in many projects where the drive to control falls into a vacuum due to the lack of a suitable control system in terms of approach, methods, and skills.

It follows that project control often turns out to be costly, ineffective, and conflict producing:

- Costly insofar as data are collected, information is processed, meetings are held, presentations are given, reports are produced, and communications are made. Considerable organizational effort is sustained in terms of the time used, resources involved, and out-of-pocket costs. The purpose of all this is to keep the project under control, in the conviction that the more spent on controlling the project, the better chance the project has of success. There is undeniably some truth in this assumption. Nevertheless, in many projects the quality of the result is not directly proportional to the intensity of the control; in fact, it may turn out to be inversely proportional. We need only think of a highly detailed control system applied to projects with a poorly defined scope and that are subject to sudden changes during the project. What should be stressed is that the cost incurred to control the project does not automatically translate into better results.
- Ineffective insofar as the control activities provide little support for the decisions that must be taken in order to complete the project. In fact, project control is effective to the extent that it allows the current state of the project to be established, the reasons for the variances

(as well as for the alignments) with respect to the initial plan to be diagnosed in a targeted way, and the decisions relative to the part of the project to be completed to be made in an informed and shared way ("we're not doing anything, as everything is going well," "we're not doing anything because things are not going well, but we are confident that they will improve in the future without the need for corrective actions," "we're implementing corrective actions to overcome the difficulties encountered to date and to relaunch the part of the project to be completed," "we're correcting some aspects of the project even if it's going well, as we are anticipating there will be problems in the part to be completed"). Unfortunately, many projects are highly controlled but poorly guided toward success.

- Conflict producing insofar as control necessarily implies an assessment of the work done by those who work on the project. Getting to the heart of the issues, assessing a situation from different points of view, representing the actual current state of play, even if negative, and investigating the reasons for the variances is conflict producing in itself. Control and conflict go hand in hand; the difference is in how conflict is interpreted and handled in projects. Some project management experts go on to state that conflict, if handled well, is the propellant that drives the project to success. The value of the conflict in the project economy should therefore be pointed out. In projects conflicts are the order of the day due to the joint presence of several stakeholders with completely different specializations, organizational placement, and reference cultures. These stakeholders, for a limited amount of time (the project duration), find themselves having to collaborate somewhat forcedly in order to achieve the project objectives, staking their interests.

10.2 PROJECT CONTROL: COMPARING MEANINGS

Projects and control are reciprocally linked: on the one hand, the project should be controlled on a regular basis in order to assess how the project is progressing; on the other hand, control should be provided with data and information that the project must be able to supply.

The success of a project is based on its capacity to provide feedback. This means going back, reviewing what was previously put down on paper in relation to the inevitable differences between what was planned and what has actually been done. Monitoring and controlling the project therefore becomes essential, precisely in order to provide feedback.

Control is therefore a systematic activity that accompanies the project from the outset until its completion. Control, in fact, provides a measure of the efficiency of our planning work and an indication of the need to review the planning in order to make the necessary adjustments.

The term *control* should be understood as "guiding, directing, driving, orienting." The project should therefore be controlled as it progresses, great attention should be paid to weak signals, and future trends should be anticipated as far as possible. The information produced by the project as it progresses should be used to reschedule the work to be completed.

The idea underlying this concept of control is that the information available on the project guides its satisfactory performance toward the achievement of the desired objectives. As in the final analysis, a project is managed by the project team (coordinated by the project manager). The collegial element ensures that the project manager can only have control over the entire project if the individual members of the project team really do have control over their work.

From this perspective we can speak about two levels of control: a micro level, which is the responsibility of the individual managers of the work packages, and a macro level, which looks at the project as a whole, coordinated by the project manager. If control is set up correctly, it should enable the project team members to perform their micro level controls and track time and costs at the project (macro) level.

Let us see how the available tools are essentially the same, just as the approach must be the same. The work breakdown structure (WBS) represents the meeting point between the two levels of control. The absolute centrality of the WBS in the overall economy of the project is highlighted once again.

10.3 PROJECT CONTROL CYCLE

The project control activities can be schematized according to a four-phase cycle, as indicated in Figure 10.1. Informing the project stakeholders of the project performance is a transversal activity.

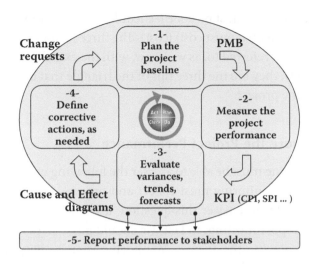

FIGURE 10.1

Project control cycle. (Adapted from Shewhart, W.A., and Deming, W.E., *Statistical Method from the Viewpoint of Quality Control*, Dover Publications, Mineola, New York, 1986.)

10.3.1 Plan the Project Baseline

In jargon we say, "Control starts with planning." The first phase of the control cycle is in fact carried out during project planning. The information and documents that will be used as a control reference are actually produced during planning. The decision on which control system should be used for the project, in relation to its profile, is also made during planning. Control that is too structured would needlessly increase the costs, while control that is too loose would dangerously increase the risks. Members of the project team, as the leading actors on the project stage (directed by the project manager), have the task of supporting the project manager in this decision by highlighting the need for control and assessing the impacts of the level of control that it is assumed will be chosen. All this information is then flowed into a single document, the project management plan. In order to carry out an effective control, the plan drawn up during planning should be "frozen" in a version called the baseline. The baseline will be the line of reference against which to exercise control. The baseline can change during the project, but only after an agreement between the stakeholders. In fact, if the baseline was freely changed during the project every time someone considered it useful to do so, it would be impossible to make an objective assessment of the project progress: Is the project ahead or behind schedule, and with respect to what? Today's plan? Yesterday's? Your version? Or mine? The baseline, in its entirety, tells us what needs doing (scope), when it must be done (schedule), and how much work must be used (or how much it must cost) (cost). The three factors—scope, schedule, and cost—are referred to, as we know, with the expression "triple constraint"; namely, they are the three tips of the triangle that define the main objectives of the project.

10.3.2 Measure the Project Performance

Project monitoring must be able to answer the following question: "Where are we at?" The monitoring must collect and process data without interpreting it. In order to answer this question, it is not always necessary to have a status report meeting; in fact, we should go to status report meetings already knowing the answer. Monitoring is an activity that should be carried out in parallel to execution and by the person responsible for the work to be done. It involves ascertaining the project's progress in an objective and consistent way in order to then compare it with the baseline. Essentially, each person accountable for a work package (WP) should provide the project manager with a project status report (on both the schedule and costs) in relation to his or her WP. Once the data have been collected, it should be summarized in specific performance indicators in order to establish whether the project is in line with the baseline or if there are variances, and if so, how large they are.

10.3.3 Evaluate Variances, Trends, and Forecasts

The assessment of the variances and estimates to complete must be able to answer the following two questions: "Why are we at this point?" and "How will the project be completed?" If the progress made is different from that expected, the causes of these detected variances should be explained and their effects on the future of the project should be evaluated in order to then make new estimates on completion.

Usually the two variables of greatest interest are the schedule and costs. With a careful eye, the project manager and the project team will be able to go beyond the commonplace and identify the true causes of the variations with respect to the baseline. It is emphasized that the variances should be investigated both in the case of negative variances, such as "we are late" or "we are spending more than expected," and in the case of positive variances, such as "we are early" or "we are spending less than expected."

10.3.4 Define Corrective Actions, as Needed

The identification of corrective actions must be able to answer the following question: What must be done between now and the next control point? The therapeutic value of this phase of the control cycle is highlighted. The fourth and last phase of the control cycle is where, with respect to project progress indicating problems, the project team, besides estimating the impact of the problems on the project costs and schedule if necessary, develops a range of possible actions to be taken to address the problems. The first rule, which may seem obvious but is not always applied, is that any actions should be taken as soon as possible. If the project progress indicates a negative trend, the sooner measures are taken to correct it, the less damage there will be at the end of the project. However, the hurry to apply corrective actions, above all in "emergency" situations, may lead to decisions that are not very effective due to their being taken in the heat of the moment and not after a structured analysis of the problem. To avoid making this kind of mistake, the project team should follow the simple rules indicated in Table 10.1.

10.4 PROJECT CONTROL IN ACTION

10.4.1 General Considerations

Control activity, despite being coordinated by the project manager, involves all the project team members. Insofar as a collective action that involves the entire project management team (PMT), control is a very important challenge for team cohesion, as all the control efforts will be aimed not so much at penalizing variances from the baseline, but rather at laying the foundations to improve project performance for the part to be completed.

Therefore, the support that a project team member can provide is essential. In fact, controlling the project means:

- Comparing the planned values against the measures taken in terms of the schedule, costs, and requirements, and assessing their variances
- Producing estimates to complete and at completion based on the data collected in order to assess progress at the time of their collection and project the measurements further ahead in time

TABLE 10.1

Rules for Effective Corrective Actions

Rule	Description
1. Stop	However serious the problem, it is always better to give everyone time to cool off so they can think about the solutions in a more detached way.
2. Look, listen, learn	It is necessary to carry out an in-depth analysis involving all the parties that may provide a contribution (sometimes even the client). This not only makes it possible to acquire several points of view before deciding how to resolve the problem, but it helps to create consensus and a sense of unity with respect to the problem ("If I've been consulted, I feel more involved in the problem, and so I'll do my best to resolve it").
3. Develop several alternatives and choose one	The more alternatives that are proposed, the more carefully considered the decision will be. If necessary, the alternative should be explored using simulations, assessing the economic impact and the value in terms of costs and benefits.
4. Get consensus on the preferred alternative	The preferred alternative must be accepted by everyone or at least by the majority of the parties involved; otherwise, its implementation can be hindered.
5. Act	Once the alternative to follow has been chosen, put it into practice as soon as possible. Hesitation in this phase may lead to greater confusion.
6. Continue to monitor	Greater control at this point makes it possible to check if the option chosen is producing the expected results.

- Identifying, on the basis of the identified or potential critical situations, the corrective or preventive measures necessary to keep the project in line with the objectives
- Approving the deliverables so that the project can move into another phase or can be closed
- Producing the necessary reports so that management can stay up-to-date on the project progress

Project team members will have a specific and defined role for each of the activities just described. For assigned activities project specialists must directly assess the variances, provide estimates to complete or at completion of the activities, identify the corrective actions, and produce the relative reports. In addition, they must support the project manager in gathering the information in order to produce an overall picture of the project.

10.4.2 Techniques for Monitoring Project Progress

During project execution, the work done to date should be periodically identified and measured so it can be compared with the project baseline.

Project team members are actively called upon to get involved for two major reasons:

- Tracking the effort made in terms of time and costs
- Measuring the progress of the activities they are responsible for

10.4.2.1 Timesheet

As regards the first aspect, time tracking, many companies apply a bureaucratic practice—the timesheet—and for this reason many are opposed to it, considering it a waste of time. The timesheet is a tool, which can even be electronic, used to collect information on the time spent each day on projects on which people are working. All the people working on a project must be required to use this tool (daily or at different intervals), as it is the only means available to the project to control the absorption of the workforce and, as a consequence, to keep the project costs under control.

If these data are not collected correctly, it will not be possible to assess the project's progress or to predict its development. This is why the whole team is required to perform this activity, also called time tracking.

The timesheet, in order to provide the project with valid administrative and control support, must be structured to obtain at least a range of information, such as the code or name of the project and the activity being worked on. It is good to share a list of the activities that can be time tracked in order to avoid difficulties in ascribing this information to the work actually carried out on the project.

The purpose of the timesheet is not to check the effective use of the full eight working hours, nor is it a system to control the presence of project team members. Rather, its purpose is to obtain information on what has been spent on a certain project. Team members must take responsibility for producing correct and accurate time and cost tracking, as the result of this work will contribute to the overall project performance. Correct time and cost tracking will make it possible to pursue project cost objectives and the prompt assessment of project progress with the possibility of taking immediate corrective actions if the project is not advancing as planned.

The information collected in the timesheet also makes it possible to carry out analyses of how the resources' time is divided over several projects, when people are assigned to several projects at the same time. This type of analysis could show us that working on several projects each day may be highly distracting, as people will have to "waste" unplanned time (setup time) switching from one project to another. In this case, an approach that provides for working, if not on one project at a time, at least on only one project per day, or better, per week, would be preferable.

10.4.2.2 Criteria for Measuring the Work Carried Out

As regards the second aspect, work progress, a question immediately arises: What should be monitored and how should monitoring be carried out?

Before getting into an examination of the different criteria for monitoring project progress, let us define what must be identified. The progress of each WP of the WBS must be identified. The more the WBS is broken down into detailed elements, the more possible it will be to apply the monitoring analytically and specifically to each element. Whereas if the WBS has only been schematized at a high level, monitoring will be applied in a more aggregate manner, and it will not be possible to understand the true pulse of the situation with regard to detailed elements of the project.

The monitoring of an element of the WBS is the responsibility of the same person that estimated and executed it, namely, the member of the PMT whose name is listed as accountable for that element in the WBS dictionary. In fact, who better than the person who planned the activity and is overseeing its execution to also define its level of completion?

However, there is a risk that team members may not be completely objective if they have to control their own work. This is why monitoring criteria should be agreed on, which are then used as a basis to produce periodic measurements of the individual elements of the WBS.

THEREFORE THE ACTIVITY IS FINISHED!

A project team unaccustomed to project management had decided to use the level of effort (LOE) technique to measure project progress. At the first status report meeting the project manager declared, "So I see things are going well. We've completed all the planned activities for this period, so next we should be able to deliver everything to the customer." This sentence generated panic among the participants who, one by one, responded that they would need at least three weeks to deliver everything that had been promised. The project manager was stunned, "How so? I have all the progress percentages at 95%. At this point we're on the home stretch." A particularly shrewd team member pointed out, "We measure progress by the hours used with respect to the budget. If the planning is perfect, this indicator is capable of showing the actual progress, but if the planning is imperfect or simply if unexpected events occur, the hours spent don't allow us to say what point we're at. We can only state how much we've worked in quantitative terms." It was only then he understood that the indicator that seemed so convenient and simple to measure was incapable of representing actual progress.

Table 10.2 sets out the main criteria for measuring project progress.

Clearly the choice of the type of measuring criteria to be adopted must be in keeping with the type of activity to be measured. This choice must be carefully agreed on within the context of the PMT, in order to monitor the project on the basis of homogeneous and shared criteria.

10.4.2.3 Comparison of the Progress Observed with Respect to the Baseline

Once collected, the project progress measurements must be compared with the baseline in order to obtain a photograph of the project's state of health, a photograph that highlights, for example, if the project is ahead of time, on schedule, or late.

Let us remember that planning not only involves financial and scheduling aspects, but also all those other aspects relating to the management of resources, risks, procurement, and quality. Last but not least, it also involves verifying the scope to assess whether what is being produced is in keeping with the requirements.

Many techniques can be used to photograph project progress, at least one for each variable considered significant (costs, schedule, scope, etc.):

- Time: One of the techniques that could be used to photograph the project progress is the Gantt chart. It can be used to highlight project planning and current progress so that it is already visually possible to observe its progress.

TABLE 10.2

Criteria for Measuring Project Activity

Criteria	Description
0–100	Also called on/off. The progress of activities is assessed as not yet begun (0%) or already finished (100%).
50–50	As soon as the activity starts, the progress percentage is set at 50%, and only after the activity is completed does the percentage assume the value of 100%. Common variants of the 50–50 criterion are 20–80 and 80–20. In the first case, little weight is given to the start of the activity, and in the second, more weight is given.
Completed units	The progress percentage is given by the total number of units completed with respect to the total to be completed. For example, imagine an activity that provides for the creation of 40 drawings. At a certain point a decision is made to control their progress, and it is noted that only 10 drawings have been done. The progress will therefore be 25%. In the case of 20 completed drawings, the progress will be 50%.
Estimated percentage	The progress percentage is estimated directly by the person whose job it is to make the assessment. In this case the team member must be aware of what many call the 90% syndrome, namely, of declaring activities to be almost complete even if they are not. This syndrome affects those in the project who do not have enough experience and fear their performance is not adequate, those who are in difficulty and wish to give the impression of confidence, relying on the remaining time to resolve the problems, and those who, with too much superficiality and trust in their methods, provide a feigned safety response. These last two elements, but especially the penultimate, tend to cover inefficiencies, shortcomings, and superficiality that will in any case be detected, even if not immediately, and that seriously compromise the achievement of project objectives.
Weighted milestones	The progress percentage is given by the achievement of milestones with defined weight. For instance, the creation of 25 drawings is planned according to a scheme with 2 milestones. Milestone 1 involves the completion of the first 5 drawings and has a weight of 30%; milestone 2 involves the subsequent 20 drawings and has a weight of 70%. If ten of the drawings have been completed by the time there is a control, the completion percentage would be 30%, given that the five additional drawings with respect to the achievement of the first milestone would not permit the second milestone to be achieved, and so they would not be considered.

- Cost: One technique that is typically used is a comparison between the budget and cost tracking values, which can be done at the level of activities, phases, or deliverables.
- Schedule/cost: One very efficient technique that integrates both the schedule and costs variables, but is not widely used due to the complexity caused by obtaining information except in big projects, is the earned value (EV) technique. The explanation of this technique

TABLE 10.2 (*Continued*)

Criteria for Measuring Project Activity

Criteria	Description
Level of effort (LOE)	This involves assigning a completion percentage based on the hours spent on the activity compared to the total estimated hours or the simple passage of time. For instance, a project that lasts 12 months was assigned a budget of 60 days/person to be allocated to project coordination activity. It is assumed that this activity is uniformly distributed over the 12 months. At the end of the third month the activity is assigned a completion percentage of 25%. This criterion is the least desirable among all those displayed and in general should only be used for project support activities, never for activities directly related to achieving the objective. In fact, it is assumed that work progress is proportional to the effort made. It is like saying, "Seeing as I estimated taking ten days/person to paint the house, having worked hard for five days/person, I have surely painted half the house and therefore I am halfway through the job."

Source: Adapted from Project Management Institute, *A Guide to the Project Management Body of Knowledge*, 4th ed., PMI, Newtown Square, Pennsylvania, 2008.

goes beyond the objectives of this book. However, we wish to explain the importance of the integrated schedule-costs view through the below example.

- Quality: In relation to the project analysis from the point of view of quality, there are more tools than in other cases. In fact, each product or service can be analyzed differently. By way of example we can mention inspections, through which it is possible to determine whether a product or process complies with the requirements; assessment questionnaires, to assess users' levels of satisfaction with the product or service; and the amount of reworking, to assess how much repair work was necessary to resolve quality issues.

- Risks: The risks defined during the planning phase must be continuously reviewed and, if necessary, redefined in order to analyze their development (increase or reduction in the probability of occurrence, increase or reduction of the impact on the project, in the case of occurrence). Furthermore, the reserves (time, money, resources) set aside at the start of the project to tackle risks identified during planning should be checked again, in order to check if the available reserves are still reasonable compared to the risks, which could have an impact on the part of the project still requiring completion.

WE'RE RUNNING AHEAD OF SCHEDULE;
ACTUALLY, NO WE'RE NOT

At a work status report meeting the project manager proudly spoke of the project progress: "By now we should have completed 60% of the project, but instead we are already at 75%. If we keep up this pace we'll finish before we planned, an exceptional result." A particularly scrupulous team member, however, had made some calculations relative to his activity and had discovered that they were indeed running ahead of schedule, but that the budget for his activity had already been almost entirely used up. The team member, in order to understand if he was the only one in this situation or others were in the same boat, asked the project manager, "Can I ask, just for information, how much of the budget assigned to the other activities has been used?" The project manager, not having the information on hand, turned the question to the other team members present. The response was chilling: almost all had spent practically the entire budget, and so what seemed to be a successful project turned into a nightmare: the remaining 25%, in fact, without a new allocation of funds, would never have been completed.

- Scope: The scope analysis makes it possible to obtain acceptance of the project scope and is done by assessing whether the deliverables correspond to the requirements, based on the acceptance criteria defined in the planning phase.

10.4.3 Techniques for Assessing Project Progress

Project monitoring produces a photograph of the project to date, in terms of the situation to date and variances/alignment with respect to the baseline.

The assessment aims to use the effects (photograph of the project to date) to trace the causes (explanation of the photograph). The assessment also aims to formulate projections to complete for the part of the project still to be completed.

It should be emphasized, provided there is a need, that project followers' contributions are essential for an accurate assessment of the project. Project followers, as members of the project management team, can and

TABLE 10.3

The Main Causes for Project Schedule and Cost Variances

Project Costs Less or Has a Shorter Duration than Planned	Project Costs More or Has a Longer Duration than Planned
Excellent project organization	Lack of project organization
Activities overestimated	Activities underestimated
Poor quality of work carried out	Excessive attention to output quality (gold plating)
Project team with above average skills, motivation, organizational intelligence	Project team with below average skills, motivation, organizational intelligence
Favorable environmental conditions	Unfavorable environmental conditions

must provide a diagnosis of the current state of play of the WPs they are accountable for.

Progress to date being equal, what are the reasons for a WP being ahead of or behind schedule, or spending more or less than was planned in the budget?

Table 10.3 sets out the main explanations for schedule and cost variances with respect to the baseline.

As Table 10.3 shows, there are many reasons for the variances, and they are not always clear. In some cases, for example, the project marks time for paradoxically positive reasons: excessive attention to the quality of the deliverables may cause delays and additional costs that seriously undermine the project.

In complex projects, different reasons for the variances coexist, in the sense that it is a set of contributory factors that determine the current state of the project.

Even where there is alignment with the baseline, in the absence of significant variances the diagnosis should be made carefully because the overall situation of the project to date may be in line with the baseline, but the alignment may only be apparent. This alignment may hide several elements of the WBS that are not aligned but nonetheless offset one another.

In fact, the following two situations may occur:

- Overall alignment on times and costs: None of the WBS activities are aligned, some are late or are spending more than planned, while others are ahead of schedule or are spending less than planned. However, due to a series of fortuitous coincidences, the overall progress of the project to date appears in line with the baseline.

- Behind schedule and over budget: One single activity of considerable duration and cost is below expectations, while all the others are in line.

Paradoxically, the second situation is, from a managerial standpoint, better than the first, even though it appears otherwise. In the first situation, in fact, the fortuitous alignment is unlikely to be seen at the next control point. Furthermore, this highlights that it is necessary to intervene simultaneously on all the activities of the WBS in order to adjust the project. Whereas in the second situation, there are greater margins for maneuver: it involves targeted intervention on a single activity to put the project back on track.

Individuals' mastery of the specific elements of the WBS and problem-solving ability at group level are the levels on which the PMT must act in order to obtain an accurate diagnosis of project progress.

Another challenge that the PMT must face during control is the formulation of "to complete" forecasts for the part of the project still to be carried out. In projects with a long duration, after a few months it is possible to start analyzing the project trends and formulate "to complete" forecasts.

Faced with these forecasts, the project team must see itself projected into the future and must see for itself what this might mean for the future of the project, the progress to date (for better, but above all for worse).

The project "to complete" forecasts are a set of predictions on the future progress of the project for the part still to be completed and that can still be affected. The forecasts are plausible provided you have set up and carried out systematic project monitoring.

On the date of the control (the so-called timenow), there are three key questions to answer as reliably as possible in terms of forecasting:

- How much is still left to do? (cost estimate to complete)
- How much will the project cost in the end? (cost estimate at completion)
- When will the project end? (schedule estimate at completion)

Answers to the three questions should be given for each activity that has been started and is not yet complete and for all activities that still have to be carried out; this way the project can be kept under control at the level of the individual elements of the WBS. These analytical data can also be used to obtain projections on the entire project as a whole.

10.4.4 Techniques to Identify Corrective Actions

In consideration of the fact that projects are rarely carried out exactly as planned, after having measured the performances and having assessed the reasons for the variances between what was planned and what has been achieved, any corrective actions must then be identified that should make it possible to bring the project back into line with the objectives.

The changes decided on by the project management team, if necessary, with the help of other experts, may aim to review the scheduled activities and the scheduling dates, review the requests of the resources, analyze the alternative risk responses, and review the cost estimates.

The identification of corrective actions may involve adjustments to the project plan and the relative deliverables, as well as the project scope. For the sake of completeness, let us examine in more detail which process should be used to make changes to the project.

In answer to the question "What are the possible corrective actions?" we can say that there are usually five options (see Table 10.4) that can be chosen to address serious problems occurring in the project. Naturally, the choice of one over another very much depends on the circumstances.

However, there is another alternative to the early closure of the project. Sometimes there are projects whose problems are linked to the proliferation of scope change requests that become so numerous that they alter the original characteristics of the project. In these cases, when confusion concerning the objectives and specifications becomes unmanageable, it is advisable to suspend the project, cancel it, and start over with a new one (it is like preferring a white sheet over a sheet full of crossings-out, at the cost of recopying something).

Team members, at this juncture, as throughout the entire project, must be supported, if not by great professionalism, by great rectitude, which leads them to pursue only the success of the project, even if it results in criticism of their work.

It should be noted that options 2, 3, and 4 mean calling the initial baseline into question and probably producing an updated version. Finally, in the project mandate and objective definition phase, the project manager and customer would normally agree, with respect to the triple constraint (scope, schedule, and time), on what importance to attribute to each of the three variables. An indication of this type is useful to guide choices when projects are in difficulties.

It should be emphasized that this phase will result, if there are corrective actions to be taken, in a return to the project planning phase.

TABLE 10.4

Types of Corrective Action Following Project Control

1. Find an alternative solution. This is by far the best option. The objective should be to adjust the project without affecting the quality, costs, schedule, and scope. Sometimes there is an alternative (for instance, doing things in a different order); you just have to be able to see it. In this sense the participation of all the parties involved in the process of analyzing and identifying the corrective actions may bring, as they say, a breath of fresh air and innovative ideas. The contribution of project followers is more often than not decisive insofar as they may have the expertise to suggest or assess the judiciousness of the alternatives relating to their area of responsibility or expertise.

2. Compromise on costs. In this option more resources are added to the project or an activity. For internal projects (where the economic margin is not an assessment parameter), this is the most frequently chosen option. However, this solution has an associated cost, which should be carefully assessed. In fact, the collateral effects should be taken into consideration, which include the learning curve for resources new to the project, the fact that certain activities should necessarily be carried out by a fixed number of people, more people only create more confusion, and so on.

3. Compromise on the schedule. This means agreeing to a delay in the delivery of the project with the project sponsor or with the client representative. It is an acceptable solution for projects where the greatest constraint is the costs.

4. Compromise on the scope. This solution essentially means reducing the quantity of the work to be done, reducing the extent of the project (not the quality of the outputs!). The result is a more reduced WBS, and therefore (presumably) savings in terms of both costs and time. The reverse side of the coin is that the project will produce a more reduced solution than the one initially planned.

5. Early closure of the project. This is the most difficult decision to make, but sometimes it is the best. It has significant implications, above all of a psychological nature, because it means disappointing the expectations of numerous people who have perhaps "given their soul" up until that point in the project or who may perceive the cancelation of the project as a personal failure ("how badly does this reflect on us?"). Nevertheless, in the most critical moments it is necessary to have the clarity and courage to ask ourselves if the project, as it is taking shape, is still worth taking through to completion. Presumably the project was started after a careful assessment of the anticipated costs and benefits. If the updated costs exceed the benefits, or if the expected benefits are no longer the same, the whole project should be called into question, and if necessary, a decision should be taken to cancel it. In these assessments how much has already been spent should not be taken into consideration, but only how much still remains to be spent ("whoever has given, has given!").

10.5 PROJECT STATUS

Project status can refer to both a meeting and a report. In both cases it is a tool, and perhaps also the most used one, to control project progress.

Proceeding by degrees, we shall define the value, the participants, or the recipients of the communications and contents.

The importance of the tool lies in the fact that it represents a moment when it is possible to exchange views with the stakeholders, meet up with the project team to address problems that may require further discussion, and define and suggest corrective measures so that the project can comply with the objectives. The project status meeting is also one of the most important moments of team building, as together the team discusses and decides how to resolve the project's problems, and has the possibility to acquire greater expertise and knowledge in the management of projects.

Team members have a duty to contribute, providing assessments of the activities they are accountable for.

The risk, however, is that the project manager will not manage to conduct the meeting effectively. Very often, in fact, meetings end up expounding on aspects that have little or nothing to do with the set scope. This creates frustration in the participants, who perceive the futility of these meetings and, most likely, will desert subsequent meetings, effectively negating all the benefits that they could have obtained from them.

On the other hand, team members must abstain from using status report meetings as individualistic moments centered around the resolution of specialist problems, thus monopolizing the meeting with subjects that may be of little importance to others. Indeed, sometimes extremely technical topics are discussed that only very few participants are interested in examining in depth, while the other participants can only hope that the meeting finishes as soon as possible.

So let us see how a team member should contribute to a project status meeting:

- Attend the project status meeting: It is regrettable and damaging when the key resources of the project do not attend the meeting. Nonparticipation has two negative consequences: (1) it means the project status meeting lacks valuable expertise in assessing the project and formulating corrective actions, and (2) it gives others the impression that the project is deemed to be of little importance ("I have other, more important things to do").

TABLE 10.5

Rules for an Effective Project Status Meeting

Before the Meeting

1. Collect all the actual progress data for the individual project activities (schedules/costs) by using a computerized or paper system.
2. Collect information, through meetings, interviews, the exchange of documents and emails, from members of the project team on: (a) completion data, (b) the qualitative progress of the activity, (c) any current and future critical situations, and (d) "to complete" estimates.
3. Prepare the project performance indexes (using, for example, those of the earned value (EV) method).
4. Prepare a list of the critical situations still open.
5. Prepare and agree on the project status meeting agenda, contacting the interested parties in advance (those who must present, those involved in the critical situations).
6. Call the project status meeting, sending the meeting information and agenda in advance to directly interested parties and other participants in the meeting.
7. Carry out the logistical tasks (book the room, prepare the material, etc.).

During the Meeting

8. Open the meeting: (a) agenda (which may be integrated with last-minute proposals) and (b) current state of the project in a short report that highlights the critical situations.
9. Conduct the meeting moderating: (a) in-depth discussions on topics that have emerged and the critical situations, (b) diagnosis of the critical situations in plenary sessions, (c) projection of the critical situations onto the future of the project, (d) identification of the corrective actions, and (e) definition of the plan of action until the next project status meeting (who will do what and by when).

After the Meeting

10. Draw up the minutes of the meeting with a summary of the action plan.
11. Circulate the minutes to all those present and to the absent stakeholders.
12. File the project status meeting documentation and minutes in the (electronic) project file, so that they can be accessed independently by the interested stakeholders.

- Come prepared: An important objective of a project status meeting is to assess project progress in order to then discuss any corrective actions. Attending the meeting without providing information on the progress of the activities one is accountable for does not allow the rest of the team or stakeholders in general to understand the status of the whole project.
- Actively contribute to the meeting: The project manager is the project coordinator, and for obvious reasons, he or she cannot have in-depth knowledge of all the activities, and therefore cannot always make decisions on an informed basis. This is why team members must

provide all the relevant information on an activity, allowing the others to understand what their colleagues are doing, how the activities are carried out, and above all, how they intend to proceed. Important events, such as risks or new information that also have an impact on the other stakeholders, must also be clearly communicated.

- Balance one's contributions: As previously mentioned, it is important for team members to contribute to the project status meeting without monopolizing the attention, for instance, by bringing up issues that should be handled at another time and with other people.

Table 10.5 states some golden rules for an effective project status meeting. These rules clearly show the decisive contribution that the project team member must be able to provide.

10.6 PERSONAL REFLECTIONS ON PROJECT CONTROL

Each project team member, during project control moments, should personally reflect on how they are working. This reflection is doubly important:

- Personal dimension. We should ask ourselves certain questions in order to gain a better understanding of our work in the project: "Are my contributions to the project always in line with the expectations?" and "Is the team collaboration effective?" By answering these questions, project team members will be able to understand if the problems detected are caused by the poor quality of their work, the structural shortcomings of the project, communication difficulties within the group, an insufficient understanding of the project, or insufficient knowledge of the topics dealt with, which are linked to the nature of the project or its management. Following these reflections, guided by the pursuit of the project objectives, project team members should be able to recognize which professional performances are not up to the task, and to act accordingly so that the problems detected do not crop up again. This action may mean: "I have understood my mistakes and I will work to ensure this does not happen again" or "I am having difficulty in understanding the working methods, rather than the contents of the project or the technology that must be used, and therefore I have to ask the project manager to organize some training sessions" or even "I realize that I can't get excited about the project, I am a negative force and I can't seem to form a team with my colleagues, and so I must ask, for the good of the project, to be replaced and to be assigned to other projects."

- Organizational dimension. Let us analyze, on the basis of our experience, how the project is proceeding and assess if its performance could be improved by suggesting the improvements that we have already been able to implement in previous projects. Surely our proactivity will allow us to grow from a project management standpoint and will benefit the project. The assessment of our performances at the end of the project will surely be positive and will mean we are given tasks with greater responsibility or interest in upcoming projects.

10.7 PROJECT FOLLOWERSHIP ACTIONS FOR PROJECT CONTROL

To summarize, here are the main project followership actions that must be performed by members of the project management team in order to add value to project control activities:

- Periodically measuring the progress of the activities under their responsibility.
- Participating in project status meetings.
- Providing information on their activities or that impacts the activities of other colleagues involved in the project.
- Not changing the facts. Any difficulties must be revealed immediately; otherwise, they may become bigger problems, even for the rest of the team.
- Suggesting improvement actions without getting into discussions that are too technical.

10.8 CONCLUSIONS

Table 10.6 summarizes the most important considerations developed in this chapter. They are divided into different phases that distinguish the project control cycle.

TABLE 10.6

The Key Principles of Project Control

Control Activity	Key Principles
Measuring	In order to be able to assess project progress we must use accurate data that are objective rather than subjective. Depending on the type of project, decisions must be made to define the criteria for measuring project progress. Once the project status information has been collected, the next step is to compare the planned values with the obtained values. The data to be taken into consideration must relate to elements where a lack of satisfaction may compromise the positive outcome of the project and, more specifically, the schedule, costs, scope, quality, and risks.
Assessment	The photograph of the project to date should be carefully diagnosed. It is necessary to understand the reasons behind the situation that has been created, whether it be positive or negative. Even perfect alignment with the baseline should be explained. The "to complete" forecasts encourage the group to share the most plausible scenario on which to establish the management of the part of the project requiring completion.
Correction	Once the reasons for the project status have been diagnosed and the "to complete" forecasts formulated, the possible options for introducing corrective actions must be assessed so that the project can be redirected toward the previously defined and approved objectives. If this is not possible, the next step is to reschedule the project or, in extreme cases, bring it to an early close.
Project status	The project status report can be both a formal meeting in which the project team and stakeholders meet to assess the progress of the work and define any corrective actions and a report that explains the key information on the progress of the work. The project status report may in any case be an output of the meeting.

See page 259 for the exercise relating to this chapter.

REFERENCE

Project Management Institute. 2008. *A guide to the Project Management Body of Knowledge.* 4th ed. Newtown Square, PA: Project Management Institute.

RECOMMENDED READINGS

Archibald, R.D. *Managing high-technology programs and projects.* 3rd ed. New York: John Wiley & Sons.

Devaux, S.A. 1999. *Total project control: A manager's guide to integrated project planning, measuring, and tracking*. New York: John Wiley & Sons.

Ghantt, T. 2012. *The lost art of project status reporting*. Melville, NY: Plumbline Publishing Group.

Gilb, T. 2005. *Project failure prevention: 10 principles for project control*. INCOSE. Available at http://citeseerx.ist.psu.edu/viewdoc/download?doi=10.1.1.87.9825&rep=repl&type=pdf.

Kerzner, H.R. 2013. *Project management: A systems approach to planning, scheduling, and controlling*. New York: John Wiley & Sons.

Meredith, J.R., and S.J. Mantel Jr. 2011. *Project management: A managerial approach*. Hoboken, NJ: John Wiley & Sons.

Pinto, J.K. 2013. *Project management*. 2nd ed. Upper Saddle River, NJ: Prentice Hall.

Shewhart, W.A., and W.E. Deming. 1986. *Statistical method from the viewpoint of quality control*. Mineola, NY: Dover Publications.

Section V

Project Followership during Project Closure

11

Projects Never Finish: The Importance of the Lessons Learned

KEYWORDS

Lessons learned
Project audit
Project postmortem analysis
Project retrospective
Project review

READER'S GUIDE

This chapter is for people who

- Have noticed that very often similar mistakes are made in projects
- Have noticed that only at the end of the project is it discovered that someone had solved a similar problem, but no one knew this
- Have noticed that only when the works are complete is it discovered that opportunities could have been seized, but the people who were aware of this did not know this information would have been useful to others

11.1 WHY THE LESSONS LEARNED ARE IMPORTANT

The expression "lessons learned" is used a lot in project management. Projects are, in fact, an interesting opportunity to test out and develop one's knowledge.

It would be good practice to ask questions like: "What has the project taught us?" "What would we do the same and what would we do differently in similar situations?" and "What tips can we give others, reinterpreting the experience that we have acquired in this project?" It would be better to ask these questions while the project is in progress, and not only at the end of the project. This is especially true for long and complex projects.

Nevertheless, for a variety of reasons, we give poor and scant attention to the lessons learned, and more generally to the management of project knowledge. This chapter aims to make project team members aware of the importance of the lessons learned, and at the same time provide some practical instructions for use.

The lessons learned draw on the experience gained in the project in order to reduce the probability of running into problems or increasing the probability of establishing virtuous circles for the benefit of the project performance and the satisfaction of stakeholders. Surveys (Knoco 2009, Thomas 2008, Ernst & Young 2007) and case studies (Abudi 2012) indicate that implementing lessons learned has positive impacts on project performance. Unfortunately, the implementation of lessons learned is still not so widespread, nor are they always adequately well developed, allowing large space for improvements in this area.

The world evolves through the accumulation of knowledge and experiences, and we, in our working activities, unconsciously draw lessons from experience. Part of the experience may be appropriated naturally, without completing any particular analysis and systemization activities (incidental learning), whereas other experiences require specific moments and techniques in order to be metabolized. A more structured approach is therefore required (intentional learning) (Watkins and Marsick 1992). The lessons learned are part of this second set, and are therefore teachings that require particular methods in order to be understood and subsequently reused.

For project team members, collaborating in the preparation of lessons learned has the following benefits:

- Understanding the project dynamics more rationally, and therefore understanding how the activities they were responsible for were influenced by other activities and how their own activities influenced the project
- Reducing the repetition of problems in the future, and therefore experiencing the project activities as less chaotic and confrontational

- Having an advance understanding of how vicious circles are generated, and thus taking the time to prepare in order to reduce the probability of their occurrence
- Accelerating the improvement process, and thus increasing the likelihood of a successful career

11.2 SOME CLARIFICATIONS ON THE CONCEPT OF LESSONS LEARNED

In the context of project management, there are many ways to refer to lessons learned (Thomas 2008). Just to mention a few, we can cite project retrospective, project postmortem analysis, post project review, and project audit. Although these expressions are often used interchangeably, there are actually differences in the activities they describe, based on when they are carried out and their aim.

Project retrospective means a set of activities aimed at understanding, analyzing, and systematizing a project's best practices and points for improvement while it is still in progress. The focus is therefore on documenting the positive factors to be reused and the mistakes to avoid in future phases of the project in progress or in future projects. This term is broadly used in agile project management (Moss 2008).

Project postmortem analysis means a set of activities aimed at understanding, analyzing, and systematizing a project's best practices and points for improvement when it is completed. This term is very often associated with projects that have not been successful. The aim is therefore to improve the performances of future projects, bearing in mind the mistakes made in the project just completed (Moss 2008).

Post project review is similar to project postmortem, but without indicating the negative outcome of the project (Projectnet Glossary 1997).

Finally, project audit means an independent assessment or analysis of a project, program, or Project Management Office (PMO) to verify compliance to company and industry standards for project and program management (IAPPM 2008). Audit is often associated with an inspection logic performed by an external resource that produces a formal output (the audit report).

11.3 VALUE OF THE LESSONS LEARNED

The above shows how the intention of activities aimed at producing lessons learned is twofold:

- To increase the value of the positive experiences, in order to make them immediately beneficial in current or future projects
- To highlight and try to rectify mistakes, so as to improve the performances of current or future projects

As said, it should be noted that the detection, analysis, systematization, and reuse of the experience gained in projects are not very widespread activities. In a survey reported by Thomas (2008), only 22% of the companies organized lessons learned information in a database. However, many companies and individuals have noticed how, once a set of problems or activities are brought together, it is clear how many problems share similar causes, and therefore how greater awareness and better monitoring of these causes can greatly simplify the development of projects (Walker 2008).

THE SLY SUPPLIER

The company SoftPro, a multinational that sells computer applications, is set up so that each product line is highly independent, in the sense that all the product managers can choose the suppliers they wish in order to get support with marketing. This philosophy comes from the conviction that each market segment has particular characteristics. Therefore, seeking synergies between products would unquestionably optimize the budget, but it would most likely be less effective, and thus, in the end, less profitable.

In order to launch a new product, an application for managing customer relations (customer relationship management (CRM)), the company decided to get support from an outside supplier whose task was to facilitate contact with potentially interested companies. During the selection of possible suppliers, a company with a very aggressive approach came forward and essentially proposed that it would receive 70% of its total fee only if the client company agreed to install the

SoftPro software demo. From SoftPro's point of view, this seemed like an excellent opportunity given that, typically, when a client agreed to install the demo, which also required time on the part of the client's staff, the purchase was practically guaranteed. Furthermore, this supplier appeared to have very interesting contacts.

During a meeting on the project to launch the new product, the person who had spoken with this supplier proposed awarding the commercial assignments to the supplier in order to increase sales of the new product. A participant at the meeting, who had participated in several other product launches, said that this approach rang a bell with him and asked the name of the supplier. The answer explained the situation: that supplier actually paid some "friends' companies" to install the demo software and then, unlike the normal chain of events, these companies never went on to buy the software, declaring that it did not meet their expectations. When the participant was asked how he had come to know about this, he replied that in another area of the company that dealt with different products the manager was a person who believed a great deal in project management, and during a meeting to detect the lessons learned, it transpired that, strangely, the demo-to-purchase conversion rate had been very low and none of the potential clients presented by this supplier had even bought a license. After this analysis a decision was made to further investigate the situation and make notes on the consulting contracts so that any collaborator, in the future, would be aware of the existence of these nontransparent practices.

11.4 FACTORS HINDERING SYSTEMATIZATION OF THE LESSONS LEARNED

Although the value of the lessons learned at the project level is positive, from a team member's point of view there may be some factors that hinder their practical application (Marlin 2008, Thomas 2008, Von Zedtwitz 2002, Busby 1999):

1. There is no time to formalize the experience. This is the most frequent issue. Although on the one hand people are theoretically aware of the importance of systematizing the lessons learned, on the other

they say there is no time. There are essentially two reasons for this perceived lack of time:

- Very often we forget to plan these formal moments of sharing and systematization from the outset. As we know, unfortunately things that are not planned cannot be organized in advance, and therefore, if they are mandatory, they become urgent, and if they are not mandatory, we skip them. Given that the lessons learned are not created to provide an answer to an immediate problem, but rather to improve the effectiveness of the project as a whole, they are often bypassed by other types of emergencies (giving an answer to a client by the evening), and therefore they are never carried out.

- The lessons learned, above all if systematized toward the end of the project, generate increased effectiveness and efficiency in subsequent projects, and therefore there is a natural tendency to postpone them (not carry them out), adopting a "one problem at a time, we'll think about the next project later" type of approach.

2. Projects are unique; thus, lessons learned are bounded to a specific project and cannot be generalized. While being unique is a typical characteristic of every project, we should not believe in the almost epic idea that each project is a separate challenge, a world unto itself, that should be managed with contingent rules and behaviors and where the information reuse rate is therefore very low. While it is certainly correct to state that each project has its distinctive characteristics, it is also true that there are similarities. So when we shift from the technical world, which can be truly different from project to project, and we enter the organizational world, many lessons learned can certainly be reused.

3. The return on investment (ROI) of these activities is not clear. Besides sporadic attempt to measure the ROI of lessons learned (Abudi 2012), there are little hard data on lessons learned returns. Moreover, lessons learned tend to benefit future projects, not the current ones. Nevertheless, since people usually works on more than one project at a time, the lessons learned from one project could also be beneficial for the other ongoing projects in which one is involved.

4. The techniques for formalizing the experience are unknown, and therefore everything risks being reduced to an almost psychotherapeutic meeting where everyone releases tensions accumulated

during the project, and thus the meeting is driven by emotions and is not very focused on rationalizing the experiences. This is why many attempts to systematize past experience went up in smoke. If a method with which to conduct lessons learned meetings is not chosen and roles are not precisely defined, in a short time everything boils down to a more or less good-natured tension-releasing session where everyone states their problems, which inevitably tend to move away from the confines of the project, even crossing over into private and sentimental areas, or the meeting may become highly confrontational, with reciprocal accusations being exchanged. Essentially, detecting and systematizing the lessons learned requires a method; it is not enough to meet in a room and "talk" about the project.

5. There is no culture of knowledge sharing. According to Busby (1999) the idea that "experience is a teacher in its own right" is very dominant. From a team member point of view there is a tendency to underestimate the importance of the lessons learned, as everyone knows their job well, and therefore everyone has already internalized the most effective way to take action. Besides the fact that this statement is questionable, as sometimes work rhythms do not allow us to stop and think if we are acting in the best way, this approach does not take into consideration the fact that people do not work in isolation but normally interact with others. When the interaction rate is high in a project, knowledge of the lessons learned also in other areas of responsibility greatly facilitates collaboration and efficiency in performing the tasks. In addition, while in daily work, as opposed to project work, it may be fairly easy to outline the perimeter of responsibilities and the type of activities carried out, in projects individuals may find themselves performing unexpected roles and tasks they have little knowledge of. Once again, we see the centrality of the lessons learned as factors for accelerating learning.

6. Open discussion. While team members are put together to work hand in hand toward the same common goal, they are often poorly suited to stand up face-to-face and give each other a piece of their mind. Frank feedback may hurt and potentially affects the relationship between individuals for years. Many people choose not to risk their social networks for the sake of project quality. However, a good project team member should learn how to speak frankly without offending the counterparts. This is a core skill in every team effort.

WHAT IS THE COST OF AN ERROR?

Mary William had just been hired by the company EsaGem as an engineer for the innovation of production processes. The company manufactures plastic die machines and is one of the largest in Europe in terms of size. Engineer William had a past record as a project management consultant, and even in the last company she collaborated with she was able to ascertain its benefits. After a few months of working at EsaGem, engineer William noticed that there were often recurrent problems in the projects, and that the company was probably not learning from past experience. After an initial analysis she reached a conclusion: EsaGem worked a great deal in quantitative terms, but much of the work done involved rectifying mistakes, which would have been avoidable if they had stopped to systematize the experiences. During an emergency meeting to respond to the umpteenth complaint by an important client, the team was considering which technical consultant to send out to Russia the next day (Saturday) to try and contain the problem. Given that problems with foreign clients cropped up very often, engineer William proposed: "OK, apart from trying to contain the problem, which has already occurred, why don't we dedicate half a day to analyzing the reasons for these ongoing emergencies with Russian clients and maybe we can try and prevent them in the future?" The team answered in unison, "But there's no time for these things, and who would pay for them? We can't add to the cost of the product. We need to work to resolve the problems. These theoretical things only work in books, etc."

Engineer William, a very calm person, absorbed the blow in the moment, but as she was sure of the effectiveness of her proposal, which had even been tested in other companies, she waited for the next emergency meeting (she didn't have to wait long) to try another strategy.

After having discussed how to resolve the emergency for two hours, engineer William asked to speak and said, "I have analyzed the last six months of work with foreign clients, who represent 70% of our turnover. In these six months we have held 30 emergency meetings, which means more than once a week. On average four people participated in the meetings, and the meetings lasted around two hours each. So we have a total person-hours cost of 240. Calculating that our average cost is 30 euros/hour, the cost of the meetings alone is 7200 euros. To resolve the emergencies we have had to send one of our technicians abroad 15 times. Given that we were responding to emergencies, the flights could not be booked in advance, and as a result we have had to pay a lot for plane tickets. So basically, travel costs for the technician have cost us 30,000 euros, for which we clearly cannot invoice the client. Then, based on our contract, machine halts during the guarantee period cost us 2000 euros a day in penalties. In total, the machines were stopped for 50 days, so we are talking about 100,000 euros. Finally, a large client, tired of ongoing problems, expected us to take back the machine, test it again, and send it back only when we were certain of the results. This little joke alone has cost us over 50,000 euros. If we add it all up, it comes to 180,000 euros, in addition to having dissatisfied clients. Given that problems with our machines only come from clients in certain countries, it means that there is a specific element related to the country variable. Perhaps we should investigate further to try to resolve the problem rather than only responding to emergencies?"

The group, impressed by the numbers and the clarity of representation, agreed to investigate further. The inquiry showed that the problem was caused by various translation errors in the user manual, especially in the setup procedure, and this led to the rapid wear of some components. The cost of definitively resolving the issue was a few hundred euros. Engineer William pointed out to everyone that if they had systematically, for instance, each month, stopped to reflect on how to improve the project, they would have incurred costs of a few thousand euros compared to savings of hundreds of thousands.

11.5 WHAT CONTRIBUTING TO WRITING THE LESSONS LEARNED MEANS

What operational contribution is required from a project team member in order to generate important lessons learned? Also, in this case there is not one single answer, as it depends on the methods used in the company or in the specific project. Let us try to systematize the cases that may occur (for a detailed review see Koners and Goffi 2007).

11.5.1 Time Dimension

As mentioned at the beginning, the identification and systematization of the lessons learned are not activities that must or can only be performed at the end of the project. If a project is to last a considerable length of time (for example, over six months), it is advisable to have formal moments to identify and formalize the lessons learned during the course of the project. The most suitable times are after achieving important deliverables or milestones. In fact, they represent important targets in the project, allowing team members to release some of the tensions they have accumulated and to systematize the events that have permitted or hindered their achievement. Formally systematizing the lessons learned during the project has the great value that team members can immediately put into practice what they have learned and thus recognize the value of this method.

11.5.2 Preparation

Similar to the kickoff meeting, the best way to fail in writing up the project lessons learned is to meet without having first defined the procedures for the meeting. Given that one of the biggest problems in lessons learned meetings is that often people do not express their opinions freely, the best thing is for the process followed, the contents, and the participants to be communicated in advance. Therefore, surprises do not generate benefits. From a team member's point of view, preparation may consist of mere mental preparation, deriving from knowing in advance what is going to be discussed, or a more formal preparation may be required by means of sending information before the meeting. Table 11.1 reproduces a form for detecting the lessons learned in preparation for a formal meeting.

TABLE 11.1

Lessons Learned Detection Form

Event Description	Positive (P) or Negative (N)?	Reasons Underlying the Event	Method of Resolution: Mitigation (if N); Enhancement (if P)

11.5.2.1 Support Questions

Thinking of activities you are directly responsible for:

- What worked particularly well?
- What caused problems?
- What were the reasons behind positive events?
- What were the reasons for the problems encountered?
- What do you suggest to further improve the positive aspects?
- What do you suggest to remove or contain the problems?

Although the most effective and traditional method is physical presence, increasingly often project teams are geographically dispersed and meeting in person is very difficult. Participation can therefore be virtual. Even purely informational participation exists at times. Therefore, there are no meetings, but instead, there is a request for information to be sent, which is then systematized and disclosed to all.

11.5.3 Discussion during a Meeting

Team members can and must provide the following contributions in a lessons learned meeting:

- An explanation of the problems encountered during the project
- An explanation of the positive aspects encountered during the project
- Detection of the reasons behind the positive and negative events
- Ideas on how to resolve the problems and how to improve the positive aspects

In this regard it is very important that team members do not immediately launch into an explanation of their best practices, i.e., "I did this or that," assuming that their behavior is successful or superior to that of their colleagues. This makes it impossible to understand the context, and furthermore, it would cause significant tension among their colleagues, who may cut themselves off from the discussion or become defiant, entering into a vicious competition to demonstrate who was the best and who, on the other hand, was damaging to the project. The best attitude is equality, and the best way to start is by announcing the positive or negative events without referring to people.

11.5.4 The Follow-Up

The added value of systematizing the lessons learned is without a doubt documenting them and making them available to everyone, but above all, putting them into practice. In a logic consistent with modern project management practices, putting the lessons learned into practice means assigning responsibilities and execution times to the people who can make them operational. Above all, if the lessons learned have already been detected during the life of the project, this aspect is crucial, as it immediately increases the value of the time invested to write up the lessons learned.

The project manager is directly responsible for some follow-up actions, but very often it is the project team members who have to contribute, so that the analysis is transformed into actual improvements.

11.6 INFORMATIONAL SOURCES FOR THE LESSONS LEARNED

Many projects are characterized by long durations and high complexity. For this reason detecting the lessons learned based only on impressions, points of view, and individuals' memories is not a good method for taking action.

The project team members called upon to help identify the lessons learned can use various documentation for support, if present obviously. Although the project documentation may be useful to identify the lessons learned, the following documents are particularly relevant:

- The Gantt chart of the project (or, more generally, other project scheduling diagrams). The project schedule, if updated, makes it possible to compare the current state of the project with the initial plan and to note where there have been significant delays. This information is useful for asking questions about the reasons for the delay and the methods of containing these occurrences.
- Risks register. The list of risks and the outcome of the response actions are valuable information for the purposes of the lessons learned, insofar as they outline if and how our actions were successful in managing risks.
- Issues log. The issue log contains information on contingent problems that have already emerged. Therefore, understanding the reason

for the existence of these issues and thinking whether any methods of resolution can be generalized is a good lessons learned exercise.

- Change requests documents. The project scope may change for various reasons: the client may request changes, there may be external factors, or we ourselves can influence and alter the scope. The scope may change continuously with small alterations, or it may occasionally undergo extensive changes. Examining the reasons underlying these changes can be very interesting in order to reduce the instability of the scope in the future.

11.7 PROJECT FOLLOWERSHIP ACTIONS FOR PROJECT CLOSURE

With reference to the lessons learned topic, here are the main actions that a project team member should implement regularly:

- Participate in meetings to identify, analyze, and systematize the lessons learned
- Actively help to document the lessons learned
- Systematically read the lessons learned documents
- If the lessons learned activities are not widespread, give simple examples to show how some serious mistakes could have been avoided with a small amount of energy

11.8 CONCLUSIONS

Although it is common opinion that the lessons learned are useful for improving individual and project performances, there are still only a few companies that draw lessons from past experiences, and therefore we content ourselves with the experiences accumulated by individuals, even unconsciously, through having been exposed to project activities.

However, many opportunities are lost like this, repeating mistakes that could have been avoided or downplaying occasions that could crop up again. If the widespread project culture is that there is no time to plan, when on the other hand planning frees up time for other activities, making them less problematic, it will be difficult for the concept of lessons learned to take hold, as it will be seen as one more burden and not as an opportunity to improve one's skills and increase project performances.

Although the optimal situation would be to work on projects that also provide for the collection, analysis, and systematization of the lessons learned, team members are advised not to wait for the organization to encourage this type of activity, but that everyone should try to analyze the events in order to draw valuable insights for future projects. If it is true that a system action brings greater benefits, it is also just as true that an individual can obtain tangible and immediate advantages.

See page 259 for the exercise relating to this chapter.

REFERENCES

Abudi, G. 2012. The ROI of lessons learned: A case study. http://www.ginaabudi.com/the-roi-of-lessons-learned-a-case-study-part-i-of-iii/.

Busby, J. 1999. An assessment of post-project reviews. *Project Management Journal* 30, 3: 23–29.

Ernst & Young. 2007. *Profiting from experience. Realising tangible business value from programme investment with lessons learned reviews.*

International Association of Project and Program Management (IAPPM). 2008. *A guide to project management auditing, assessments and recommendations.* http://www.iappm.org/pdf/CIPAGuide_03Feb08.pdf.

Knoco. 2009. *The status of lessons learning in organisations.* http://www.knoco.com/Knoco%20White%20Paper%20-%20Lessons%20Learned%20survey.pdf.

Koners, U., and K. Goffi. 2007. Learning from post-project reviews. A cross-case analysis. *Journal of Product Innovation Management* 24, 3: 242–258.

Kotnour, T.G. 2000. Organizational learning practices in the project management environment. *International Journal of Quality and Reliability Management* 17, 4–5: 393–406.

Marlin, M. 2008. Implementing an effective lessons learned process in a global project environment. *PM World Today.*

Moss, L. 2008. Project retrospectives ... post-mortems revisited. *EIMI Archives* 2, 5. http://www.eiminstitute.org/library/eimi-archives/volume-2-issue-5-august-2008-edition/project-retrospectives-post-mortems-revisited.

ProjectNet Glossary. 1997. Project Manager Today. http://www.pmtoday.co.uk.

Thomas, W.H. 2008. *A metaevaluation of lessons learned repositories evaluative knowledge management practices in project management.* Western Michigan University.

Von Zedtwitz, M. 2002. Organizational learning through post-project reviews in R&D. *R&D Management* 32, 3: 255–268.

Walker, L.W. 2008. *Learning lessons on lesson learned. PMI Global Congress North America.* Newton Square, PA: Project Management Institute.

Watkins, K.E., and V.J. Marsick. 1992. Towards a theory of informal and incidental learning in organizations. *International Journal of Lifelong Education* 11, 4: 287–300.

RECOMMENDED READINGS

Ayas, K., and N. Zeniuk. 2001. Project-based learning: Building communities of reflective practitioners. *Management Learning* 32, 1: 61–76.

Collier, B., T. DeMarco, and P. Fearey. 1996. A defined process for project postmortem review. *IEEE Software* 13, 4: 65–72.

Duffy, P., and R. Thomas. 1989. Project performance auditing. *International Journal of Project Management* 7, 2: 101–104.

Edmondson, A.C., and I.M. Nembhard. 2009. Product development and learning in project teams: The challenges are the benefits. *Journal of Product Innovation Management* 26, 2: 123–138.

Glass, R.L. 2002. Project retrospectives, and why they never happen. *IEEE Software* 19, 5: 111–112.

Gulliver, F. 1987. Post project appraisals pay. *Harvard Business Review* 87, 2: 128–132.

Jugdev, K. 2012. Learning from lessons learned: Project management research program. *American Journal of Economics and Business Administration* 4, 1: 13–22.

Keegan, A., and J.R. Turner. 2001. Quantity versus quality in project-based learning practices. *Management Learning* 32, 1: 77–98.

Kotnour, T.G. 1999. A learning framework for project management. *Project Management Journal* 30, 2: 32–38.

Martin, P., and K. Tate. 2002. Close out, the forgotten phase. *Chemical Engineering Progress* 98, 1. http://www.highbeam.com/doc/1P3-103423492.html.

Maya, I., M. Rahimi, N. Meshkati, D. Madabushi, K. Pope, and M. Schulte. 2005. Cultural influence on the implementation of lessons learned in project management. *Engineering Management Journal* 17, 4: 17–24.

Newell, S. 2004. Enhancing cross-project learning. *Engineering Management Journal* 16, 1: 12–20.

O'Dell, C., and C.J. Grayson. 1998. *If only we knew what we know.* New York: The Free Press.

Williams, T. 2008. How do organizations learn lessons from projects—And do they? *IEEE Transactions on Engineering Management* 55, 2: 248–266.

12

Personal Assessment

12.1 WHY YOU SHOULD PARTICIPATE IN PROJECTS

We are coming to the end of the book. When reaching the end of something it is customary to make an assessment or evaluate whether the experience has been positive or negative.

In this case, we are not interested in assessing whether it is worth reading this book or not; in fact, we would be the least suitable people to perform this task. Instead, we wish to make an assessment of project followership, to evaluate how it can generate value for those that practice it.

In order to do this, let us start with that which gives rise to the idea of project followership, namely, projects, now ever more present in companies. We want to start with projects because, irrespective of project followership, participating in projects may be the source of important benefits.

What benefits could a project team member obtain from participating in a project? We have already partly answered this question in various sections of the book; now we wish to systematize what we have stated and add some more information.

- Assessing our managerial skills. Participating in projects does not only require specialist skills, which is very hard to ignore. Projects require specialist skills to be included in a broader system where, in order to function, different contributions must coexist in harmony. In classic project management literature the creation of this harmony has always been proposed as the project manager's responsibility. While we agree with this view, we also consider it unbalanced. In any project, willingly or unwillingly, project team members perform coordination activities. The weight of these activities, in terms of a percentage of the total time dedicated to the project, may vary based on the characteristics of the activities and in relation to personal inclinations and attitudes. For instance, project team members must in any case coordinate with the project manager to assess when specific activities should be performed, and must coordinate with other people in their specialization area as well as interact with specialists in other areas. These coordination activities, even if on a smaller scale than those performed by the project manager, are an excellent test to assess their attitudes toward holding project coordination roles and, in the future, managerial positions. In fact, if we notice that we are excellent at performing specialist activities, but at the same time we have difficulty in organizing the work of others and in making decisions that affect others, then we have valuable information on the most suitable directions in which to develop our career. Sometimes the best specialists in one area are then promoted to managerial roles, underestimating the profound difference in skills and behaviors required. All this generates discontent in both the company and the collaborator. This is why projects can represent both an aptitude test and a training ground where we can start, in a small way, to practice our managerial skills. Projects are therefore a valuable school of management.

- Comparing ourselves with others. In a project, comparison with others is the rule rather than the exception. Comparison is often difficult, it's true. Different mindsets, experiences, skills, and knowledge cause us to see reality from different points of view and to interpret it very differently, which are at times complementary and other times confrontational. Comparing ourselves with others, however, enables us to improve ourselves. It is not news that companies invest a lot in working methods based on the diversity of views and expertise. The best decisions, as you can imagine, can arise from assessing information from other sources and listening to opinions, even conflicting, that nonetheless can contain interesting winning insights. How many times have you heard: "I just didn't think of that." So comparison with others often leads to this positive reaction, as it shows us a part of the world that, due to history, knowledge, or attitudes, we had not considered, namely, to explore a part of the project world that until recently was unknown.

- Networking. "We are what we network." This phrase was coined by George Cybenko to emphasize how the world has changed radically in recent years. In an increasingly complex environment, it is rare that personal skills alone allow us to achieve important goals. These goals can only be reached with the support of a network of acquaintances that can help us to obtain information, collaborate on specific themes, and develop contacts with people of interest to us. Projects are a natural arena in which to network insofar as they involve people from different company areas and external parties.

- Self-efficacy. As stated several times in this book, projects are characterized by deviation from more traditional work methods: innovation, orientation toward objectives, and the capacity to analyze and resolve problems, even outside of our typical skills, are all elements that form part of the project world. A typical comment of someone who has participated in a project, perhaps for the first time, is this: "At the start it took me a while to understand how to behave and what contribution I had to give. However, after a little initial difficulty I then got into the swing of things. Looking back, I'm really satisfied with myself and with what I have accomplished. It was tiring, but I discovered I know how to do more things and knew how to manage more situations than I realized." Projects allow us to test ourselves in different situations, to test our skills, and when we have reached the required objectives, they provide a strong sense of satisfaction related to the gratification that what has been achieved also depended on our efforts.
- Putting ourselves in the limelight. Why not? There's nothing wrong with it. Projects are great occasions for shining the spotlight on ourselves and demonstrating our skills to the full. In fact, many projects enjoy a great deal of attention from company management, as they are important for the future of the company. It follows that individuals who actively contribute to projects enjoy a visibility that they would not otherwise have had. It is not uncommon to find people who, when explaining the fundamental steps of their career, say they had the opportunity to be noticed and to demonstrate their skills through an important project. Projects can therefore be excellent launch pads.

12.2 WHY YOU SHOULD ADOPT A PROJECT FOLLOWERSHIP APPROACH

What we have said so far suggests that projects can represent excellent opportunities to enrich and improve our working life. With this book we have gone a step further, proposing methods and approaches that increase the potential benefits of participating in projects. If the end of the project is a time for making evaluations, we would instead like satisfaction to emerge throughout the entire project. So let us see how project followership can contribute to satisfaction by participating in projects.

In Table 12.1 we go over the previous chapters and compare the vision of a team member who works with a too specialized approach with the vision of a team member who puts project followership principles into practice. Naturally, we have taken the concepts to the extreme and the approach cannot be considered scientific, but we are sure that many of you will recognize yourselves in one approach or the other.

This summary shows that the level of satisfaction, personal growth, and the creation of a positive working environment arise from not only the technical characteristics of a project, but also the way in which it is approached. It is not so much the "doing" but "how it is done" that creates the difference between working and working with satisfaction. Of course, working life is not only made up of projects, but at least in this area, following the principles of project followership, we can try and improve for ourselves and for the organization we collaborate with.

TABLE 12.1

Comparison between the Specialist Approach and the Followership Approach

Topic	Specialist Approach	Project Followership Approach
Kickoff meeting	The kickoff meeting is a simple meeting where someone presents slides. If I am busy, I prefer not to go; at most, I will read the documentation afterward or ask someone for a summary.	In the kickoff meeting I had the chance to meet and converse with the main parties involved in the project. I was able to ask for clarification on some parts that were not very clear and better define my role and the expectations that others had of me. I then had the opportunity to understand the strategic vision of the project sponsor, which had quite often escaped me or I had interpreted wrongly. Now the company's choices are much clearer to me and I can understand the importance of my contribution.
Requirements analysis	The people who should provide me with the project requirements don't know what they want and they don't know how to express it well. It almost seems like they are not part of this company. Since I have good experience, I often prefer to decide the project requirements myself. In any case, somehow or other, something will go wrong, so it's worth it in order not to waste time.	Analyzing the requirements is one of the most complex tasks in a project. There was a time when I trivialized this activity, thinking that it was enough to ask a couple of questions in order to receive all the useful answers, but this did not happen regularly. Then I realized that the way I asked the questions was difficult for others to understand, and this further reduced the quality of their answers. So I learned to communicate more clearly, to ask what the problems were, and not to propose solutions immediately. I learned to listen. I then learned to use different information sources to identify the requirements, and thus discover any inconsistencies between the sources in advance. This allows me not to drag out problems for a long time that sooner or later must find a solution.

Continued

TABLE 12.1 (*Continued*)

Comparison between the Specialist Approach and the Followership Approach

Topic	Specialist Approach	Project Followership Approach
WBS	I have never actually seen the WBS. I'm usually informed of the activities I have to work on, but I'm not clear what's going on around me and I'm not even interested, I don't have time to waste on these organizational issues.	Participating in writing up the WBS was not easy. I would have taken around a third of the time by myself, but I have also understood that I never would have reached that level of completeness and clarity. I now fully understand my role in the project and which other activities I have to interface with. So, if need be, I'll immediately know who to turn to. I have to say that having a vision of the whole project really helps me to steer my efforts in the right direction.
Planning and estimates	If there's one thing that gets on my nerves, it's people who tell you what to do and how and when to do it, without having the slightest idea of what work there is to be done. If I can demonstrate that their estimates are wrong, I'll be happy; that way the next time perhaps they'll ask the real experts for advice. Then if the accounts don't add up, thanks to the numbers they threw down at random, they can't expect me to stay here past my working hours to solve the problems they have caused.	Thinking about the correct amount of time to dedicate to an activity has been a useful exercise. In fact, very often there is a tendency to provide instinctive estimates without considering what's actually behind a figure. I have realized that estimating activities makes one much more aware of the actual time available and increases one's ability to organize the work. Accordingly, I have noticed that my reputation has considerably improved as colleagues trust me and my ability to bring the work to completion in the time stated. Then participating in writing up the Gantt and the logical dependencies between the activities has been very useful insofar as it has enabled me to understand my network of relations within the project, and this has facilitated communication and the exchange of information a great deal.

Risks	We should think about substituting the word *project* with the word *emergency*. Every day something unexpected happens and I lose an enormous amount of time chasing after problems. At the end of the day I realize that I have not done many or any of the things that I planned to do. Perhaps working like this has become physiological, but I must adapt.	Thinking in terms of risks is not simple at all, especially at the start. Even colleagues have not shown much support and are often dismissive, saying, "We'll think about it when it happens, but for now we'll keep on working." Then I realized that thinking in terms of risks enables you to make better decisions, to go around the obstacle rather than going against it, and therefore to significantly reduce the rate of emergencies. I feel more the master of my time and much more effective in my work, as well as being less stressed.
Change	In my opinion they don't have a clear idea of what they want. If I act as required, undoubtedly the outcome will not be satisfactory. It's better that I do it my way. This way they'll see the difference in quality and my real skills. Then if they don't like it, they'll just have to adapt. I don't have time to lose.	I have learned that, when faced with a change where I don't understand the underlying logic, if I ask for explanations, justifying my requests, I get many more answers than I thought. Consequently, I manage to establish very transparent relationships with my colleagues, and I have often seen that, because of my questions, decisions are discussed for the purpose of arriving at better conclusions. Other times, I have discovered that if I had acted as I thought right, I would have actually created problems for other colleagues and the project as a whole.

Continued

TABLE 12.1 (*Continued*)

Comparison between the Specialist Approach and the Followership Approach

Topic	Specialist Approach	Project Followership Approach
Control	If instead of continuing to ask me what point I'm at they concentrated on the work to be done, we would take half the time and have fewer problems. In the final analysis a task has either been done or it hasn't; the rest is superfluous.	True, sometimes there is no full awareness of the benefits of project control. Everything becomes clear, however, when your actions depend on those carried out by others, and not knowing what point they're at and when they will finish does not enable you to organize your work and make decisions. If everybody provided truthful information, the work would be much simpler. Then I discovered that understanding what point we are at and how much I still have left to do is an excellent exercise for improving my ability to organize the work, and therefore reduce the level of urgencies and stress.
Lessons learned	Once they suggested we meet to review a project that was not successful. I didn't go. I know my job and what I do well enough. If something went wrong, it is surely someone else's responsibility. I can't understand what I am supposed to learn by talking to people who don't even deal with my subject area.	I learned that very often we overestimate our skills. As we have been dealing with a certain subject matter for some time, we think we know it all. However, very often we operate automatically, without reflecting on and systematizing our experience. During lessons learned meetings I understood many of the mistakes made, which at first did not seem to be such. I even discovered successful actions that I was not even fully aware of. Then hearing the opinions and analyses of colleagues from other areas made me understand how my point of view was relative and not absolute. It even enabled me to acquire a more systematic vision in my work, and one that is more integrated with the work of my colleagues.

Exercises

CHAPTER 1

The exercise consists of a test of eight multiple choice questions. The questions concern the key concepts addressed in the chapter, and are expressed adopting the perspective of the project team member. The test takes a few minutes. Answer each question without consulting the book. At the end, check your answers and reread the paragraphs corresponding to any answer you got wrong.

Question	Possible Answers	Your Answer
1. The success of a project depends on	A. The project management strategy B. Success evaluation criteria C. The project's degree of complexity D. All three aspects	
2. A key characteristic that distinguishes a project is the fact of it being	A. Organized B. Unique C. Challenging D. Costly	
3. The PMT (project management team)	A. Includes the project team B. Overlaps with the project team C. Accounts to the project sponsor D. Is part of the project team	
4. The complexity of a project does *not* depend on its	A. Dimension B. Innovation C. Importance D. Hostility	
5. CSFs (critical success factors) of a project are	A. Parameters that measure its success B. Conditions to achieve the success C. The most critical aspects to avoid D. External factors that cannot be influenced by the PMT	

Continued

Question	Possible Answers	Your Answer
6. Project management should be applied to the project	A. As much as possible B. As little as possible C. As needed D. Only if required	
7. Which of these is a perspective of evaluating the success of the project?	A. Impacts on the business B. Corporate climate C. Profit for the year D. Efficiency in production processes	
8. The project is collaborative by nature insofar as	A. Working well together is desirable B. The responsibilities fall to everyone C. It brings together several heterogeneous parties D. It is based on hierarchy	

CHAPTER 2

The exercise consists of a test of eight multiple choice questions. The questions concern the key concepts addressed in the chapter, and are expressed by adopting the perspective of the project team member. The test takes a few minutes. Answer each question without consulting the book. At the end, check your answers and reread the paragraphs corresponding to any answer you got wrong.

Question	Possible Answers	Your Answer
1. Which of these is not a distinctive feature of project followership?	A. Initiative B. Rigidity C. Adaptability D. Influence	
2. As a distinctive feature of project followership, professionalism includes	A. Ethics B. Working overtime C. Delegating tasks D. Challenging the project manager	
3. During project initiation, the PMT member is called upon to	A. Share the project mandate B. Define the project mandate C. Negotiate the project mandate D. Present the project mandate	

Continued

Question	Possible Answers	Your Answer
4. During project planning:	A. The contribution of project specialists is not important since the project manager has to develop the project plan B. It is better that every project team member works in isolation C. It is better that PMT members work together directed by the project manager D. It is better that PMT members work together without the presence of the project manager	
5. During project execution a good project team member should	A. Be focused as much as possible on the execution of technical tasks B. Coordinate the work of internal specialists and external suppliers under his or her responsibility C. Work in isolation: it is the mandate of the project manager to coordinate people and tasks D. Speak with the project manager at least once a day	
6. In performing project control:	A. The role of project team members is secondary B. The main task of project team members is to fill the timesheet C. Project specialists should communicate to the project manager only in case of deviations from the plan D. Project specialists should report the actual values for both time and cost of each individual WP	
7. During project closing:	A. Project team members have no role since closing a project normally involves administrative tasks that are under the responsibility of the project manager B. Project specialists should contribute to the production of lessons learned C. Project specialists should not contribute to the production of lessons learned since they may have a distorted vision of what happened during the project D. Project team members should ask the client the acceptance of the deliverables	

Continued

Question	Possible Answers	Your Answer
8. During project initiation, the most important feature of project followership is	A. Openness B. Professionalism C. Influence D. Global vision	

CHAPTER 3

The company Wirecom, a mobile phone market leader, decided to embark on a new project that should have enabled it to improve its use of the payment instruments provided by the banking system.

However, we must make the premise that the organization had a poor project management culture despite the company managements being convinced otherwise.

The company rules for a project of this kind provide for the nomination of an account, namely, of the person who within the organization of the IT department manages relations with the internal client, which, in this case, was represented by the sales department.

The account, with the collaboration of the sponsor, organized the kick-off meeting, after having defined the steering committee, which was to be comprised of the sponsor, the IT director, and the account manager (the account's manager). Representatives of the IT department, representatives of the department that would have managed the telecommunications, and those who would have managed the product at the end of the project were invited to the meeting.

The organization of the meeting included:

- Preparing slides presenting the steering committee, the sponsor, the project objectives, and the team that would have carried out the project
- Deciding on the date and booking a spacious meeting room
- Sending the sponsor and project team a communication about the meeting by using the message contained in the screen shown below.

The project was presented and barely discussed, planned, carried out, and put into production, but the objectives for which it was requested failed miserably, as contracts with the banks that would have had to accept the new payments had not been signed.

The roots of this failure were clearly there from the outset. Can you list at least three factors that ensured the project would fail?

CHAPTER 4

4.1. Here is a short story of a project. Identify and classify the stakeholders according to the diagram in Figure 4.2. Have fun!

"Everyone should remember this party for years to come," thought the enthusiastic Sara White. Sara had recently moved to a country town, leaving the city and her parents behind. She had fallen in love with a small farmhouse on the edge of the town and had renovated it, taking care of everything down to the smallest detail. She had used local suppliers for the renovation, and this choice had enabled her to make herself known and be accepted as "a citizen" by the community of the town where she had decided to go and live, and in particular by the families who lived in the nearby farmhouses. Sara was overjoyed with her new house. The time had now come to share her joy with others: first of all, her dearest friends, but also her brother and his family, her parents, and a select group of relatives. Even a few nice work colleagues that Sara wanted to become more friendly with. And finally, the local suppliers with whose help she had set up house, the people from the nearby farmhouses who helped her to integrate into the community, and the most prominent people of the town. Sara decided to organize a farmyard party, in the traditional farmer's spirit: a large table outside with wholesome food, an accordion playing, freestyle dancing, open-air games for children, and a final surprise of fireworks, which Sara loved. The preparations were numerous and varied: getting authorization from the municipality for the fireworks, agreeing on the type and sequence of the fireworks with the specialist company, asking John, an accordion teacher, to find a way to come and play at the party, making arrangements with her friends Laura and Patricia from the town kindergarten to organize games for the children (there would have been around 30, including grandchildren and the children of relatives, work colleagues, and people from the town), and preparing a peasant's menu with seasonal produce (Anthony and Mary, owners of the local town restaurant the Chicken and the Egg, cared a great deal about the party and had offered to help her with the cooking). Sara's mom and dad were immediately enthusiastic about the idea and couldn't wait to give her a hand. In the end around 100 people were invited and Sara's dad suggested hiring a couple of waiters to help out.

4.2. Here are some project requirements. Distinguish the well-formulated requirements from the badly formulated ones.

Requirement	Good	Bad
1. The electrical system must comply with current regulations.		
2. The party atmosphere must be welcoming.		
3. The system must be easy to use.		
4. The concert ticket may be refunded up to a week before the event, but this will incur a 40% penalty, and it must be presented at authorized retail outlets.		
5. The teaching materials for the training course must be updated to the latest international standards.		
6. The external supplier instructed to build the air conditioning plant for building A must be on the company's list of qualified suppliers.		
7. The restore times in the event of malfunction must be less than two days in 90% of the cases.		
8. The references that can be ordered on the Internet (online shopping) must be selectable based on the type of promotion and discount percentage.		
9. No more than ten adults at a time in each exhibition room, on weekends or public holidays.		
10. Foreign nationals may enter the selection process.		
11. The new machine must be used for a trial period by a production line.		
12. Training on the new machine should be provided for two operators per shift; five days of training per person to be carried out in the second half of 2013.		
13. It must be possible for the entire sales network to enter orders quickly and directly.		

CHAPTER 5

The figure below sets out the organization of a party WBS. From a first reading it seems correct, but looking at it more carefully, it is only partly

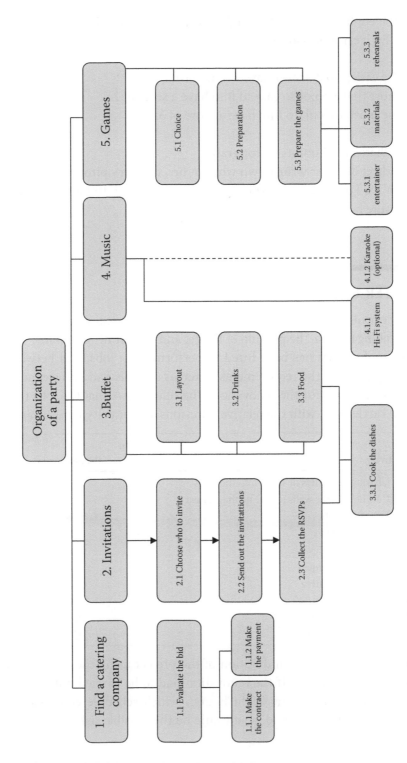

Organization of a party WBS.

correct: it contains no less than eight errors concerning the logical structuring! Each error is associated with a score:

- The easiest to discover have a score of 1.
- Those that are not so easy to find have a score of 2.
- The most difficult to find have a score of 3.

In total there are 14 points up for grabs.

On a sheet of paper write down what errors, in your opinion, are found in the WBS. For each error explain why you consider it to be such. Enjoy the treasure hunt!

CHAPTER 6

An apartment must be renovated in terms of the electrical wiring system, the plumbing system, the planing of floors, and the painting of walls.

A team of experts has been hired to perform these jobs, and between them they cover all the requirements in terms of skills and knowledge in the areas necessary for the renovation. The offer shows that the jobs that must be carried out, with the relative durations and priority reports, are:

Activity	Duration (hours)	Predecessors
A: Chasing new wires or tubes into the walls	4	None
B: Cutting into the walls (to create the chases)	8	A
C: Laying the tubes	16	B
D: Laying the wires	16	B
E: Closing the holes	10	C, D, L
F: Planing the parquet	24	E
G: Planing the marble	24	E
H: Filling the walls	3	E
I: Painting the walls	16	H, F, G
L: Testing the system	3	C, D

Determine the minimum duration of the project using the start-finish dependency relationship. If the renovation had to be carried out in nine days (each working day has eight hours), which schedule compression techniques could be used and what would be the possible risks?

CHAPTER 7

The company GovWeb had won a tender to develop new e-government services (public services for citizens available through the Internet) for Slovakia. The company had acquired a great deal of experience in this type of project in Italy and was considered a leader in its field. The customers were extremely satisfied with the quality of the work and recognized the people at GovWeb had great expertise and experience.

In fact, the company had followed a very organic process of growth without making reckless choices and had paid great attention to the management of human relations. This led to a high level of satisfaction among the collaborators and a very low rate of turnover. It can be said that each collaborator was a piece of important history for the company.

To draft the project plan, in response to a call for tenders, the company had relied on its leading expert, engineer Saladini, who had practically created most of the services offered by the company and was considered by all the collaborators as a point of reference for technical problems.

An initial analysis showed that the services to be implemented in Slovakia were less complicated than similar services developed in Italy. For the estimates, engineer Saladini always used two methods: on the one hand, he used a model developed over the years that had turned out to be reliable enough, and on the other, he readjusted the estimates based on his experience.

The model took into consideration the type of service (for example, the payment of taxes, the issuing of certificates, bookings, etc.) and the features requested, and generated an estimate based on the effort required.

Then budget and time estimates were generated by correlating these data with the cost of the resources and the time available.

In this case, the model generated a duration of around one year and three months. However, engineer Saladini considered this estimate to be very cautious and so corrected it downward, suggesting the duration of one year.

Considering the relative simplicity of the project and the fact that many collaborators, in addition to not speaking English, did not wish to relocate to Slovakia for one year, it was decided to hire an ad hoc team of computer experts from companies operating in the private sector.

The required qualifications, based on the expert's analyses, were a brief working experience (even a few months was enough) and knowledge of the English language.

The search was not very difficult, as many people wanted to include a significant experience abroad on their CV in the hope that it would make a positive contribution to their career.

The project started on February 10, 2010, but it quickly became apparent that the estimated time of one year had been greatly underestimated: in practice, the works proceeded at just over half the anticipated speed.

An initial analysis revealed that this extension to the schedule could not be attributed to incorrect behavior on the part of the client, who had in fact been highly collaborative.

Instead, the problems seemed to be linked to some specific aspects in Slovakian legislation, which should have been reflected in the proposed services and the very high rate of error on the part of the Italian team.

What were the likely problems?

CHAPTER 8

The company QuintLab must undertake a project that involves moving its 2000 employees from one building to another, 20 miles apart.

The company conducts research in the biotechnologies sector and handles confidential information, much of which is stored on paper documents.

In addition to all the office furniture and equipment, QuintLab also had to move the laboratories.

For the move an external company well known worldwide was chosen, which had only just started operating locally, but it seemed that there was already a high level of demand for its services.

The diagram in the figure below shows the risk management plan for the QuintLab project.

Although we know the perfect analysis does not exist, insofar as there are always margins for interpretation, you are asked to identify any errors and gaps in the plan and to suggest what changes should be made to the plan.

CHAPTER 9

John was a team member on the project for the development of a new high-power industrial air-conditioning unit for a shopping mall. Within

Risk Management Plan for the QuintLab Project

#	Risks: Given that …	There is the risk that …	Resulting in …	Analysis: Probability	Impact—Schedules	Impact—Budget	Impact—Scope	Impact—Quality	Score (PXI)	Response Strategy	Management: Owner	Resources Involved	Contingency Plan
1	There is confidential information in the offices	The removal company will come into possession of it	Its communication to competitors or the media	5				9	45	Have the removal company sign a letter of confidentiality	Managing director	Legal office	Immediate dismissal of the removal company
2	There are delicate pieces of equipment in the laboratory	During the transportation something will break	The new premises not being fully operational	3		5			15	Pack the most delicate pieces of equipment so that they do not break if dropped	Managing director	Project manager	
3	The supplier has only been operating for a short time and the demand is already high	There are not enough employees	Delays to the project	7	3				21	Make a contract with penalties in the event of delays	Manager	Legal office	

the scope of the project he manages customer relations. One day he met the project manager at the company's bar and said, "Listen, Barbara, as you're here I want to tell you something. I was on the phone ten minutes ago with a client who told me that the air conditioning system will be placed in an area where it will also be visible to customers. So he asked me if it would therefore be possible to color the external metal not with the usual white, but with a color that would integrate into the existing infrastructure better, in this case, red. I replied that it was feasible in principle and it seemed like a good idea; in fact, a touch of color would also make our machines less anonymous. I wanted to talk to you about it; will you inform the person responsible for the painting?"

What mistakes did the team member make in this project as regards change management?

CHAPTER 10

You are part of the project team for a new project. The project manager is involved in defining the project management plan—in other words, defining the rules with which the project will be managed. Taking into consideration the control actions that must be carried out as part of the management of schedules and costs, how can you help the project manager?

CHAPTER 11

A formalized system for the assessment of project performances was implemented in your company three years ago. The parameters assessed included the variations in the planned delivery dates (in days) and the satisfaction of the other team members in having collaborated with you (measured on a scale of 1 to 10, where 1 represents the lowest level of satisfaction and 10 represents the highest). In order to carry out the tasks you are responsible for, you must have external suppliers to support you; however, you will not be able to select them. Given that you suspect some suppliers are not up to the job, during a lessons learned meeting present the data contained in the following table in reference to the analysis of 21 activities. What lessons can you learn?

Activity	Gap from Planned Delivery Date	Project Team Satisfaction	Supplier
1	8	5	Cable & Co.
2	−1	9	Wire
3	10	4	Network Ltd.
4	0	8	Systems
5	5	7	Systems
6	2	7	Network Ltd.
7	3	8	Network Ltd.
8	10	3	Cable & Co.
9	12	3	Cable & Co.
10	1	7	Systems
11	2	6	Network Ltd.
12	4	7	Network Ltd.
13	3	8	Systems
14	8	5	Cable & Co.
15	8	5	Systems
16	5	6	Network Ltd.
17	9	4	Cable & Co.
18	10	3	Cable & Co.
19	12	4	Sys Ltd.
20	13	3	Cable & Co.
21	15	3	Cable & Co.

Solutions

CHAPTER 1

   1. D
   2. B
   3. D
   4. C
   5. B
   6. C
   7. A
   8. C

CHAPTER 2

   1. B
   2. A
   3. A
   4. C
   5. B
   6. D
   7. B
   8. A

CHAPTER 3

Some of the mistakes made in managing the project were

- Project manager: The project was managed by an account that due to the particular type of assignment was not in a position to have the necessary skills to manage the projects and very likely not the time, as the account also had to manage the customer's requirements for new projects. Not having a project manager dedicated to the project or a person capable of coordinating the activities undermined the project's foundations. The project manager, thanks to his experience and skills, would have managed the project differently (support in preparing the kickoff meeting).
- Stakeholders: There was no clear identification of the stakeholders. Only the technical departments were involved in organizing the meeting without giving importance to the other departments of the company. The project must rely on the collaboration of all the stakeholders and not just those involved in achieving it. If the sponsor or account had also distributed the project requirements or description to the other departments, the shortcomings that only became apparent at the end would have been identified from the outset and correctly addressed. If the requirements had reached the finance department (responsible for the contracts with banks), the fact that its involvement was not planned would have been noticed (kickoff objectives).
- Invitation to the meeting: The invitation to the meeting did not provide all the information that would have made it possible to conduct a constructive discussion on the requirements. The invitation to the meeting only provided information on the location and duration of the meeting but did not say anything about its contents. A correct meeting invitation should have at least specified the agenda and the main characteristics of the project (response to the invitation and receipt of information).
- Documentation: To allow the project management team members to participate constructively, information should have been distributed, in this case the slides and the document containing the

requirements, well in advance of the date of the meeting. A preliminary analysis of the documentation makes it possible for individuals to participate in the meeting asking specific questions on the requirements or the organization in order to gain a better understanding of the content and context (response to the invitation and receipt of information).

In addition to these four possible mistakes we can mention the fact that a large part of the failure of the project could also be attributed to the project team members who did not delve into the project scope before the kickoff (nor most likely afterwards), thereby demonstrating superficiality and a lack of professionalism. If this had happened during the meeting the debate would certainly have been more heated and interesting, and most likely the factors that brought about its failure would have come to light.

CHAPTER 4

4.1. Sara's Party: Stakeholders' Matrix

High power over the project	Municipality	Anthony and Mary (restaurant)
	John the accordion player	Sara's parents
	Prominent people from the town	Laura and Patricia (kindergarten)
Low power over the project	Fireworks company	Children
	Work colleagues	Brother and family
	Waiters	Select group of relatives
	Local suppliers	Friends
		Neighbors
	Low interest in the project	**High interest in the project**

4.2. Good requirements: 4, 6, 7, 8, 9, 12.
Bad requirements: 1, 2, 3, 5, 10, 11, 13.

CHAPTER 5

Error	Explanation	Score
Error 1 1 Find a catering company	Ideally the first level of the WBS should state the project deliverables, and the tasks that need to be performed to achieve those deliverables should be listed gradually as one goes down through the levels. The deliverables should be expressed with nouns (focus on what to produce) and not with verbs (focus on what to do). Do not forget the PMI's definition of the WBS: "a deliverable-orientated hierarchical decomposition of the work to be executed by the project team to accomplish the project objectives and create the required deliverables." In our case, activity 1 should be replaced by a deliverable such as "catering service."	2
Error 2 1 Find a catering company 1.1 Evaluate the bid	The WBS is a decomposition structure in which level N + 1 provides a more detailed description of what is stated in level N. Therefore, a 1:1 connection between elements of different levels cannot exist. Do not forget the PMI's definition of the WBS: "Each descending level represents an increasingly detailed definition of a project component." In our case either activity 1.1 was done away with because it coincided with activity 1 or it is necessary to add other activities at the same level as 1.1 (1.2, 1.3, etc.).	1
Error 3 2 Invitations 2.1 Choose who to invite 2.2 Send out the invitations 2.3 Collect the RSVPs	The WBS does not provide any indication of the sequence project activities should be performed in. The sequence is described by the schedule network diagram. In our case the arrows should not appear.	1

Continued

Error	Explanation	Score
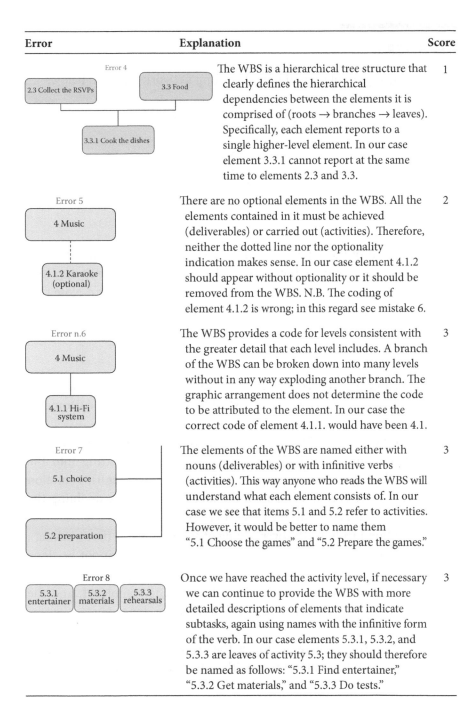	The WBS is a hierarchical tree structure that clearly defines the hierarchical dependencies between the elements it is comprised of (roots → branches → leaves). Specifically, each element reports to a single higher-level element. In our case element 3.3.1 cannot report at the same time to elements 2.3 and 3.3.	1
	There are no optional elements in the WBS. All the elements contained in it must be achieved (deliverables) or carried out (activities). Therefore, neither the dotted line nor the optionality indication makes sense. In our case element 4.1.2 should appear without optionality or it should be removed from the WBS. N.B. The coding of element 4.1.2 is wrong; in this regard see mistake 6.	2
	The WBS provides a code for levels consistent with the greater detail that each level includes. A branch of the WBS can be broken down into many levels without in any way exploding another branch. The graphic arrangement does not determine the code to be attributed to the element. In our case the correct code of element 4.1.1. would have been 4.1.	3
	The elements of the WBS are named either with nouns (deliverables) or with infinitive verbs (activities). This way anyone who reads the WBS will understand what each element consists of. In our case we see that items 5.1 and 5.2 refer to activities. However, it would be better to name them "5.1 Choose the games" and "5.2 Prepare the games."	3
	Once we have reached the activity level, if necessary we can continue to provide the WBS with more detailed descriptions of elements that indicate subtasks, again using names with the infinitive form of the verb. In our case elements 5.3.1, 5.3.2, and 5.3.3 are leaves of activity 5.3; they should therefore be named as follows: "5.3.1 Find entertainer," "5.3.2 Get materials," and "5.3.3 Do tests."	3

CHAPTER 6

The graphic representation of the scheduling network is shown below.

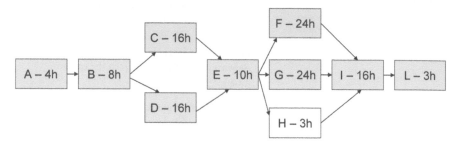

The duration of the activities overall is 81 hours, and considering that a working day is comprised of 8 hours, the work will last for 10 days and 1 hour. The activities highlighted in gray are on critical paths. Note that there are four critical paths out of a total of six paths.

If the renovation must not exceed nine days, three techniques can be applied:

- Reduction of the scope: Leads to customer dissatisfaction, as the desire to renovate cannot be satisfied in this way and the customer is therefore reluctant to choose this type of solution.
- Schedule compression (crashing): There are various activities that can be compressed by increasing the resources (cutting into the walls, laying tubes and wires, and painting). However, this solution may involve extra costs due to the fact that generally doubling the resources does not half the execution time.
- Execution involving the overlapping of some activities (fast tracking): This involves risks, however. In fact, the painting cannot be done in advance as the risk of the planing work dirtying the walls is very high, the system cannot be tested before it is completed, and the holes cannot be closed before the test has been done.

The best solution is therefore to use the crashing method, as it ensures execution within the required time with only an extra cost.

Risk Management Plan for the QuintLab Project

	Risks			Analysis						Management			
	Given that …	There is the risk that …	Resulting in …	Probability	Impact—Schedules	Impact—Budget	Impact—Scope	Impact—Quality	Score (PXI)	Response Strategy	Owner	Resources Involved	Contingency Plan
1 (1)	There is confidential information in the offices	The removal company will come into possession of it (2)	Its communication to competitors or the media	5 (3)				9 (4)	45	Have the removal company sign a letter of confidentiality	Managing director	Legal office	Immediate dismissal of the removal company
2	There are delicate pieces of equipment in the laboratory	During the transportation something will break	The new premises not being fully operational	3		5 (6)			15	Pack the most delicate pieces of equipment so that they do not break if dropped	Managing director	Project manager (7)	(8)
3 (5)	The supplier has only been operating for a short time and the demand is already high	There are not enough employees	Delays to the project	7	3				21	Make a contract with penalties in the event of delays	Manager	Legal office	

CHAPTER 7

1. Unsuitable estimation model for the specific situation. The project, although technically similar to others, did not take into consideration the major novelty of a team composed of external personnel with little experience, and the fact that the project was managed in another language, in a different country, with a different culture.
2. An expert who makes estimates for other people with much lower skill sets. The company's leading expert on technical matters was involved in the estimation process. His mindset led him to underestimate the difficulties that a newly hired person, even from another sector and with little working experience, would have faced in performing the project activity.
3. The context information was not taken into consideration. Engineer Saladini, as well as having underestimated the difficulties that collaborators would have faced, made a superficial analysis of the problem, trivializing and underestimating the distinctive features of the project environment that made unforeseen changes necessary, also due to different regulations.

CHAPTER 8

The table below shows the changes to be made to QuintLab's project risk management plan in order to make it more responsive to the need to manage the portfolio of risks affecting the project.

1. Internal personnel should also be included as a source of risk.
2. The true final effect is missing, which in this case is damage to the image or competitiveness of the business.
3. In general, it is always a good idea to add notes that explain why certain values have been chosen.
4. While it is true that there is an impact on the quality of the project (in fact, confidentiality should be a very important quality criterion), the real impact is on the business, whose image would be tarnished,

and it would lose information that could be used by its competitors. If the company allows the template to be customized, a new column for "Business Impact" should be added that encompasses the broadest concept of the impact on an individual project.

5. Only indicating the supplier company in general could lead to misunderstandings if other companies are also involved in the project. It would therefore be necessary to indicate that it is a removal company. The same consideration goes for the comment on personnel, as it is not clear who is being referred to.

6. The risk has been assessed concerning the project's budget. In actuality the budget is determined by the cost to move, and therefore the impact is on the quality.

7. It seems very strange that the managing director is dealing with this activity and that the project manager is the executor of the activity. It is more likely that the logistics manager (if there is one) would be in charge of the risk and the removal company would be the resource involved.

8. It is better never to leave columns empty, as it is not possible to understand if they have been left empty due to forgetfulness or because it was not deemed necessary to fill them in. In our example, where the contingency and fallback plans have often not been filled in, we can add "this cell has been left blank intentionally" or explain the reason why it was not filled in.

CHAPTER 9

1. The impact of the change has not been assessed, but it has been trivialized due to the lack of specific expertise (the color has an impact on the machine's performances as it changes its external temperature due to sun rays).

2. The change did not follow a formal process, which would have enabled it to be analyzed and the impacts to be assessed.

3. The decision was made independently; the project manager was only informed of it, thus bypassing the project manager's responsibility for it.

CHAPTER 10

The support you can give the project manager in terms of controlling the scheduling and costs of the project can be defined as follows:

- Define the rules to measure project progress.
- Define the control parameters to assess the status of the project.
- Define the tools and techniques that must be used to ascertain project progress.
- Collect information to determine project progress.
- Identify the experts that could help the team to assess how the project is developing.
- Define the information that must be distributed to stakeholders and the communication tools and techniques.
- Define the rules with which to correct the project development.

CHAPTER 11

Undoubtedly the supplier Cable & Co. is not capable of bringing benefits to the project, as the timings and level of satisfaction are always low.

Nothing can be said about Sys Ltd. for now, as although it is true that the performances were negative, it is also true that it has only collaborated once. The same can be said for Wire, Inc., even if the performances were positive.

The suppliers Network Ltd. and Systems, Inc., on the other hand, are inconsistent, as they show both positive and negative performances. It is therefore necessary to investigate further in order to be able to make rational decisions.

So the only clear thing to emerge is that Cable & Co. is not a suitable supplier.

Index